STOCK MARKET POLICY SINCE THE 1987 CRASH

STOCK MARKET POLICY SINCE THE 1987 CRASH

A Special Issue of the Journal of Financial Services Research

edited by

Hans R. Stoll
Vanderbilt University

Reprinted from the
Journal of Financial Services Research
Volume 13:3 (1998)

KLUWER ACADEMIC PUBLISHERS
Boston/Dordrecht/London

Distributors for North, Central and South America:
Kluwer Academic Publishers
101 Philip Drive
Assinippi Park
Norwell, Massachusetts 02061 USA
Telephone (781) 871-6600
Fax (781) 871-6528
E-Mail <kluwer@wkap.com>

Distributors for all other countries:
Kluwer Academic Publishers Group
Distribution Centre
Post Office Box 322
3300 AH Dordrecht, THE NETHERLANDS
Telephone 31 78 6392 392
Fax 31 78 6546 474
E-Mail <orderdept@wkap.nl>

Electronic Services <http://www.wkap.nl>

Library of Congress Cataloging-in-Publication Data

A C.I.P. Catalogue record for this book is available from the Library of Congress.

Printed on acid-free paper.

Printed in the United States of America

Journal of Financial Services Research

Volume 13, Number 3, June 1998

Journal of Financial Services Research 13:3 183–186 (1998)

Special Issue: Ten Years Since the Crash of 1987

Guest Editor: HANS R. STOLL
The Anne Marie and Thomas B. Walker Professor of Finance and Director of the Financial Markets, Research Center, Owen School, Vanderbilt University

Introduction

Monday, October 19, 1987, marked the largest single-day decline in stock-market history as the Dow Jones Industrial Average (DJIA) fell 508 points—nearly 23%—to close at 1738. The decline between the close on the preceding Tuesday, October 13, and the close on October 19 totaled 30.6%. By Tuesday, October 20, market participants and regulators feared defaults on outstanding transactions that could bring gridlock in financial payments, trigger a financial crisis, and propel the economy into a recession. Market observers recalled the crash of October 29–30, 1929, which had been followed by the severe depression of the 1930s and by continued stock price declines that totaled 89% from the market's high in September 1929 to its low in July 1932. Would the crash of 1987 lead to a similar economic crisis? Fortunately the answer to this question was in the negative. Stock prices recovered sufficiently by year-end to post a positive return for calendar 1987, although they did not reach their prior high until the second half of 1989.

Sources of the crash

Analysts pointed to several factors that could have triggered the crash. Legislative actions, such as antitakeover legislation passed in October 1987, were identified as trigger that adversely affected the prices of stocks. Index futures and options, combined with index arbitrage that transmitted derivative markets shocks to the cash markets, were blamed for the crash. Portfolio insurance, a trading technique that replicated put options and required stocks to be sold when stock prices fell, was thought to accentuate the crash. However, since the crash was common to world markets, trading techniques and legislation particular to the United States seem unlikely culprits. Most likely were macro-economic factors, in particular the significant increase in interest rates in the six months prior to the crash, that easily would justify a major downward adjustment in stock prices.

Do the events of 1987 imply that the stock market exhibited irrational exuberance in the six months prior to the October crash? With the benefit of hindsight, perhaps so; for stock prices continued to rise in spite of interest rate increases. Between March 1987 and September 1987 the long-term government bond rate rose by about 200 basis points (from about 7.6% to about 9.6%) without an apparent adverse effect on stock prices, which rose by 10%. Such an increase in rates normally would lower stock values substantially unless anticipated earnings and dividend growth increased dramatically. For example, if the discount rate for stocks were 5% over the long-term government rate and if the dividend growth rates were an unchanged 9% in March and September, an application of the simple dividend growth model would imply a stock price decline of 36%.[1] The crash of 1987 may simply have been the result of the market's realization that earnings and dividends were not going to grow by enough to offset the interest rate increase. In this sense the market reacted rationally to changing economic conditions, albeit quite abruptly.

Chance events, combined with unfulfilled expectations, finally led to a massive correction on October 19. There is some evidence of overreaction, since the market recovered somewhat by year-end. However, the S&P 500 Index finished at only 247, considerably below its level of 322 at the end of September, and part of the bounce back can be explained by a drop in long-term rates to 9.12% and an increase in dividends.

Studies of the crash

The crash of 1987 probably is the most analyzed event in financial history.[2] The Presidential Task Force on Market Mechanisms (Brady Commission) published its one-inch-thick volume in January 1988. The SEC followed with a two-inch-thick volume in February. Other government reports were prepared by the Commodity Futures Trading Commission and the Office of Technology Assessment. Think tanks, futures exchanges, and stock exchanges prepared their own reports. The president appointed a Working Group consisting of the Under Secretary of the Treasury, the chairman of the Commodities Futures Trading Commission, the chairman of the Federal Reserve Board, and the chairman of the Securities and Exchange Commission to assess the studies and make recommendations for regulatory changes. In its Interim Report of May 1988, the Working Group concluded (1) that coordinated circuit breakers should be implemented with ''limits broad enough to be tripped only on rare occasions''; (2) that the credit, clearing, and settlement system should be improved; (3) that current minimum margins for stocks, stock index futures, and options are adequate (although the SEC disagreed with this conclusion); (4) that markets should enhance the operational capacity of trade processing and improve the quality of executions; (5) that capital adequacy be reviewed and improved as necessary; and (6) that contingency planning and the Working Group continue on an ongoing basis.

Ten years after the crash

In April 1997, the Financial Markets Research Center (FMRC) at Vanderbilt University's Owen Graduate School of Management held a conference, Ten Years Since the Crash, to consider the lessons of the crash and review developments over the past 10 years. The conference was sponsored by the FMRC with the help of a special grant from the NYSE. The articles in this volume were selected after review from those presented at the conference.

One of the recommendations of the Working Group was for coordinated circuit breakers to halt trading in case of exceptional price declines. The circuit breakers existing in April 1997 called for a market shut down of a half-hour if the DJIA fell by 350 points and a shutdown of one hour if the DJIA fell by 550 points. In "Setting NYSE Circuit Breaker Triggers," Booth and Broussard criticize these fixed-point circuit breakers as too small in light of the current value of the DJIA. Their analysis is based on the stochastic behavior of the DJIA over a period of 67 years. Their criticism hit home on October 27, 1997, when the DJIA triggered the 550 point breaker and closed the market for the remainder of the day. In February 1988, the NYSE enlarged the circuit breakers significantly to halt trading for one hour if the market declines 10% and for two hours if the market declines by 20%.[3] According to Booth and Broussard, circuit breakers of 10% and 20% would be hit every 6.45 years and 70 years respectively, more in keeping with the original intent that the circuit breakers be rarely triggered.

Another major issue examined by the postcrash studies and the Working Group was the quality of executions and the capacity of markets. Nasdaq market makers, in particular, were criticized for failing to answer phones and for technology that allowed trading systems to lock. In the postcrash period, the Nasdaq Stock Market implemented a number of changes aimed at improving market making. Christie and Schultz investigate the behavior of market makers in "Dealer Markets Under Stress: The Performance of Nasdaq Market Makers During the November 15, 1991, Market Break." They conclude that the performance of Nasdaq market makers was much improved in 1991 over 1987.

The crash of 1987 also rekindled a long-standing debate about the efficacy and desirability of government-regulated initial margin requirements. Margin for stocks has been regulated by the Federal Reserve Board under the 1934 Securities Exchange Act, and in 1992 Congress gave the Fed authority to regulate margins on futures contracts as well. Kupiec's paper, "Margin Requirements, Volatility, and Market Integrity: What Have We Learned Since the Crash?" provides a comprehensive review of the margin literature. Kupiec examines in detail whether margin policy can be used to limit volatility of the type seen in the crash of 1987. He concludes that margin regulations do not affect the volatility of the stock market.

One of the dramatic changes in financial markets over the past 20 years has been the growth in mutual funds. At present over 5,500 equity mutual funds are operating according to Lipper Analytical Services. This compares with about 2,900 companies listed on the NYSE. Some observers argue that investors in mutual funds are unsophisticated and that fund inflows and outflows are subject to instabilities that have large effects on stock prices. These observers are concerned that this instability will be a source of the next crash. Edwards and Zhang analyze this issue in "Mutual Funds and Stock and Bond Market Stability." They conclude that mutual fund inflows and redemptions have no material effect on stock values.

In the 10 years since the crash, regulators have worked to improve the functioning and safety of the financial system. If the market sometimes (albeit rarely) makes large unanticipated mistakes, the most important task for policy makers is not to eliminate crashes—they are unavoidable random events—but rather to structure financial markets to withstand future price changes without adding to market stress. In the parlance of policy makers, the idea is to avoid systematic risk arising out of failures in the financial system. In "Ten Years After: Regulatory Developments in the Securities Markets Since the 1987

Market Break,'' Lindsey and Pecora analyze the many regulatory changes implemented in the last 10 years in areas such as market structure, automation, clearing and settlement, risk controls, capital requirements, and international coordination.

While the debate continues as do the importance of regulation to the stability of financial markets, most observers would agree that financial markets, at least in the developed world are more resilient today than in 1987. The articles in this volume provide important new research in the ongoing effort to improve the functioning of financial markets.

Acknowledgments

I thank Bill Christie for his helpful comments.

Notes

1. The constant growth dividend model is $P = D/(k - g)$, where D is the current dividend, k is the discount rate, and g is the constant growth rate of dividends. If D is unchanged, if g is unchanged at 9%, and if k is the T-bond rate plus 5%, the proportional stock price change is

$$\frac{\Delta P}{P_0} = \frac{k_0 - k_1}{k_1 - g} = \frac{0.126 - 0.146}{0.146 - 0.09} = -0.36$$

which is close to the actual decline in stock prices.

2. The list of major government and exchange studies includes the following:

   - The Chicago Board of Trade's *Response to the Presidential Task Force on Market Mechanisms*, December 1, 1987.
   - *Preliminary Report of the Committee of Inquiry Appointed by the Chicago Mercantile Exchange to Examine the Events Surrounding October 19, 1987*, December 22, 1987.
   - *Report of the Presidential Task Force on Market Mechanisms* (Brady Commission), January 1988.
   - *Final Report on Stock Index Futures and Cash Market Activity During October 1987, Report to the CFTC from the Division of Economic Analysis and the Division of Trading and Markets*, January 1988.
   - *The October 1987 Market Break, a Report by the Division of Market Regulation, U.S. Securities and Exchange Commission*, February 1988.
   - *Interim Report of the Working Group on Financial Markets*, May 1988.
   - *Trading Analysis of October 13 and 16, 1989, Report by the Division of Market Regulation, U.S. SEC*, May 1990.
   - *Report on Stock Index Futures and Cash Market Activity During October 1989 to the U.S. CFTC, Division of Economic Analysis*, May 1990.
   - *Market Volatility and Investor Confidence, Report to the Board of Directors of the NYSE*, June 7, 1990.
   - *Electronic Bulls and Bears: U.S. Securities Markets and Information Technology*, Office of Technology Assessment, U.S. Congress, September 1990.

3. However a 10% drop after 2:30 would not halt trading; a 20% drop between 1 PM and 2 PM would halt trading for one hour only; a 20% drop after 2 PM would close the market for the day; a 30% drop would close the market for the day whenever the drop took place.

Journal of Financial Services Research 13:3 187–204 (1998)

Setting NYSE Circuit Breaker Triggers

G. GEOFFREY BOOTH
Eli Broad Graduate School of Management, Michigan State University

JOHN PAUL BROUSSARD
School of Business, Rutgers University—Camden, New Jersey

Abstract

This paper investigates the stochastic behavior of large movements in the Dow Jones Industrial Average and applies the results to estimate the probability that the circuit breaker mechanism employed by the New York Stock Exchange will be activated. This is accomplished using extreme value statistics. In addition, the results confirm the inflexibility of a fixed-point circuit breaker.

In the aftermath of the October 1987 stock market crash, the New York Stock Exchange (NYSE) established a set of rules, dubbed *circuit breakers*, designed to halt trading during periods of excessive marketwide price movements. This action was in response to the suggestions by the Presidential Task Force on Market Mechanisms (1988), commonly referred to as the *Brady Commission*, and the Working Group on Financial Markets (1988) that such rules are necessary to dampen market overreactions and permit orders to be efficiently processed.[1] According to Lindsey and Pecora (this issue), circuit breakers are designed to replace spontaneous trading halts with planned ones. The extant rules, which are based on the behavior of the Dow Jones Industrial Average (DJIA), affect not only the NYSE but also other stock markets, such as the American Stock Exchange and Nasdaq, both of which have agreed to follow NYSE trading halts.

Evidence supporting the efficacy of circuit breakers is mixed, only usual with the most popular opposing argument being that these rules simply impede the inevitable price discovery process.[2] Nevertheless, circuit breakers remain a high-profile component of NYSE's market architecture. The current focus is not whether a circuit breaker should exist but at what point it should be triggered. This concern was brought about largely by the trigger being defined in terms of the DJIA's level rather than its relative change. Therefore, although NYSE has not experienced a marketwide circuit break, the bull market of the 1990s has made this possibility much more likely. As a result, in late 1996, the U.S. Securities and Exchange Commission (SEC) requested that NYSE widen its circuit breakers to guard against a stoppage caused by a ''normal'' market fluctuation. In response to the SEC request, NYSE eased its requirements. Until the beginning of 1997, circuit breaker rules shut the market down for one hour if the DJIA fell 250 points from its previous day's close. If, after reopening, the market fell another 150 points (400 points in total), trading was halted for an additional two hours. In mid-1996, the cooling off periods were reduced to 30 minutes and one hour, respectively; and in early 1997, the triggers were raised to 350 and 200 points (550 points in all).[3] In discussing NYSE's action, Edward A. Kwalwasser, the exchange's regulatory chief, maintained that "[t]here isn't any magic as to what the right number is, but we think that this is pretty close to [it]" (McGeehan, 1996b).

The purpose of this paper is to provide new insights into the probability that a prespecified circuit breaker trigger will cause a trading halt. The focus of the analysis contained here is on the initial trigger and is accomplished using extreme value statistics to estimate the probability that this trigger will be activated. To facilitate this estimation, the trigger is expressed not in points but as a percentage of the previous day's close. Thus, the task is equivalent to determining the probability that a particular extreme negative return will occur sometime during the day.[4]

Extreme value statistical theory relies on the notion, first articulated by Bortkiewicz (1922), that the statistical properties of extreme observations are different from those of observations usually experienced. As Kinnison (1985) points out, accurate probabilities of observing extreme values may be obtained only by exploring the statistical nature of these observations by themselves. Although extreme-value statistic applications to financial issues have begun to emerge, the techniques have been examined extensively in the statistical inference literature and have been used on numerous occasions in engineering, meteorological, and biological studies.[5] Key finance applications pertaining to market-wide movements of common stock prices have been presented by Jansen and de Vries (1991), Longin (1996), and Booth et al. (1997).

This study concludes that the NYSE fixed-point circuit breaker is an inflexible tool that, over time, may lead to unwanted triggering of the circuit breaker mechanism. Given a DJIA level in the 6,000 to 7,000 range, the increase in the initial trigger from 250 to 350 points decreases the probability of halting trading by approximately two thirds. Nevertheless, even at the higher trigger level, it can be expected that the circuit breaker will be activated about once in every 8 to 13 months. Whether this frequency is acceptable depends on full consideration of the costs associated with a market shutdown and the related benefits, an exercise beyond the scope of this research effort.

The remainder of the paper is arranged in the following five sections. Section 1 briefly introduces the basics of the relevant extreme-value distributions. Section 2 describes the data and the construction of the return series. Section 3 provides the mechanics of estimating extreme-value distribution parameters and discusses their use in calculating the probability of an excess. Section 4 presents the statistical results and their implications. Section 5 offers concluding remarks.

1. Extreme-value distributions

Castillo (1988) demonstrates that, to determine the probability of a specific extreme value of a variable occurring using order statistics, it is sufficient to know only the variable's cumulative distribution function and the corresponding sample size. In many instances, especially for stock prices, this is not the case. As subsequently mentioned, the "true" stochastic process of stock prices is a hotly debated issue. Moreover, it is not straightforward to ascertain the number of observations even if the time series is not infinite. For example, even high-frequency data such as transaction prices may be used to only approximate the sample size because the "true" price may have changed without a transaction occurring.

One way to overcome this lack of knowledge is provided by Fisher and Tippet (1928), who derive three asymptotic distributions that describe extreme value behavior, one of which replicates the contribution of Fréchet (1927). These distributions are applicable to all data generation processes and mimic the tail behavior of the parent distribution, after suitable transformations to avoid degeneracy. For proofs of this assertion, see Fisher and Tippet (1928) and Galambos (1978, pp. 51–57). Some general concepts related to the behavior of maximal extreme values follow. The protocol for minimal excesses is analogous, since these can be converted to maximal exceedences by multiplying them by -1.

Consider a sequence of a stationary variable $X_1, X_2, \ldots, X_n$ with a cumulative probability density function F.[6] Suppose that the probability that the maximum

$$M_n = \max(X_1, X_2, \ldots, X_n) \tag{1}$$

value of the first n variables is below a certain level, x, is given by

$$Pr\{M_n \leq x\} = F^n(x). \tag{2}$$

Extreme-value statistics investigates the asymptotic distributional properties of the scaled order statistic M_n. Its objective is to find values of a_n and b_n that satisfy

$$Pr\{a_n(M_n - b_n) \leq x\} \xrightarrow{w} D(x) \tag{3a}$$

or in terms of F,

$$F^n(x/a_n + b_n) \xrightarrow{w} D(x). \tag{3b}$$

$D(x)$ is one of Fisher and Tippet's (1928) three distributions; a_n measures dispersion, b_n is a location parameter, and $\xrightarrow{w}$ denotes "to weakly converge."

If eq. (3b) holds, F belongs to D's domain of attraction, where D is one of the following types:

$$\text{Type I}: \quad D(x) = \exp(-e^{-x}), \quad -\infty < x < \infty \tag{4a}$$

$$\text{Type II}: \quad D(x) = 0, \quad x \leq 0 \tag{4b}$$
$$= \exp(-x^{-\alpha}), \quad x > 0$$

$$\text{Type III}: \quad D(x) = \exp[-(-x)^{\alpha}], \quad x < 0 \tag{4c}$$
$$= 1, \quad x \geq 0$$

where α denotes the tail shape of the parent distribution. Type I (Gumbel) and Type II (Fréchet) distributions are similar in that right-hand side tails are asymptotic. The Gumbel distribution approaches its asymptote exponentially. The Fréchet distribution, however, decays by a power and, therefore, does not decay as rapidly as the Gumbel distribution. In contrast to these two distributions, the Weibull distribution's right-hand side tail is finite, as is the case with a truncated process. For the Gumbel and Weibull distributions, all moments are well-defined. However, for the Fréchet distribution, α

denotes the highest defined moment with moments greater than α being infinite (Hols and de Vries, 1991).

The seminal works of Bachelier (1990) and Mandelbrot (1963) spawned a vast literature describing the efforts modeling the stochastic behavior of asset returns.[7] The preponderance of these attempts center on fitting a parent process with either Gumbel or Fréchet tails to the data. Popular distributions, which are contained in the Gumbel family, include Gaussian, finite mixture of Gaussians, and mixed diffusion-jump process (Leadbetter, Lindgren, and Rootzèn, 1983). Sub-Gaussian stable laws, Student t, and ARCH models also often are used to model parent distributions. These processes belong to the Fréchet group. For sub-Gaussian stable distributions, $0 < \alpha < 2$. Student t and most ARCH processes exhibit $\alpha > 2$. A special ARCH model, IGARCH, is described by $1 < \alpha < 2$ (Ghose and Kroner, 1995).

Despite these extensive and creative efforts, the issue of the "true" distribution remains unresolved. Nevertheless, because this paper's purpose can be accomplished by knowing only tail properties, it is not necessary to model the stochastic behavior of the DJIA as a whole. Instead, the crux of the analysis is to determine which of the three distributional types conforms to the DJIA series used to activate the circuit breaker and then to estimate the relevant distributional parameters and the resultant probabilities of extremal occurrences. Danielson and de Vries (1997) point out that, since excesses in financial returns appear to be random, the use of these unconditional distributions is appropriate for decisions involving risk.

2. Data

The data consist of daily close DJIA values and the following day's low for the 67+ year period beginning October 1, 1928, and ending July 7, 1995. These are provided by CSI Data Corporation. The data begin when the DJIA first appeared in its current 30-stock format and end when this study was started. These stocks are purported to provide a broad measure of the U.S. stock market's performance. The index is price weighted and adjustments are made routinely to account for technical changes such as stock splits, spinoffs, and substitutions that would distort its value.[8] Over time these adjustments have reduced the DJIA's divisor from 30 to less than 1, making the divisor a de facto multiplier. In other words, a one-point price change in one of the component stocks results in a greater than one-point movement in the index. However, if change is expressed in percentage terms, this multiplier effect disappears.

Following the NYSE's circuit breaker rules, the price drop (DROP) for each day is calculated as

$$\mathrm{DROP}_t = 100(\mathrm{CLOSE}_{t-1} - \mathrm{LOW}_t)/\mathrm{CLOSE}_{t-1} \qquad (5)$$

where CLOSE is the daily closing index value and LOW is the lowest index value during a day. In this calculation the largest daily decline is expressed in positive terms. This convention is used because the circuit breaker trigger is stated as a positive number. Only those days for which DROP is positive are included in the distributional analysis. For the period under study, CSI and other popular data sources provide the "theoretical" LOW and not the "actual" LOW. The "theoretical" LOW is calculated using the lowest intraday price of each of the DJIA stocks. Therefore, the "theoretical" LOW generally is smaller than the "actual" LOW, providing a more conservative measure of DROP. In either case, the use of this measuring scheme, assuming that the time frame from which to extract an excess is one day and that the parent stochastic process in intraday cumulative returns with the cumulation period beginning with the previous day's close, results in DROP being the minimal excess.[9]

Table 1 presents the 10 largest DROPs for the full sample as well as for the period following the establishment of the circuit breaker. A review of the table indicates that the 10 largest DROPs occurred before the circuit breaker took effect (see panel A). Moreover, although the post-circuit breaker DROPs are not among the 10 all-time largest, the absolute price declines, with one exception, are larger. For instance, the October 13, 1989, mini-crash's DROP is 7.8% (rank 21), which was brought about by a price decline of 214.3 points (rank 2). In contrast, the October 29, 1929, crash's corresponding numbers are 18.5% (rank 2) and 48.3 points (rank 254). This phenomenon manifests the difficulty of relying on a circuit breaker activated by an absolute rather than relative price decline.

Table 1. Largest price declines (October 1, 1928–July 27, 1995)

	DROP		Absolute decline	
Date	Rank	Percent	Rank	Points
Panel A. Full data series (October 1, 1928–July 27, 1995)				
10/19/87	1	25.3	1	569.1
10/29/29	2	18.5	254	48.3
10/28/29	3	14.7	302	44.4
7/21/33	4	12.3	3,096	11.8
10/5/31	5	11.8	3,228	11.4
11/6/29	6	11.4	873	29.3
10/24/29	7	11.0	641	33.6
5/21/40	8	9.6	3,095	11.8
10/22/87	9	9.4	3	190.0
8/12/32	10	9.3	5,737	6.4
Panel B. Post-circuit breaker data series (October 19, 1988–July 27, 1995)				
10/13/89	21	7.8	2	214.3
8/3/90	125	5.0	8	142.6
8/6/90	165	4.5	12	126.5
8/19/91	168	4.5	9	132.6
7/23/90	179	4.3	10	128.4
11/15/91	209	4.2	11	127.4
8/23/90	232	3.9	23	100.8
10/5/92	306	3.5	17	113.2
10/24/89	319	3.5	28	92.6
10/9/90	337	3.4	35	85.9

Note: This table presents results of the largest DJIA daily declines. DROP represents the percentage of the price decline in the DJIA from the previous day's close to the current day's low expressed as a positive. Only those observations where DROP is positive are considered. *Rank* refers to the rank in the full sample, which contains 15,427 observations.

To highlight this difficulty, consider figure 1. Panel A displays the DJIA levels in the post-circuit breaker period. Panel B provides a plot of the 250-point trigger expressed as a percentage of the DJIA. (The corresponding percentages for the 350-point trigger are 1.4 times those of the 250-point trigger.) An examination of these two panels reveals that the level of the DJIA has increased from the circuit breaker's initiation to the end of the period (2,137 to 4,732). As a result, the 250-point trigger, being constant, decreased from 11.7% to 5.3% of the DJIA. By way of contrast, corresponding DROPs are presented in panel C. This series is mean stationary and its maximum is 7.8%.[10]

3. Probability estimation

According to Maritz and Munro (1967), eq. set (4) can be operationalized to estimate empirically the cumulative probability distributions for negative and positive extreme values. In the case of the DROP series, which by construction contains only positive observations, the cumulative distribution function is specified as

$$F = \exp[-\exp\{-(\text{DROP} - \lambda)/\delta\}], \quad \tau = 0 \tag{5a}$$

$$F = \exp[-\{1 - \tau(\text{DROP} - \lambda)/\delta\}^{1/\tau}, \quad \tau \neq 0 \tag{5b}$$

where τ, δ, and λ are the tail index, dispersion, and location parameters, respectively. $(\text{DROP} - \lambda)/\delta$ may be thought of as the deviation of DROP from its location standardized by its dispersion. The tail index determines the type of distribution from which the DROPs are drawn and is related to the tail shape of the parent distribution, such that for $\tau \neq 0$, $\tau = -(1/\alpha)$. If $\tau = 0$, the limiting distribution is Gumbel. If $\tau < 0$, the Fréchet distribution obtains; while if $\tau > 0$, the limiting distribution is Weibull. For $\tau < 0 (\tau > 0)$, DROP is bounded from below (above) by $\delta + \lambda/\tau$.

As Gumbel (1958) suggests, a straightforward way to obtain estimates of τ, δ, and λ is to solve the following nonlinear least squares regressions:

$$-\ln\{-\ln[m/(N+1)]\} = \delta^{-1}(\text{DROP}_m - \lambda) + e_m, \quad \tau = 0 \tag{6a}$$

$$-\ln\{-\ln[m/(N+1)]\} = \tau^{-1}\{\ln\delta - \ln[\delta - \tau(\text{DROP}_m - \lambda)]\} + e_m, \quad \tau \neq 0 \tag{6b}$$

where m is the rank assigned to each return after ordering all observations from the lowest to the highest value, N is the number of observations with $m/(N+1)$ measuring the observed cumulative probability.[11] Thus, eq. set (6) is the empirical analog of eq. set (5), constructed by twice taking the logarithm, rearranging the right-hand side terms, twice multiplying by -1, and adding the obligatory disturbance term, e_m. Equation (6a) is estimated only if the eq. (6b) estimate of τ is not significantly different from 0.

Substituting the parameter values found from estimating eq. set (6) into eq. set (5) provides an estimate of the probability that a DROP value less than or equal to a specified value occurs. The probability of exceeding this specified value, which may be considered the circuit breaker trigger, is the complement of F; that is, $P = 1 - F$. This probability, however, is predicated on the assumption that a positive DROP occurred, an assumption made to lessen the possibility of violating the DROP boundary conditions.[12] Therefore, if it is to be used as an input to the normative setting of a circuit breaker trigger, a

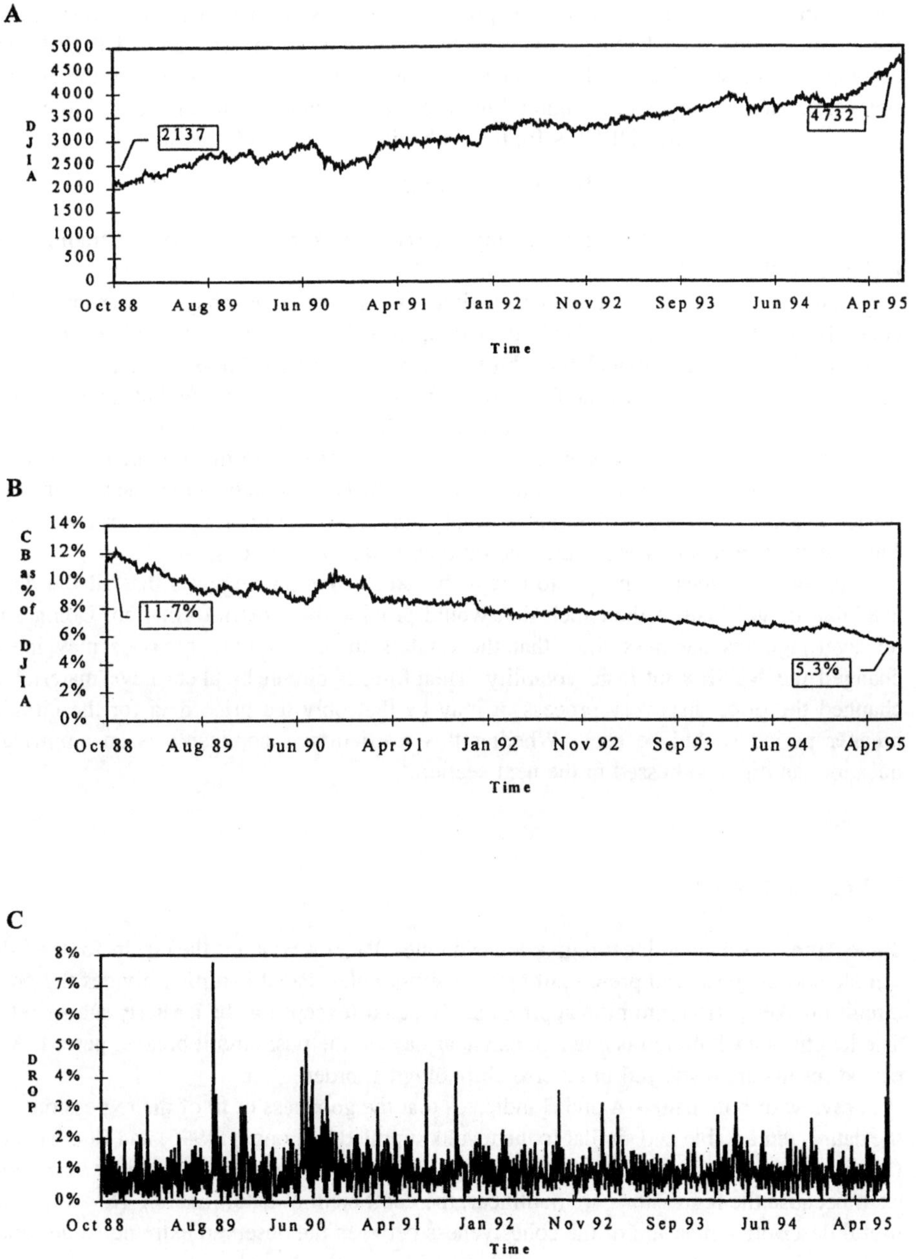

Figure 1. Plots of DJIA, fixed-point trigger and DROP for the post-circuit breaker period.
Note: Panel A, DJIA closing value in points; Panel B, 250-point circuit breaker as a percentage of DJIA; Panel C, DROP, the largest decline during a day expressed as an absolute percentage of the previous DJIA closing value. Dates are provided at 200 trading day intervals.

modification is necessary. A plausible approach is to consider that there are two states of nature, one characterized by a positive DROP and the other by a nonpositive DROP. From an empirical perspective, the latter state of nature represents the case where the circuit breaker cannot be triggered. Defining T to be the total number of trading days (N plus the number of days in which DROP ≤ 0), the probability is modified such that

$$P* = (N/T)P + [(T - N)/T](0) = (N/T)P \tag{7}$$

where $P*$ is the probability of exceeding a circuit breaker trigger when all trading are included in the calculus.

Before continuing, a brief digression into probability philosophy is warranted. As cogently pointed out by Weatherford (1982), probability may be viewed in different contexts. For instance, logical probability asserts that the likelihood of a future event depends on the information available. This information set may include, but is not limited to, the nature of the structure of the process or mechanism that has the potential to produce the event and the event's historical frequency. The latter information set typically is referred to as *relative probability*, which holds that the best estimate of the true probability, if such probability exists, is the most current cumulative relative frequency of the event. Thus, relative probability is conditional on only what has been observed.[13]

Application of these concepts to circuit breaker activation suggests that all the data available be used, since their inclusion would provide the most information. Doing so, however, ignores the possibility that the establishment of circuit breakers may have changed the NYSE's intrinsic volatility. Therefore, if circuit breakers have materially changed the price discovery process, it may be that only the price data for the circuit breaker period should be used. Whether this restriction is applicable is an empirical question, and it is addressed in the next section.[14]

4. Empirical results

Table 2 presents the nonlinear regression estimates. Panel A contains the results for the full sample and the post- and pre-circuit breaker subsamples. Panel B further divides the pre-circuit breaker period into nine approximately equal (except for the earliest) subperiods. The length of each period is equal in calendar days to the post-circuit breaker period. All period results are displayed in reverse chronological order.

A review of both panels A and B indicates that the goodness of fit of the regressions to the data is remarkable and similar to the results supplied by Longin (1996) and Booth et al. (1997). To illustrate, although an overall goodness-of-fit measure technically does not exist because the regressions are nonlinear, the coefficient of determination (R^2) still is a useful descriptive measure of the cohesiveness between the observed extreme values and those predicted by the regression model. In all cases, the R^2 values are extremely high, with the lowest being 0.9884 for the total sample regression. Moreover, on an individual basis, the estimates for τ (tail index), δ (dispersion), and λ (location) in every case are statistically significant at p-values less than 0.0001. Similar to most previous financial investigations, all of the τ values are negative, signifying that the tail distributions of the

Table 2. Nonlinear regression results

Sample	Dates	N	Maximum drop	τ	δ	λ	R^2
Panel A							
Full	10/1/28–7/7/95	15,427	25.3	−0.273	0.409	0.546	0.9884
				(0.0003)	(0.0002)	(0.0002)	
Post-circuit breaker	10/19/88–7/7/95	1,673	7.8	−0.133	0.371	0.642	0.9926
				(0.0028)	(0.0011)	(0.0011)	
Pre-circuit breaker	10/1/28–10/18/88	13,754	25.3	−0.287	0.412	0.535	0.9987
				(0.0003)	(0.0002)	(0.0002)	
Panel B							
Pre-circuit breaker	10/19/81– 10/18/88	1,687	25.3	−0.235	0.413	0.658	0.9796
				(0.0031)	(0.0019)	(0.0021)	
	10/19/74–10/18/81	1,696	4.2	−0.044	0.428	0.641	0.9986
				(0.0009)	(0.0000)	(0.0000)	
	10/19/67–10/18/74	1,680	4.4	−0.053	0.428	0.695	0.9900
				(0.0008)	(0.0000)	(0.0000)	
	10/19/60– 10/18/67	1,723	6.3	−0.118	0.308	0.495	0.9959
				(0.0015)	(0.0000)	(0.0000)	
	10/19/53–10/18/60	1,641	8.4	−0.160	0.312	0.431	0.9940
				(0.0020)	(0.0000)	(0.0000)	
	10/19/46–10/18/53	1,579	5.3	−0.234	0.284	0.377	0.9981
				(0.0016)	(0.0000)	(0.0000)	
	10/19/39–10/18/46	1,433	9.6	−0.323	0.297	0.363	0.9973
				(0.0016)	(0.0000)	(0.0000)	
	10/19/32–10/18/39	1,407	12.3	−0.281	0.629	0.689	0.9921
				(0.0031)	(0.0000)	(0.0000)	
	10/1/28–10/18/32	908	18.5	−0.196	1.095	1.213	0.9925
				(0.0035)	(0.0001)	(0.0000)	

Note: This table presents the estimated extreme value parameters for the complete data series and selected subperiods, all of which are presented in reverse chronological order. The following regression is used:

$$-\ln\{-\ln[m/(N+1)]\} = \tau^{-1}\{\ln\delta - \ln[\delta - \tau(\mathrm{DROP}_m - \lambda)]\} + e_m, \qquad \tau \neq 0 \tag{6b}$$

where τ (tail index), δ (dispersion), and λ (location) are extreme-value parameters. DROP is the percentage decrease from the DJIA's previous day's close to the current trading day's low expressed as a positive; and $m/(N+1)$, the observed cumulative probability, is the order rank (m) of a specific DROP divided by the total number (N) of observations plus 1. Asymptotic errors are in parentheses and all parameter values are significant at p-values < 0.0001. Equation (6a) is not used because $\tau \neq 0$. In each case, the extreme value distribution is Fréchet and the relevant boundary condition is met.

full sample and the various subsamples are Fréchet.[15] In all cases the boundary conditions imposed by the Fréchet distribution are met.

To address the probability issue raised in the previous section, it is instructive to compare the post-circuit breaker parameter values to their pre-circuit breaker counterparts. Comparing first the post- and pre-circuit breaker parameter values reported in panel A, indicates that the former's location is somewhat more positive, its dispersion is slightly smaller, and its tail thickness is noticeably thinner (but still not as thin as the tails of a Gaussian distribution). A review of the coefficient estimates in panel B, however, indicate that the post-circuit breaker period estimates are not atypical. For instance, for the 10 subperiods (1 post-circuit breaker and 9 pre-circuit breaker), the post-circuit breaker τ, δ, and λ values rank fourth, sixth, and fifth, respectively, when the coefficients are ranked from the largest to the smallest. Therefore, it is sensible to base the analysis of the probability of triggering the NYSE circuit breaker on the full data set.

Two points concerning the full sample parameter estimates merit mention. First, τ is significantly less than 0 but greater than -0.5, indicating that the parent stochastic process is neither Gaussian nor some type of Gaussian mixture nor is it sub-Gaussian stable. Instead, $\tau = -0.273$, which denotes a Fréchet distribution, suggests that the parent may be either ARCH or Student *t*. The relevant parent series of the DJIA intraday returns is not contained in this study's data set. Nevertheless, Lagrange multiplier (LM) tests indicate that DROP and close-to-close returns, both being censored representatives of the parent process, exhibit ARCH effects, supporting the notion that the parent process is ARCH.[16] Second, according to the parameter values, DROP is bounded from below by -0.952; that is, $0.546 + [0.409/(-0.273)]$. Since, by construction, DROP > 0, the requisite boundary condition is met.

Since the probability is conditional jointly on the estimates of τ, δ, and λ, it is instructive to examine how these parameters interact and how the probability of a DROP exceedence reacts to a change in one or more of the parameter values. Figure 2 provides some insights into these questions. Panel A holds τ constant and permits δ and λ to vary. Panels B and C hold δ and λ, respectively, constant while allowing the other two parameters to assume different values. Each panel assumes DROP to equal 5%. An inspection of these panels indicates that, as τ decreases (becomes more negative), the probability of exceedence increases, ceteris paribus. This is expected, since τ measures tail thickness and the smaller is the τ value, the thicker the tail. Under the ceteris paribus conditions, this probability is positively related to δ and λ. However, ceteris paribus conditions need not hold.

Table 3 presents the calculated extreme value probabilities for various circuit breaker triggers ranging from 1 to 30%. These probabilities are derived by solving eqs. (5b) and (7). The full sample parameter values are used in eq. (5b). The resulting DROP exceedence probabilities are transformed in circuit breaker trigger probabilities using eq. (7), where $N = 15{,}427$ and $T = 16{,}770$, indicating that there are 1,343 trading days in which DROP is not positive. For ease of exposition, these daily probabilities are converted to units of time by assuming a 12 month, 250 trading day year.

Before illustrating the interpretation of these probabilities, it is useful to explore their accuracy. Information relevant to this task is provided in figure 3, which contains plots for the 5th and 95th percentiles plus the mean of 1,000 trading day probability forecasts for each DROP. These forecasts are created using Monte Carlo simulation, where the regression parameters are perturbed and a set of random error terms is generated. A review of this figure indicates that the variation of the forecasts from the mean is not large. Although, as expected, the dispersion of the forecasts increases as DROP increases, the 5th and 95th percentiles expressed as a percentage of the mean forecast ranges (in absolute terms) from 7 to 9%.

Keeping in mind the Monte Carlo results, now consider the largest DROP reported in table 1. The frequency in the probability that this DROP, 25.3%, is exceeded is once every 39,561 days, which is equivalent to once in every 1,899 months or 158 years. In other

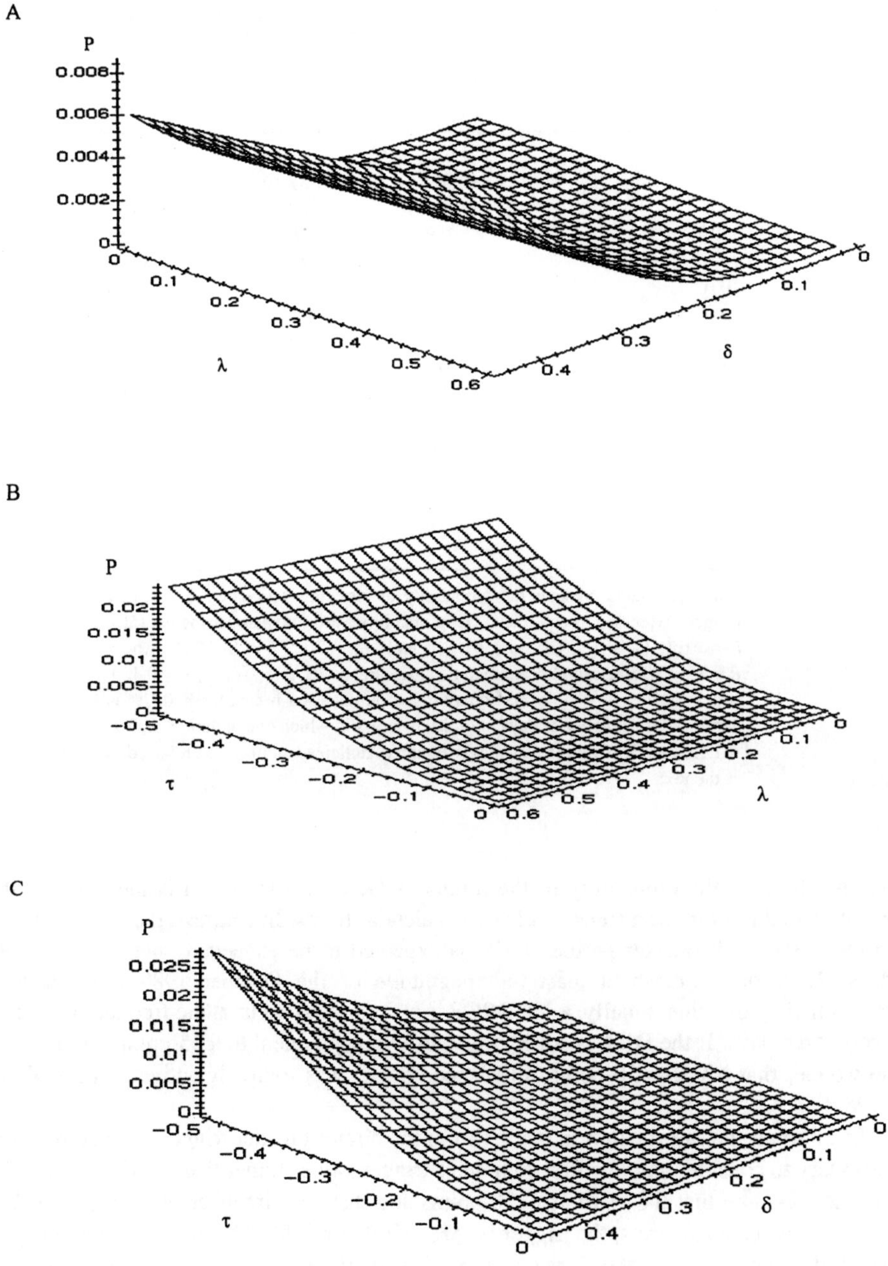

Figure 2. Sensitivity of the probability (P) of exceeding a DROP to changes in probability parameter values. *Note:* $P = 1 - F$, where as expressed in eq. (5b), $F = \exp[-\{1 - \tau(\text{DROP} - \lambda)/\delta\}^{1/\tau}]$. Total sample parameter values are used and DROP = 5.0%. Panel A, λ vs. δ and $\tau = -0.273$; panel B; τ vs. λ and $\delta = 0.409$; panel C, τ vs. δ and $\lambda = 0.546$ (see table 2). Equation (5a) is not used because $\tau \neq 0$.

Table 3. Probability analysis of violating a percentage circuit breaker trigger

	Violation probabilities		
Circuit breaker (%)	Days	Months	Years
30.0	72,077	3,459.7	288.31
25.3	*39,561*	*1,898.9*	*158.24*
20.0	17,228	826.9	68.91
15.0	6,388	306.6	25.55
11.8	*2,789*	*133.9*	*11.16*
10.0	1,596	76.6	6.38
9.0	1,124	54.0	4.50
8.0	762	36.6	3.05
7.8	*693*	*33.3*	*2.77*
7.0	494	23.7	1.98
6.0	*302*	*14.5*	*1.21*
5.0	*171*	*8.2*	*0.68*
4.0	*87*	*4.2*	*0.35*
3.0	39	1.9	0.16
2.0	14	0.7	0.05
1.0	3	0.1	0.01

Note: This table presents the probability of violating various circuit breaker triggers expressed as a percent. The probabilities are calculated using eq. (5b), $F = \exp[-\{1 - \tau(\text{DROP} - \lambda)/\delta\}^{1/\tau}]$, and eq. (7), $P^* = (N/T)P$, where $P = 1 - F$. Total sample parameter values are used: $\tau = -0.273$, $\delta = 0.409$, and $\lambda = 0.546$ (see table 2). Equation (5a) is not used because $\tau \neq 0$. P^* is expressed the number of days, months, or years in which one violation occurs. A 12 month, 250 trading day year is assumed. Italicized numbers are referred to in the text.

words, although the probability of the infamous October 1987 crash is measurable, the event indeed is a rare occurrence, at least in calendar terms. In contrast, the largest DROP in the post-circuit breaker period, 7.8%, is expected to be exceeded once in every 693 days. Therefore, a crash at least the magnitude of the October 1989 mini-crash is probablisticly overdue. Finally, a 1% DROP is estimated to occur at the frequency of once every three days. If the DJIA is 6,500, this DROP is equivalent to a 65 point decline. It is no wonder that NYSE's 50-point Collar (see note 3) was routinely activated throughout 1996.

To interpret the information in table 3 from the circuit breaker trigger perspective, it is necessary to consider only the first column as trigger values rather than DROP values. For instance, assume that the DJIA is 6250 points and that the circuit breaker trigger is 250 points. In percentage terms, the trigger is 4%, (250/6,250)100. The probable frequency at which this trigger is activated is once every 87 days. If the trigger is set at 350 points, the frequency decreases to between once in every 302 days if the DJIA is 5833 (a 6% trigger) and once in 171 days if the DJIA is 7000 (a 5% trigger).

Figure 4 presents the excess probability analysis from a different perspective. For the post-circuit breaker period, it shows the probable frequencies of triggering the 250-point

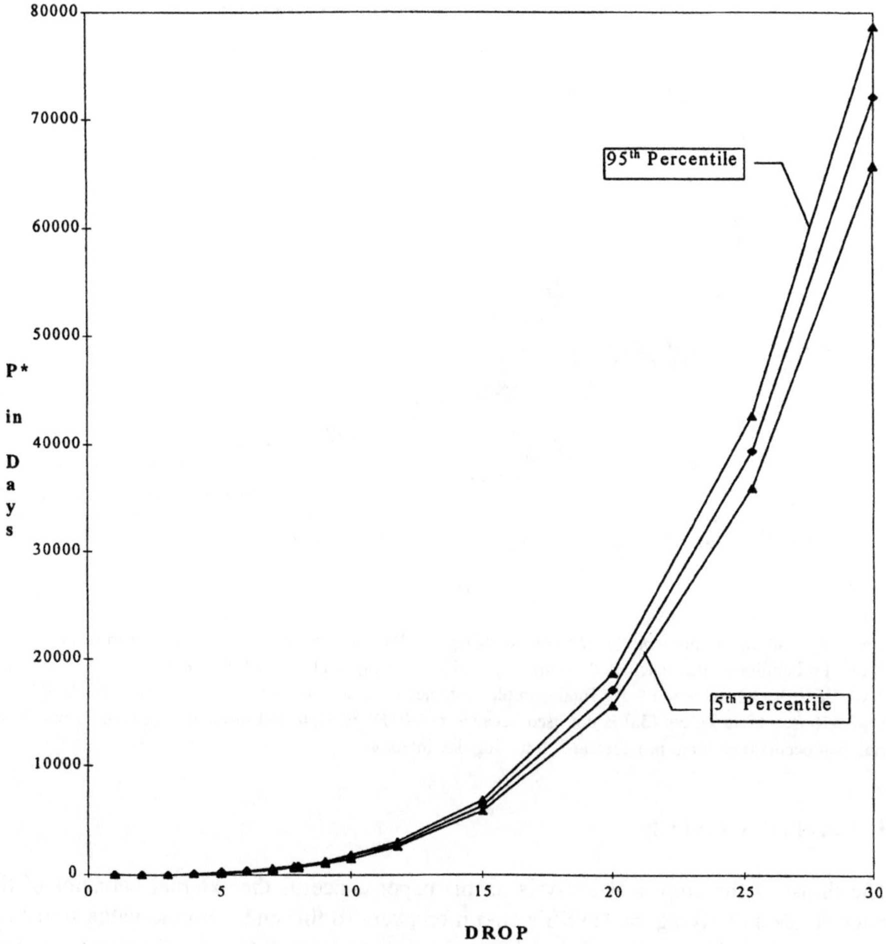

Figure 3. Forecast confidence 5th and 95th percentiles.
Note: These percentiles plus the mean of 1,000 trading day probability forecasts for each DROP in table 3 are plotted. The forecasts are created using Monte Carlo simulation. The probabilities are calculated using eq. (5b), $F = \exp[-\{1 - \tau(\text{DROP} - \lambda)/\delta\}^{1/\tau}]$, and eq. (7), $P^* = (N/T)P$, where $P = 1 - F$. Total sample parameter values are used: $\tau = -0.273$, $\delta = 0409$, and $\lambda = 0.546$ (see table 2), eq. (5a) is not used because $\tau \neq 0$. P^* is expressed in number of days in which one violation occurs.

and 350-point circuit breaker limits over time. The increase in frequency is dramatic. For example, at its inception the probable frequency of activating the 250-point trigger is only once every 2,789 days (11 years). This is in stark contrast to once in every 87 days for a DJIA of 6250. One further point needs to be made in this regard. To obtain the same level of risk present at the 250-point trigger's inception, the current value of the fixed activation point should be in the neighborhood of 750 points, not 350, for a DJIA of 6500.[17]

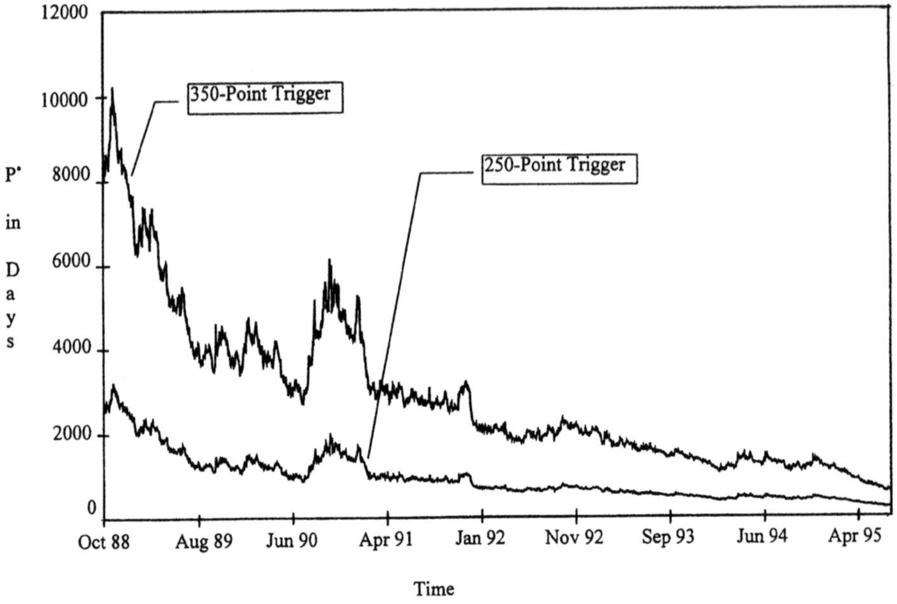

Figure 4. Trading day probabilities (P^*) of exceeding the 250- and 350-point circuit breaker triggers.
Note: Probabilities are calculated using eq. (5b), $F = \exp[-\{1 - \tau(\text{DROP} - \lambda)/\delta\}^{1/\tau}]$, and eq. (7), $P^* = (N/T)P$, where $P = 1 - F$. Total sample parameter values are used: $\tau = -0.273$, $\delta = 0.409$, and $\lambda = 0.546$ (see table 2), eq. (5a) is not used because $\tau \neq 0$. P^* is expressed in number of days in which one violation occurs. Dates are provided at 200 trading day intervals.

5. Concluding remarks

The thrust of the empirical analysis in this paper concerns the external behavior of the price series underlying the NYSE's circuit breaker. To this end, extreme-value statistical theory is applied to estimate the probabilities that negative extreme values are exceeded. Applying the statistical results to the issue of setting a value for the circuit breaker trigger suggests the following. First, it confirms the often-stated notion that a fixed-point circuit breaker trigger is inflexible to changes in the DJIA. This inflexibility may be overcome by expressing the trigger in relative terms or by changing its point value periodically (perhaps annually) to reflect new market levels. Second, it demonstrates the way in which extreme-value theory can be used as a decision-making tool. As an example, it shows that an increase in the trigger from 250 to 350 points does not restore the environment to the point where it was when the 250-point circuit breaker was started.

The research results, however, are not limited to circuit breaker trigger setting, since other mechanisms are used to ensure market stability. Indeed, as Lindsey and Pecora (this issue) extensively report, numerous reforms have been made in this regard. For instance, information transfer among regulators and financial markets has been enhanced by the establishment of the WAFM and other rapid communication channels. The SEC now has the power, subject to the approval of the president of the United States, to employ emergency authority under extreme conditions to calm the markets. Clearance and settlement procedures have been restructured. For instance, many trades are routed and executed electronically and the settlement time shortened in an effort to "smooth" the trading procedure. Cross-margining among financial markets now exists and there are cross-guarantees among clearing agencies. These agencies also have bolstered their capital reserves. Broker/dealers also have increased their capital and have become active in the commercial paper market, reducing their reliance on banks for their short-term fund requirements.[18]

That these market changes may have changed the need for a circuit breaker system is an unresolved issue. Kwalwasser's previously cited quote asserting that there is no precise way to determine the level where the circuit breaker trigger should be set is insightful and correct. An important ingredient, however, in deliberating the viability and nature of the extant circuit breaker rules is plausible estimates of the probabilities of large price changes. These estimates are the natural province of extreme-value theory.

Acknowledgments

Our interest in extreme value statistical theory and its applications to finance was (re)ignited by the participants of the Conference on Multivariate Extreme Value Estimation with Applications to Economics and Finance, Erasmus University, Rotterdam, 1994. We thank the participants of the Conference on Ten Years Since the Crash, Vanderbilt University, Nashville, TN, April 10–11, 1997, and of the Visiting Scholar Program, Office of the Comptroller of the Currency, Washington, DC, March 19, 1997.

Notes

1. The Working Group on Financial Markets (WAFM) was established on March 18, 1988, to provide a focal point for considering, resolving, recommending, and acting on the market issues raised by the October 1987 crash. The four principles of WAFM are the chairman of the U.S. Securities Exchange Commission, chairman of the Commodity Futures Trading Commission, chairman of the Board of Governors of the Federal Reserve System, and the U.S. Secretary of the Treasury. These individuals meet approximately every six weeks but their staffs meet more often.
2. For instance, that circuit breakers do what they are intended to do is supported by Ma, Rao, and Sears (1989a, 1989b) and Betero and Mayer (1990). Opposing empirical evidence is provided by Roll (1988), Santoni and Liu (1993), and Lauterbach and Ben-Zion (1993). On the theoretical level, Greenwald and Stein (1991) argue in favor of the circuit breaker principle while Subrahmanyan (1994) develops a model in which circuit breakers can exacerbate price movements, a possibility empirically supported by Kuhn, Kurserk, and Locke (1991).
3. The NYSE also has two mechanisms to regulate program trading that are similar to, but are not, circuit breakers in the marketwide sense. The Collar limits this type of trading when the DJIA either falls or rises 50 points from its previous day's close. It remains in effect for the rest of the trading day or until the DJIA moves to within 25 points of its previous day's close. The Sidecar essentially stops program trading whenever the S&P 500 futures contract declines 12 points, which is roughly equivalent to 100 DJIA points.
4. From a circuit breaker design perspective, this formulation has the benefit of explicitly incorporating a changing reference level, thereby highlighting the difficulty of using a fixed-point rule in a strongly trending

market. The formulation also is consistent with rational choices from either the perspective of utility theory's relative risk aversion or prospect theory, as promulgated by Kahneman and Tversky (1979).

5. See Gumbel (1958) for a statistical inference exposition, Galambos (1978) for engineering applications, Jenkinson (1955) for a meteorological example, and Maritz and Munro (1967) for several biological uses.
6. What follows assumes that this sequence is independent and identical (i.i.d.). However, the limiting distributions, which subsequently are described, are robust to i.i.d. violations such as linear (Berman, 1964) and nonlinear (de Haan et al., 1989) dependence. Violations of this type are often found in asset return series, the DJIA being no exception.
7. Bachelier's contribution first appeared as a doctoral dissertation, which he submitted to the Faculty of Sciences of the Academy of Paris on March 29, 1900. An accessible English translation by James Boness is provided in Cootner (1964).
8. The component stocks of the DJIA have changed over time. These changes have been brought about not only by mergers but also by the need to keep the DJIA a representative stock index. It is implicitly assumed that these changes are part of the stochastic process that is modeled. This assumption is made in the spirit of Ross's (1996) observation that, regardless of natural and human-made changes over thousands of years, the Nile River is still the Nile River.
9. If $CLOSE_t = LOW_t$, DROP measures the conventionally calculated daily return. This typically is not the case, highlighting the difficulty of using daily returns to infer intraday return relationships.
10. According to the conventional unit root tests, the null hypothesis that DROP contains a unit root is rejected. The ADF calculated t statistic with a constant and trend is -5.363; p-value 0.01 equals -3.96. As expected, however, this null hypothesis cannot be rejected for either the close or low DJIA daily series (ADF $t = 0.59$ and 0.18, respectively). This implies that the null also cannot be rejected for any fixed-point circuit breaker expressed in terms related to the DJIA.
11. An alternative of this approach is to estimate the parameters using the maximum likelihood method, which is described by Hosking (1985), Macleod (1989), and Harter and Balakrishnam (1996) among others. Both approaches yield consistent estimates, and Longin (1996) reports in his analysis of the tail shape properties of the returns on NYSE stocks that the methods provide similar results, although the maximum likelihood method provides somewhat smaller standard errors. However, as subsequently reported here, the parameter t-values are very large, rendering this statistical issue moot.
12. It is possible to ensure that the trading behavior exhibited on all days is considered by decreasing the frequency of measurement from daily to, say, weekly. As pointed out by Feller (1971), among others, doing so will not affect the magnitude of α because it is independent of temporal aggregation. But, as subsequently shown, this change may affect the relevant cumulative probability calculation. Since the NYSE rules state that the circuit breaker trigger mechanism is restarted daily, it appears to be more sensible from a normative perspective to handle the impact of the missing observations in a different manner. Also see note 9.
13. In Weatherford's (1982) hierarchy, relative probability subsumes classic probability and logical probability is subsumed by subjective probability. Frankfurter and McGoun (1996) provide an excellent discussion of these probability theories and their implications for empirical financial research.
14. After reviewing the literature since the October 1987 crash on a similar issue, Kupiec (this issue) asserts "that no substantial body of scientific evidence supports the hypothesis that margin requirements can be systematically altered to manage the volatility in stock markets."
15. That the underlying distributions are thicker tailed than a Gaussian distribution serves to underscore the difficulties of relying only on a standard mean/variance analysis of the DJIA to determine the probability of triggering the circuit breaker. Such reliance would result in severely underestimating the probabilities of an excess.
16. LM(1) statistics are 824.4 and 422.4 for DROP and close-to-close returns, respectively. Both are significant at the $p < 0.0001$ level.
17. According to McGeehan (1996a), the National Association of Securities Dealers has suggested setting the initial trigger at 10% of the DJIA. At the time of the suggestion, this trigger was equivalent 540 points.
18. Greenwald and Stein (1988) offer an alternative to increased capitalization. They suggest that the NYSE engage in an insurance scheme with a consortium of insurance companies. The idea is that the consortium would buy a portion of the specialists' inventory, an action triggered by a large market decline on heavy volume.

References

Bachelier, L.J.B.A., *Theorie de la Speculation*, Paris: Gauthier-Villars, 1900.

Berman, S.M., ''Limiting Theorems for the Maximum Term in Stationary Sequences,'' *Annals of Mathematical Statistics* 35 (1964), 502–516.

Bertero, E., and C. Mayer, ''Structure and Performance: Global Interdependence of Stock Markets Around the Crash of October 1987,'' *European Economic Review* 34 (1990), 1155–1180.

Booth, G.G., J.P. Broussard, T. Martikainen, and V. Puttonen, ''Prudent Margin Levels in the Finnish Stock Index Futures Market,'' *Management Science* 43 (1997), 1177–1188.

Bortkiewicz, L. von, ''Variationsbreite und mittlerer Fehler,'' *Sitzungsberichte den Berliner Mathematik Gessellschaft* 21 (1922), 3–11.

Castillo, E., *Extreme Value Theory in Engineering*, San Diego, CA: Academic Press, 1988.

Cootner, P.H. (ed.), *The Random Character of Stock Market Prices*, rev. ed. Boston: Massachusetts Institute of Technology, 1964.

Danielson, J., and C.G. de Vries, ''Extreme Returns, Tail Estimation, and Value-at-Risk,'' Working paper, Erasmus University, Rotterdam, the Netherlands, 1997.

Feller, W., *An Introduction to Probability Theory and Applications*, vol. 2. New York: John Wiley, 1971.

Fisher, R.A., and L.H.C. Tippett, ''Limiting Forms of the Frequency Distribution of the Largest and Smallest Member of a Sample,'' *Proceedings of the Cambridge Philosophy Society* 24 (1928), 180–190.

Frankfurter, G.M., and E.G. McGoun, *Toward Finance with Meaning*, Greenwich, CT: JAI Press, 1996.

Fréchet, M., ''Sur la loi de probabilité de l'écart maximim,'' *Annals de la Société Polonaise de Mathematiques* 6 (1927), 93–116.

Galambos, J., *The Asymptotic Theory of Extreme Order Statistics*, New York: John Wiley, 1978.

Ghose, D., and K.F. Kroner, ''The Relationship Between GARCH and Symmetric Stable Processes: Finding the Source of Fat Tails in Financial Data,'' *Journal of Empirical Finance* 2 (1995), 225–251.

Greenwald, B., and J. Stein, ''The Task Force Report: The Reasoning Behind the Recommendations,'' *Journal of Economic Perspectives* 2, no. 3 (1988), 3–23.

Greenwald, B., and J. Stein, ''Transactional Risk, Market Crashes and the Role of Circuit Breakers,'' *Journal of Business* 64, no. 4 (1991), 443–462.

Gumbel, E.J., *Statistics of Extremes*, New York: Columbia University Press, 1958.

de Haan, L., I.S. Resnick, H. Rootzèn, and C.G. de Vries, ''Extremal Behavior of Solutions to a Stochastic Difference Equation with Applications to ARCH Process,'' *Stochastic Processes and Their Applications* 32, (1984), 213–224.

Harter, H.L., and N. Balakrishnan, *CRC Handbook of Tables for the Use of Order Statistics in Estimation*, Boca Raton, FL: CRC Press, 1996.

Hols, M.C.A.B., and C.G. de Vries, ''The Limiting Distribution of Extremal Exchange Rate Returns,'' *Journal of Applied Econometrics* 6 (1991), 287–302.

Hosking, J.R.M., ''Maximum-Likelihood Estimation of the Parameters of the Generalized Extreme-Value Distribution,'' *Applied Statistics* 34 (1985), 301–310.

Jansen, D.W., and C.G. de Vries, ''On the Frequency of Large Stock Returns: Putting Booms and Busts into Perspective,'' *Review of Economics and Statistics* 73 (1991), 18–24.

Jenkinson, A.F., ''The Frequency Distribution of the Annual Maximum (or Minimum) Values of Meteorological Elements,'' *Quarterly Journal of the Royal Meteorological Society* 7 (1955), 145–158.

Kahneman, D., and A. Tversky, ''Prospect Theory, an Analysis of Decision Under Risk,'' *Econometrica* 47, no. 2 (1979), 264–291.

Kinnison, R.R., *Applied Extreme Value Statistics*, Columbus, OH: Battelle Press, 1985.

Kuhn, B.A., G.J. Kuserk, and P. Locke, ''Do Circuit Breakers Moderate Volatility? Evidence from October 1989,'' *Review of Futures Markets* 10 (1991), 136–175.

Lauterbach, B., and U. Ben-Zion, ''Stock Market Crashes and the Performance of Circuit Breakers: Empirical Evidence,'' *Journal of Finance* 48, no. 5 (1993), 1909–1925.

Leadbetter, M.R., G. Lindgren, and N. Rootzèn, *Estimates and Related Properties of Random Sequences and Processes*, New York: Springer Verlag, 1983.

Longin, F.M., ''The Asymptotic Distribution of Extreme Stock Market Returns,'' *Journal of Business* 69 (1996), 383–408.

Ma, C., R.P. Rao, and R.S. Sears, ''Limit Moves and Price Resolution: The Case of the Treasury Bond Futures Market,'' *Journal of Futures Markets* 9, no. 4 (1989a), 321–335.

Ma, C., R.P. Rao, and R.S. Sears, ''Volatility, Price Resolution, and Effectiveness of Price Limits,'' *Journal of Financial Services Research* 3 (1989a), 165–199.

Macleod, A.J., ''Comment on 'Maximim-Likelihood Estimation of the Parameters of the Generalized Extreme-Value Distribution','' *Applied Statistics* 38 (1989), 198–199.

Mandelbrot, B., ''The Variation of Certain Speculative Prices,'' *Journal of Business* 36 (1963), 394–419.

Maritz, J.S., and A.H. Munro, ''On the Use of the Generalized Extreme-Value Distribution in Estimating Extreme Percentiles,'' *Biometrics* 23 (1967), 79–103.

McGeehan, P., ''Other Changes in Circuit Breakers are Likely,'' *Wall Street Journal* (July 22, 1996a), C1.

McGeehan, P., ''Big Board Raises 'Circuit Breaker' to 350 Points,'' *Wall Street Journal* (December 6, 1996b), C1.

Presidential Task Force on Market Mechanisms, *Report of the Presidential Task Force on Market Mechanisms*, Washington, D.C.: U.S. Superintendent of Documents, January 1988.

Roll, R., ''The International Crash of October 1987,'' *Financial Analysts Journal* (September–October 1988), 19–35.

Ross, S., ''Keynote Address, Conference and Annual Membership Meeting, International Association of Financial Engineers, New York, 1996.

Santoni, G.J., and T. Liu, ''Circuit Breakers and Stock Market Volatility,'' *Journal of Futures Markets* 13, no. 3 (1993), 261–277.

Subrahmanyam, A., ''Circuit Breakers and Market Volatility: A Theoretical Perspective,'' *Journal of Finance* 49, no. 1 (1994), 237–254.

Weatherford, R., *Philosophical Foundations of Probability Theory*, London: Routledge and Kegan Paul, 1982.

Working Group on Financial Markets, *Interim Report of the Working Group on Financial Markets*. Washington, DC: May 1988.

Journal of Financial Services Research 13:3 205–229 (1998)

Dealer Markets Under Stress: The Performance of NASDAQ Market Makers During the November 15, 1991, Market Break

WILLIAM GARY CHRISTIE
Owen Graduate School of Management, Vanderbilt University, Nashville, TN

PAUL HARVEY SCHULTZ
College of Business Administration, University of Notre Dame, IN

Abstract

The liquidity of the NASDAQ market was seriously undermined during the crash on October 19, 1987, when bid-ask spreads widened dramatically and dealers reputedly withdrew from market making. This paper studies the liquidity of 36 NASDAQ issues on November 15, 1991, when average prices fell over 4%, representing the first major correction in the post-crash era. We find that bid-ask spreads, the percentage of dealers posting inside quotes, and trading volume remained virtually unaffected. Effective spreads were also largely unaffected, except for trades in excess of 1,000 shares among issues whose market makers avoided odd-eighth quotes. Our evidence implies that, unlike October 1987, the liquidity of the NASDAQ market did not deteriorate appreciably during this episode of unusual market stress.

October 19, 1997, marked the 10-year anniversary of the crash of 1987, when the prices of U.S. and international stocks fell over 20% in one trading session.[1] During the crash, many investors experienced delays in the execution of orders, and the reporting infrastructure could not keep pace with the trading volume. The apparent inability of the world markets to cope with such extraordinary volume and price volatility resulted in the adoption of numerous institutional changes, including circuit breakers and restrictions on program trading, intended to enhance the liquidity of financial markets when faced with unusual price pressures.

The NASDAQ market received especially strong criticism for its performance during the 1987 crash. For example, the Brady Commission report stated "For many investors, both large and small, the over-the-counter market broke down when it failed to perform its function of providing liquidity for buyers and sellers, and many customers and dealer orders did not get promptly executed if they were executed at all" (*Report of the Presidential Task Force on Market Mechanisms*, 1988, p. VI-49). The reported lack of liquidity among NASDAQ market makers led the National Association of Securities Dealers (NASD) to implement regulatory changes designed to ensure the integrity of the market during periods of market stress.

This paper studies whether market reforms adopted subsequent to the crash helped to avert similar declines in liquidity when the market faced unusual periods of market stress. The second largest one-day percentage decline in U.S. financial markets between 1974 and

1995, excluding October 1987, occurred on Friday, November 15, 1991, when the NASDAQ value-weighted index declined 4.38%. An important feature of this market break was that the decline was concentrated in the final hour of trading, heightening concerns over the direction of the market the following Monday. The presence of a large nontrading interval provides an additional opportunity to explore the liquidity of the market when uncertainty over equilibrium prices is particularly high.

Our empirical analysis examines the liquidity of the NASDAQ market using individual-dealer bid and ask quotes and trades for a sample of 36 NASDAQ issues. In contrast to the performance of the NASDAQ market during the severe market break in 1987, we find that inside spreads, individual-dealer spreads, the number of dealers at the inside market, and the size and number of trades were not materially affected by the extraordinary price declines.

To confirm our inferences, we pursue three forms of sensitivity analysis. First, we expand our sample by examining the intraday pattern of inside bid-ask spreads for the broader set of 100 large and actively traded NASDAQ issues studied by Christie and Schultz (1994). Second, we compare the liquidity of our expanded NASDAQ sample with that of the 100 comparable New York Stock Exchange (NYSE) and the American Stock Exchange (AMEX) stocks used by Christie and Schultz (1994). We find that, for the broader sample of NASDAQ stocks, bid-ask spreads did not widen significantly, independent of the propensity of market makers to use or avoid odd-eighth quotes. Therefore, in contrast to October 1987, the width of NASDAQ spreads did not appear to have been compromised during high levels of price uncertainty. In contrast, the Amex and NYSE issues *did* experience a significant widening of spreads, particularly during the final 30 minutes of trading. Finally, we compute effective spreads, which use the location of trade prices relative to the inside spread, for the sample of 100 NASDAQ stocks on November 15, 1991, and compare these estimates to those obtained during the preceding 22 trading days. Our analysis shows that, for most investors, the price pressure did not materially affect effective spreads on November 15. We did, however, observe a modest increase in effective spreads for trades in excess of 1,000 shares among stocks whose dealers avoid odd-eighth quotes, implying that the ability to obtain price improvement within the inside spread declined slightly.

These results are open to a number of alternative explanations. The improved performance of participants in the NASDAQ market might be tied to the affirmative obligations faced by market makers, who were required to continue participating in the market or face significant costs of withdrawal. An alternative explanation is that the more restrictive rules imposed on market makers following the crash of 1987 led to a widening of spreads as a defense mechanism against unanticipated market movements that the dealers could no longer escape. Consistent with this hypothesis, Huang and Stoll (1996) report that quoted spreads increased from approximately $0.30 per share in 1989 to between $0.40 and $0.45 by 1992. Under this hypothesis, the price decline in November 1991 might not have been sufficiently severe to require a further widening of spreads. However, market makers would have had to anticipate severe losses during periods of market stress to warrant such large increases in spreads tied to affirmative obligations that arose after the crash of 1987. An additional hypothesis is that NASDAQ spreads were not determined competitively and the competitive level of spreads did not widen sufficiently to reach the posted quotes. Whatever the explanation, our results consistently indicate that, during an episode of abnormal price pressure, the performance of the NASDAQ market was much improved over predictions that might emerge based on inferences drawn from October 1987.

The remainder of the paper is organized as follows. Section 1 describes the performance of the NASDAQ market during the crash in 1987 and summarizes the ensuing market reforms. Section 2 describes the price pressure that emerged during trading on November 15, 1991. Section 3 characterizes our data; while section 4 contains the quote, trade, and market maker participation results for our sample of 36 issues. Section 5 examines the intraday bid-ask spreads for a broader sample of 100 NASDAQ stocks and a matched sample of 100 NYSE/AMEX securities. Section 6 estimates the impact of market stress on effective spreads. Section 7 summarizes our findings.

1. Liquidity among NASDAQ issues during the crash of October 1987

The general consensus during the 1987 crash was that the NASDAQ market failed to provide liquidity to investors. The report of the U.S. Securities and Exchange Commissions (Section 9-2) concludes that

> These problems—unreliable quotations, delayed transaction reports, reduced market maker participation, and increased manual handling of orders coupled with greater telephone inquiries—all combined to reduce dramatically the liquidity and orderliness of the OTC market during the October market break.

The total volume in the OTC market fell to less than 40% of the order flow for listed stocks on October 19. Prior to the week of the market break, this ratio consistently reached 80%. This dramatic retreat in NASDAQ volume relative to listed stocks was attributed to an array of factors: withdrawal of market makers, abandonment of the small order execution system, market makers executing only small orders, and market makers increasing the inside spread.

Withdrawal of market makers

Unlike the NYSE or the AMEX specialists, NASDAQ market makers do not have an exclusive franchise to make a market in a particular stock nor an affirmative obligation to maintain an orderly market. In 1987, market makers could withdraw from the market at any time, for any reason, and be subject to only a two-day penalty before they could again act as a market maker in that issue. Therefore, during periods of stress, NASDAQ dealers could cease making markets at little professional cost. In light of the potentially large benefits from removing their exposure to a volatile market, it is not surprising that the total number of dealers declined during the period of greatest price pressure. The Brady report estimates that, on average, the number of market makers for large securities declined by 6.8% and the number of dealers in the smaller stocks fell by 16%. Some of the dealers who continued to make markets did so in name only. Numerous reports found that dealers failed to answer their telephones or refused to trade. The NASD deemed that the overall performance of their market makers warranted stiffer penalties for the voluntary withdrawal of market making services. Therefore, the NASD Board of Governors recommended that firms who "voluntarily withdraw as a market maker in an issue will be prohibited from re-entering quotations in that security for 20 business days."[2]

Abandonment of the Small Order Execution System

The automated execution of orders for 1,000 shares or fewer was accomplished through the small order execution system (SOES). Orders entered into SOES were executed against either the best bid or offer. The dealer on the opposite side of the trade was selected from all dealers posting quotes at the inside bid or asks using a rotational algorithm. Alternatively, an order may be "preferenced" to a specific dealer, who agreed to execute the order at the inside market, independent of the dealer's current quotes. The Division of Market Regulation at the SEC indicated that approximately 40% of the SOES volume was preferenced.

In 1987, participation in the SOES network was voluntary. Dealers could withdraw from SOES without cause or notice and then resume SOES activity with no mandatory waiting period. So, the easiest avenue for dealers to reduce their exposure during the market break was to withdraw from SOES. As the Brady Commission report indicates, this factor was not lost on the market makers:

> Prior to October 19, 46 of the 50 top market makers were active SOES participants in at least some securities. During the week of October 19, many of them dropped out of SOES entirely. On the 19th, four of these 46 firms did not participate in any SOES trades as a market maker. On the 20th, the number of such firms leaped to 18.

The lack of SOES trading implied that trades that would be executed automatically now required negotiation among dealers, exacerbating the backlog of unfilled orders.

An additional feature of SOES allowed dealers to bypass SOES during the market break. SOES was designed to protect market makers from losses arising from quotes that did not reflect the current market by automatically shutting down SOES when the new quote would result in a locked or crossed quote. According to the Brady Commission report (p. VI-55), dealers "put quotes into the system with the intent of deliberately closing down trading in those stocks." The shutdown of SOES system left traders with little alternative except to execute trades through phone contact.

The NASD, in its recommendations to reform the NASDAQ market, made participation in SOES mandatory for all market makers in NASDAQ/National Market System (NMS) stocks. In addition, the NASD mandated that the SOES market must continue to operate when an inside quotation became locked or crossed.[3] The continuous operation of SOES, coupled with the mandatory participation requirement, would be expected to improve liquidity during periods of market stress.[4]

Only small orders executed by market makers

While a portion of the decline in NASDAQ volume relative to that on the NYSE can be attributed to a reduction in the number of market makers, a more relevant factor was the decay in market depth. As the Brady Commission report wrote (p. VI-51),

> It has been widely reported that during the market break, many market makers fulfilled only their minimum obligation, refusing to buy or sell any more than 100 shares at their quotes, while other firms which would normally trade thousands of shares with their better institutional customers at their quotes were only willing to trade hundreds of shares.

Thus, the market break witnessed a dramatic decline in the average trade size. This practice aggravated the already overloaded phone networks, since trades that normally would be executed in one transaction were divided among a number of dealers, each requiring a phone contact.

Increase in the inside spread

The increased price uncertainty and the withdrawal of market makers resulted in an increase in the inside bid-ask spread for NASDAQ/NMS stocks. The SEC report (pp. 23–24) indicated that

> During the week immediately preceding the market break, the average inside spread increased 20.2% to 60.1 cents per share. From Monday to Wednesday of the market break week, that average increased an additional 13.5% to 68.2 cents per share. Thus in total the average inside spread in NASDAQ securities increased by 36.4% from September to October.

These four factors all contributed to the illiquidity of the NASDAQ market during October 1987. The proposed changes implemented by the NASD were intended to alleviate these problems when the market again faced abnormally high levels of price uncertainty, volatility, and volume.

2. Description of the market break on November 15, 1991

On November 15, 1991, the DJIA fell 120.31 points (3.93%) for its fifth largest point decline in the history of the index. The Standard and Poor's 500 also declined by 3.66%. The average price declines on NASDAQ were even sharper. As shown in table 1, the decline in the Center for Research in Security Prices (CRSP) NASDAQ value-weighted index on November 15, 1991, was −4.38%, making it the ninth largest price change in either direction in the 5,057 trading days between December 15, 1974, and December 31, 1991. When the month of October 1987 is excluded, November 15, 1991, had the second

Table 1. The 10 largest one-day returns in absolute value for the CRSP NASDAQ value-weighted portfolio during the 4,810 trading days between December 15, 1972 and December 31, 1991

Rank	Date	CRSP NASDAQ value-weighted index return
1	10/19/1987	– 11.37%
2	10/26/1987	– 8.95%
3	10/20/1987	– 8.78%
4	10/21/1987	7.42%
5	3/27/1980	– 5.88%
6	10/29/1987	5.44%
7	10/30/1987	5.34%
8	10/22/1987	– 4.44%
9	*11/15/1991*	*– 4.38%*
10	8/06/1990	– 4.17%

largest price change in the 20-year period. Clearly, this was a day of unusual stress for NASDAQ market makers. On November 18, 1991, the *Wall Street Journal* characterized trade in the afternoon of November 15 as "panic selling." The OTC FOCUS column quoted Amy Foster, who traded approximately 25 biotech stocks, as saying "It was fairly much of a nightmare. I can't imagine anything worse."

As in October 1987, the source of the price decline was elusive. One possible explanation attributed the price declines to statements made by President Bush concerning the continued high level of credit-card interest rates despite significant declines in short-term rates. On Wednesday, November 13, President Bush urged banks to reduce their credit-card interest rates to help stimulate the economy. The following day, as the *Wall Street Journal* reported

> Senator Alfonse D'Amato poured on the gasoline by going to the Senate floor and pushing a measure that would force credit-card interest rates down to 14% from their current average of 18.9%. His surprised fellow senators quickly recognizing the political appeal of the move, voting 74–19 to support him. Not to be outdone, a House subcommittee is scheduled to consider an interest rate cap today with the possibility of passing something this week.

An article that appeared in the *Wall Street Journal* on November 18 stated that the sell-off was precipitated by the previous day's "congressional reaction to the President's spectacularly inane remark about stimulating the economy by having banks shave interest rates on credit card balances."

3. Data

All quote and trade data for Friday, November 15 and Monday, November 18, 1991, were downloaded from the Bridge Quotation System. This real-time quotation service has been used as a source of data by Blume et al. (1989); Schultz and Zaman (1994); Chan, Christie, and Schultz (1995); and Christie, Harris, and Schultz (1994). Trade data consist of volume and prices, but the identity of the dealer executing the trade is unavailable. Quote data consist of every bid and ask from every market maker throughout the day and include the prevailing inside quote. Quotes and trades are time-stamped to the minute.

Firms are selected randomly from stocks that would have resided in the top three size deciles of NYSE/AMEX firms for 1990 as computed by the CRSP. Our sample is restricted to large stocks to alleviate potential biases that result from infrequent quote revisions or trading activity. However, the sample size is limited by the time required to download data from the computer screen to disk. The sample, which is described in table 2, contains 36 stocks, including Apple Computer, Lotus Development, and MCI Communications. The table also provides summary statistics for the mean bid price over the two-day period, the average inside spread, and the average number of dealers at the inside market. The average prices range from a low of \$0.75 for Alta Gold, to a high of \$56.50 for Roadway Services. Inside spreads range from \$0.061 for Alta Gold to a high of \$1.375 for Electro Rent. In addition, the average number of market makers posting inside quotes ranged from 3.2 for Environmental Elem. to 18.5 for Apple Computer.

Figure 1 plots the cumulative percentage change in prices at one-minute intervals on November 15, 1991, for our sample of 36 stocks. The figure shows that the major losses are concentrated during three separate periods: 11:30 AM to 12:30 PM (– 0.52%), 1:30 PM to 2:30 PM (– 1.05%), and 3:00 PM to 4:00 PM (– 1.63%). Indeed, the trading interval between 1:30 PM and the close results in a cumulative price decline of 2.5%. Therefore, the selling pressure is concentrated during the two and one-half hours prior to the close of trading. In addition, the average price decline of 4% mimics the overall NASDAQ market, which fell 4.38%. For comparison purposes, figure 2 plots the cumulative average percentage price changes for our sample on Monday, November 18. Figure 2 highlights the absence of any significant price movements after the nontrading interval, despite the rapid decline in prices during the final minutes of trading on November 15.

4. Results using data at the dealer level

Unlike other sources of intraday data, the Bridge Quotation System provides both individual dealer quotes and the prevailing inside quotes. Indeed, one of the unique features of our analysis is the examination of the behavior of individual dealers and not just those electing to post inside quotes. Our study of the relation between the inside spread and the dispersion of individual dealer quotes is similar to that of Chan et al. (1995), who study the intraday pattern of bid-ask spreads for NASDAQ issues. We compute inside spreads and average dealer spreads nearest the end of each one-minute interval. The average spread across all dealers measures the distance between the average bid and ask prices.

In light of the reported sources of illiquidity among NASDAQ dealers during the October 1987 market break, our empirical analysis focuses on the following four hypotheses:

Table 2. Identity and summary statistics for the 36 NASDAQ firms in the November 15, 1991 sample

Ticker symbol	Firm	Mean inside bid price	Mean inside spread	Mean number of dealers at the inside
AAPL	Apple Computer	$51.84	$0.31	18.5
ALDC	Aldus Corp.	$37.37	$0.43	6.6
ALFA	Alfa Corp.	$11.14	$0.50	6.6
ALGR	Allied Group	$19.20	$0.92	6.5
ALTA	Alta Gold	$0.75	$0.06	7.7
ANDW	Andrew Corp.	$32.73	$0.66	6.7
APOG	Apogee Enterprises	$12.71	$0.75	16.0
BIGB	BigB Corp.	$12.03	$0.25	6.3
BMET	Biomet	$42.62	$0.37	14.3
BRAN	Brand Companies	$16.63	$0.38	5.5
CDMS	Cadmus	$6.00	$0.65	7.0
CHRS	Charming Shoppes	$21.92	$0.20	10.8
DHTK	DH Technology	$11.14	$0.47	11.0
ELPA	El Paso Electric	$4.08	$0.20	13.0
ELRC	Electro Rent	$19.25	$1.38	4.5
ERTS	Electronic Arts	$32.24	$0.25	5.7
FSCO	First Security Corp.	$26.84	$0.46	7.9
GARN	Garnet Resources	$13.75	$0.75	4.0
LOTS	Lotus	$15.07	$0.27	5.0
MCIC	MCI Communications	$27.36	$0.17	11.8
MNPI	Microcom	$12.85	$0.41	8.2
MOLX	Molex	$30.12	$0.49	9.2
MTWN	Mark Twain Banks	$22.81	$0.58	5.9
NELL	Nellcor	$27.85	$0.23	7.8
NLCO	Environmental Elem.	$14.99	$0.48	3.2
RESC	Roanoke Electric St	$6.93	$0.43	3.8
RIGS	Riggs National	$5.32	$0.13	4.5
ROAD	Roadway Services	$56.50	$0.40	10.0
SMCR	Summcorp	$25.95	$0.61	7.9
SONO	Sonoco	$33.22	$0.48	8.4
SPCO	Software Publishing	$14.38	$0.40	10.8
SSAX	Systems Software	$24.43	$0.62	11.3
SWIS	St. Ives	$8.26	$0.31	6.6
TRUK	Builder's Transport	$6.12	$0.31	6.5
WTHG	Worthington Inds.	$21.44	$0.30	9.4
YELL	Yellow Freight	$29.67	$0.24	5.6

Note: The firms were selected randomly from issues that would have qualified for inclusion among the top three size deciles of NYSE/AMEX firms for 1990 as computed by the Center for Research in Securities Prices. The mean inside bid, inside spread, and number of dealers at the inside are averages computed using the inside quote prevailing at the end of each five-minute interval on both November 15 and 18. The mean number of dealers at the inside includes the number at the inside bid or at the inside ask.

1. To avoid trading during periods of market stress, individual dealers will move their bid and ask quotes away from the inside market. The simultaneous withdrawal of quotes from the previous inside bid or ask quote will result in a widening of the inside spread.

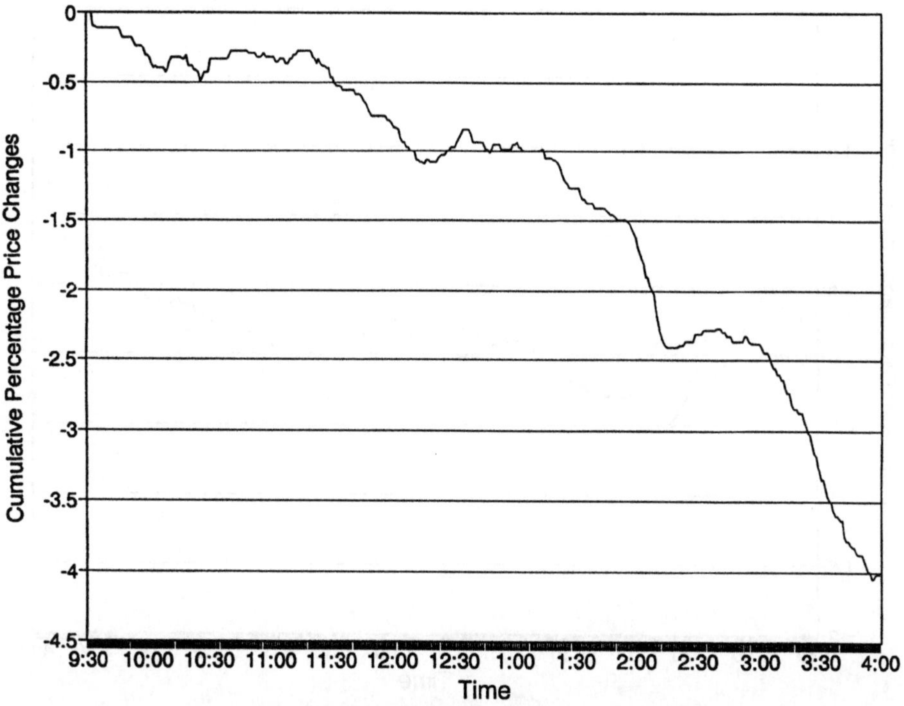

Figure 1. The cumulative intraday average percentage price changes for a sample of 36 NASDAQ issues on Friday, November 15, 1991. The firms were selected randomly from stocks that would have resided in the top three size deciles of NYSE/AMEX firms for 1990.

2. While market makers can withdraw from the inside and maintain a constant dealer spread, the increased risks inherent in posting inside quotes in a "fast market" may force dealers to increase the width of their quotes to compensate for the increased price uncertainty. Therefore, we would expect to observe an increase in the average dealer spread.
3. The withdrawal of dealers from the inside also would be reflected in a decline in the number of dealers posting inside quotes. Thus, the depth of the inside market, as measured by the number of dealers posting inside quotes, might decline in the presence of extreme price volatility. In addition, the lack of a "downtick" rule for NASDAQ market makers might induce dealers who are willing to trade to be concentrated at the inside ask rather than at the inside bid.
4. The crash of October 1987 indicated that some dealers were unwilling to answer their phones or withdrew from making markets. If these patterns persisted on November 15, 1991, the number of trades would be expected to deteriorate significantly.

This section reports the empirical results for the intraday patterns for inside spreads, average dealer spreads, the number of dealers posting inside quotes, and the number of

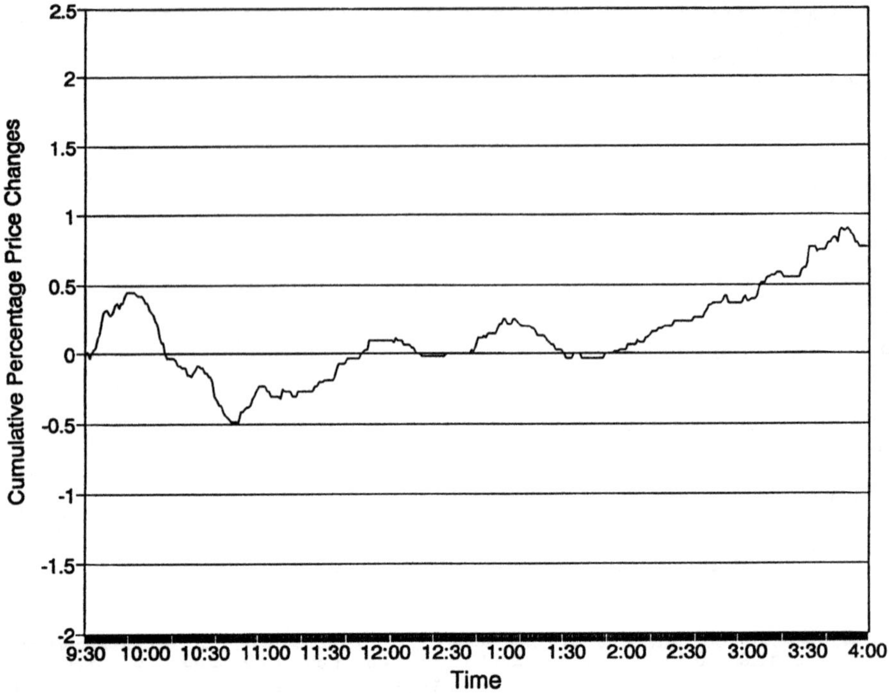

Figure 2. The cumulative intraday average percentage price changes for a sample of 36 NASDAQ issues on Monday, November 18, 1991. The firms were selected randomly from stocks that would have resided in the top three size deciles of NYSE/AMEX firms for 1990.

trades. For comparison, we also include the intraday patterns for these variables on the subsequent trading day. The addition of the trading day following the period of market stress increases our ability to draw inferences from the results, since Figure 2 confirms that this trading day was relatively calm with regard to price pressure.

Average inside and average dealer spreads

The pattern of intraday average inside spreads for the sample of 36 NASDAQ stocks for November 15 and 18, 1991, is provided in figure 3. The series is computed by averaging the inside spread for the 36 stocks at the end of each one-minute interval. In interpreting the results, recall that the periods of market stress on November 15 is concentrated between 11:30 AM and 12:30 PM, 1:30 PM and 2:30 PM, and most notably between 3:00 PM and the close of trading.

Figure 3 shows that the average inside spread *declines* during the day, particularly during the intervals associated with the most severe price declines. For example, the average inside spread fluctuates between \$0.44 and \$0.48 between the open and approximately 1:00 PM. The inside spread then narrows sharply, moving between \$0.40

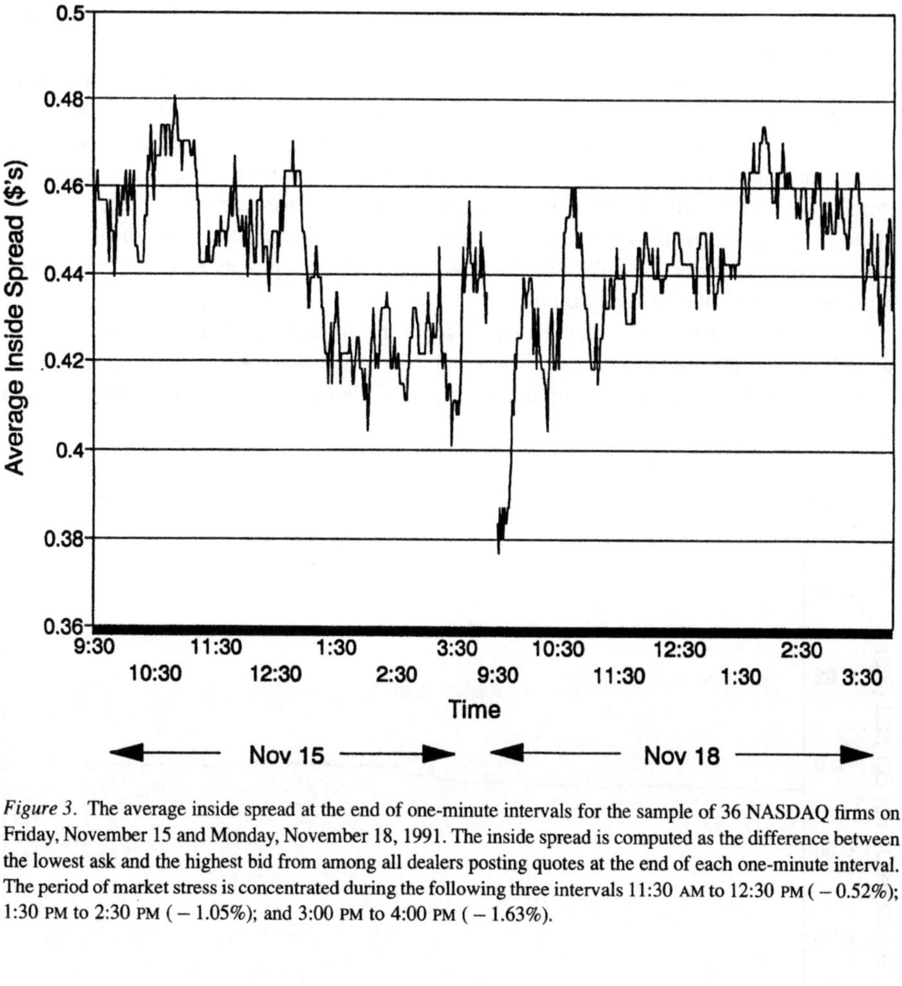

Figure 3. The average inside spread at the end of one-minute intervals for the sample of 36 NASDAQ firms on Friday, November 15 and Monday, November 18, 1991. The inside spread is computed as the difference between the lowest ask and the highest bid from among all dealers posting quotes at the end of each one-minute interval. The period of market stress is concentrated during the following three intervals 11:30 AM to 12:30 PM (− 0.52%); 1:30 PM to 2:30 PM (− 1.05%); and 3:00 PM to 4:00 PM (− 1.63%).

and \$0.44 for the remainder of the afternoon, with some values exceeding \$0.44 in the final half-hour of trading. These patterns contradict the hypothesis that NASDAQ market makers responded to this extraordinary price decline by widening the inside spread.

Additional evidence on the liquidity that was available in the NASDAQ market after the November 15 break is obtained by examining the average inside spread at the onset of trading on November 18. Since the steepest decline in average prices occurred immediately prior to the close of trading on the Friday, there was a heightened degree of uncertainty concerning the direction that prices would follow after the open on Monday. This increased price uncertainty could lead to a widening of inside spreads. However, figure 3 indicates that the average inside spread near the opening on November 18 actually is narrower than at the close of trading on the preceding Friday. Indeed, the average inside spread near the opening on November 18 is the narrowest of any trading interval observed during the two-day period. Therefore, NASDAQ market makers did not pursue a strategy of increasing trading costs near the open on November 18 despite the apparent increase in price uncertainty.

Although figure 3 indicates that the average inside spread did not widen, the figure does not address whether individual dealers moved away from the inside market by widening their bid-ask spreads. In 1991, market makers had some latitude in quoting unusually wide spreads during periods of heightened price uncertainty. At the time of the crash, the excess spread rule required that individual dealers post quotes that were no greater than 200% of the average spread of the three market makers with the narrowest spread.[5] Thus, market makers were afforded considerable latitude to exercise their option to minimize their exposure to unwanted trading activity.

We study this issue in figure 4, which plots the intraday pattern of average dealer spreads. The scale used in figure 4 is identical to that of the average inside spread used in figure 3. The hypothesis that individual dealers widened their spreads to reduce their

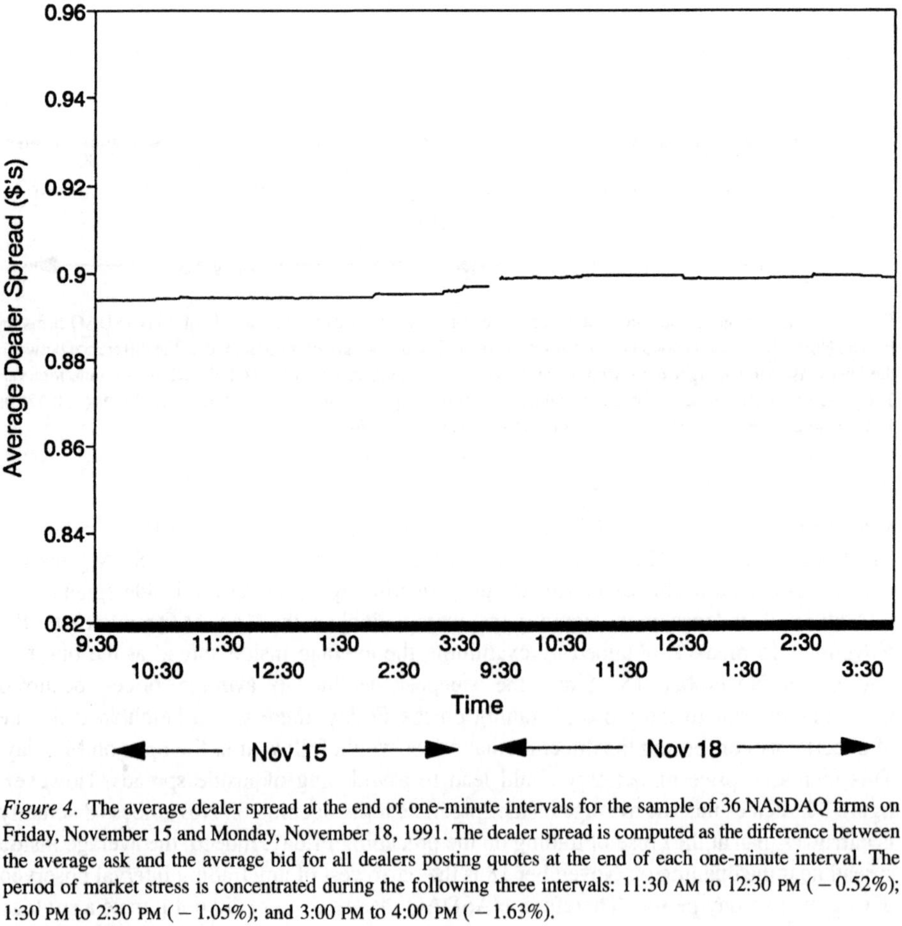

Figure 4. The average dealer spread at the end of one-minute intervals for the sample of 36 NASDAQ firms on Friday, November 15 and Monday, November 18, 1991. The dealer spread is computed as the difference between the average ask and the average bid for all dealers posting quotes at the end of each one-minute interval. The period of market stress is concentrated during the following three intervals: 11:30 AM to 12:30 PM (– 0.52%); 1:30 PM to 2:30 PM (– 1.05%); and 3:00 PM to 4:00 PM (– 1.63%).

potential exposure to trades implies that the average dealer spread would widen during the afternoon trading hours. However, figure 4 shows that the variation in the average dealer spread is trivial relative to the variation in the inside spread, ranging between $0.894 to $0.8995, or approximately one-half of one cent per share. In essence, the average dealer spread across all dealers remains virtually unchanged during this period. This result reinforces the conclusion that NASDAQ market makers continued to provide liquidity despite the increased risks inherent during the market break and the price uncertainty present at the onset of trading on November 18. These results are important both from an economic and public policy perspective, since they suggest that the changes to the NASDAQ market appear to have enhanced the liquidity of that market when unusual price uncertainty arises.

The number of dealers posting inside quotes

Although the previous section provides evidence that inside spreads were not materially affected by the rapid erosion of prices, the number of dealers willing to trade at these quotes may have diminished. This section explores whether there was an appreciable decline in the number of dealers posting inside quotes during the period of market stress.

Figure 5 presents the intraday pattern of the average number of dealers at the inside bid or the inside ask at the end of each one-minute interval. The figure shows that the average number of market makers at the inside fluctuates between 8.5 and 10.5 from the opening on November 15 through approximately 1:00 PM. The period of greatest market stress, which occurs after 1:30 PM, is met with a reduction in the average number of dealers posting inside quotes. The average number of dealers at the inside varies between 7 and 9.5 for the remaining trading intervals on November 15. So, figure 5 suggests that, on average, one market maker ceased posting inside quotes during the afternoon. This evidence does not support the conclusion that market makers abandoned the inside market when price uncertainty reached unusually high levels.

The number of dealers posting inside quotes on November 18 further supports this conclusion. Recall that the period surrounding the Monday opening was characterized by heightened uncertainty concerning the direction of prices. Figure 5 shows that the average number of dealers posting inside quotes near the opening on November 18 was 1.5 dealers lower than that observed at the close on November 15. Thus, the figure provides some evidence that dealers avoided posting inside quotes during the opening minutes of trading on November 18. However, the figure also reveals that the number of dealers at the inside bid or inside ask varies between 7.5 and 9.5 throughout November 18, which was tranquil in comparison with the preceding day. Therefore, the variation in the number of dealers at the inside market near the close of trading on Friday, November 15 is consistent with the levels observed on a more typical trading day and may simply reflect random variation.

Additional evidence on the possible source of the decline in the number of dealers posting inside quotes is obtained by separating the dealers at the inside into those that post bid or ask prices. In light of the severe decline in average prices, individual dealers may have been reluctant to post inside bid prices, thus removing themselves from the additional uncertainty of purchasing securities while prices were tumbling. Therefore, we might

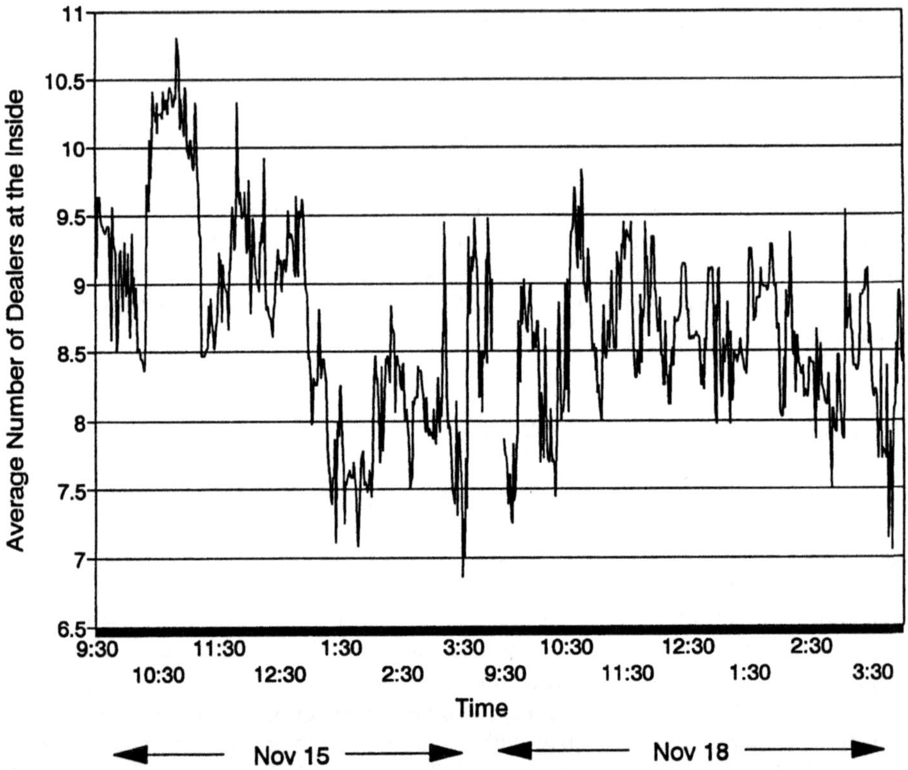

Figure 5. The average number of dealers posting inside quotes for the sample of 36 NASDAQ firms on Friday, November 15 and Monday, November 18, 1991. The figures are computed at the end of each one-minute interval and include both the number of dealers posting quotes at the inside bid and the number of dealers posting quotes at the inside ask. The period of market stress is concentrated during the following three intervals: 11:30 AM to 12:30 PM (– 0.52%); 1:30 PM to 2:30 PM (– 1.05%); and 3:00 PM to 4:00 PM (– 1.63%).

expect the number of dealers posting inside ask quotes to exceed inside bid quotes. Figure 6 provides direct evidence on this issue by reporting the intraday pattern in the ratio of the number of dealers posting inside bid quotes to the number posting inside ask quotes. A ratio of less than 1 indicates that a larger number of dealers were attempting to sell rather than purchase shares. The evidence in figure 6 indicates that this ratio is centered around 1.0 throughout November 15. While the ratio falls below 1.0 during the majority of the afternoon hours, values under 1.0 are not confined just to this interval. Indeed, the ratio lies below 1.0 during the first hour of trading, yet prices had fallen only slightly. In addition, the ratio exceeds 1.0 for much of the final 30 minutes of trading even though this period coincides with the steepest decline in average prices. Overall, the evidence in figure 6 indicates that dealers were positioned almost equally at the inside bid or ask during the period of market stress. This result further supports the hypothesis that the reduction in the average number of dealers at the inside can be attributed to random variation.

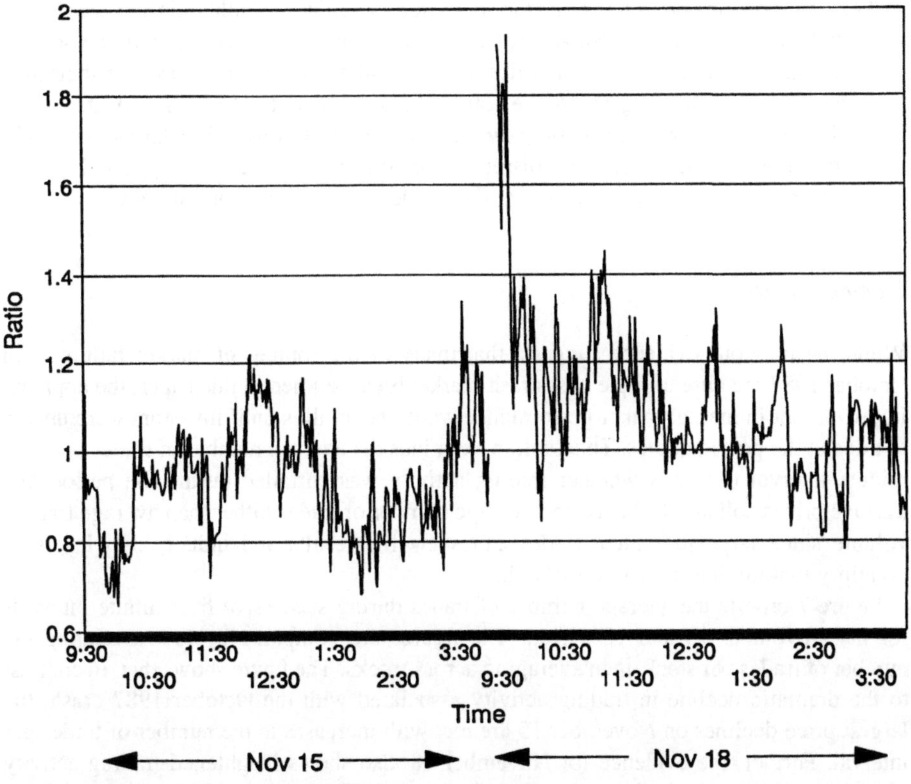

Figure 6. The ratio of the number of dealers at the inside bid divided by the number of dealers at the inside ask for the sample of 36 NASDAQ firms on Friday, November 15 and Monday, November 18, 1991. The figures are computed at the end of each one-minute interval. A ratio of less (greater) than 1.0 indicates that there are more dealers willing to sell (purchase) shares than purchase (sell) shares at the inside market. The period of market stress is concentrated during the following three intervals: 11:30 AM to 12:30 PM (– 0.52%); 1:30 PM to 2:30 PM (– 1.05%); and 3:00 PM to 4:00 PM (– 1.63%).

The most striking result in figure 6 is the intraday pattern near the opening of trading on November 18. Figure 5 indicates that near the opening, the average number of dealers at the inside bid or ask is lower by approximately 1.5 relative to the close on November 15. However, figure 6 shows that the number of dealers posting inside bids is almost twice as large as the number of dealers posting inside asks. Therefore, the opening of trading on November 18 was characterized by a disproportionate number of dealers seeking to purchase rather than sell shares. This ratio quickly returns to levels that are similar to those observed on November 15 within the first 30 minutes of trading.

The continued participation of market makers at the inside quotes throughout November 15 is insightful in light of the alleged activity of day traders (SOES activists or bandits) or who use the SOES system to take advantage of dealers who are slow to update their quotes. Day trading was very active in 1991, and we might expect a reduced willingness of market makers to post inside quotes in the presence of SOES bandits during large and unpredictable price declines. However, we observe no serious deterioration in the number of market makers at the inside quotes, despite the rapid movement in prices over short time intervals. These results suggest that the potential trading activity of SOES activists did not dissuade market makers from participating in the market. In this light, claims that SOES activists were a major source of disruption in the market are not supported by the continued presence of market makers at the inside quotes throughout the day.

Trading activity

While the previous evidence suggests that many of the sources of market failure from October 1987 are absent in the post-crash market break studied in this paper, the apparent improvement in market maker performance would be an illusion if investors were unable to trade at the posted quotes. This section examines the average number of trades per five-minute interval to assess whether trading activity was curtailed during the period that average prices collapsed. We use the average number of trades rather than average trading volume since large individual trades can skew the results and induce high levels of volatility making interpretation difficult.

Figure 7 reports the average number of trades during successive five-minute intervals for the November 15 and 18 period. The figures are computed by first averaging the number of trades per stock, then averaging across stocks. The figure shows that, in contrast to the dramatic decline in trading activity associated with the October 1987 crash, the largest price declines on November 15 are met with increases in the number of trades per interval. Further, the evidence for November 18 also shows heightened trading activity after the opening, when price uncertainty is elevated. Therefore, we find no evidence that market makers were unwilling (or unable) to complete transactions at the quoted prices.

5. Results based on a broader sample of NASDAQ stocks

The previous section demonstrates that the liquidity of the NASDAQ market was not harmed by a 4% decline in securities values. One potential criticism of these findings is that our sample is confined to 36 securities. To address this issue, we studied the intraday patterns for inside spreads for a larger sample of NASDAQ stocks. Specifically, we use the sample of 100 active NASDAQ stocks compiled by Christie and Schultz (1994), in which they identify a scarcity of odd-eighth quotes for 70 of these issues. Their sample selection criteria identified the 50 largest NASDAQ stocks measured at the end of 1991 and also included a random sample of 50 NASDAQ issues whose market capitalization exceeded $100 million. If the absence of wider spreads on November 15, 1991, arises from our small sample size, the study of 100 large, active NASDAQ issues might detect the expected widening of spreads.

The first issue that we explore in the context of our wider sample is whether the incidence of locked or crossed quotes rose on November 15. While not directly testable, the absence of an increase in spreads might be due to trading systems that were upgraded

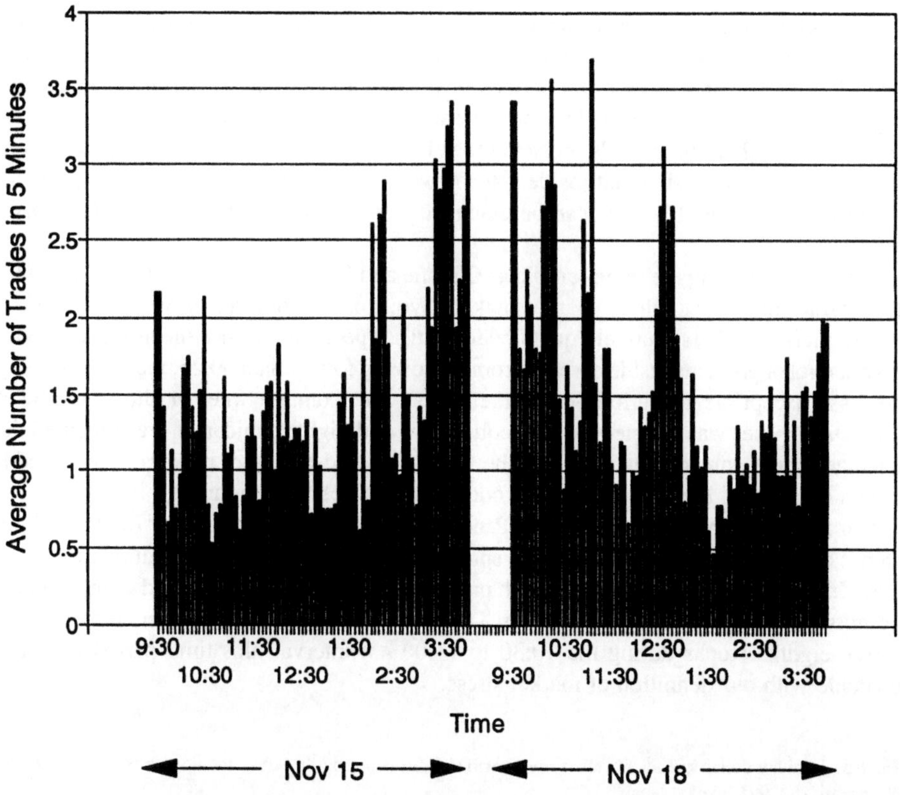

Figure 7. The average number of trades per stock during each five minute interval for the sample of 36 NASDAQ firms on Friday, November 15 and Monday, November 18, 1991. The figures are computed first for each stock within each five minute interval, and then averaged across stocks. The period of market stress is concentrated during the following three intervals: 11:30 AM to 12:30 PM (−0.52%); 1:30 PM to 2:30 PM (−1.05%); and 3:00 PM to 4:00 PM (−1.63%).

following the 1987 crash. One characteristic of such improvements would be the lack of locked (inside ask = inside bid) or crossed (inside ask < inside bid) quotes. To test for the presence of nonequilibrium inside spreads, we compare the average frequency of locked or crossed quotes on November 15 relative to the average computed during the preceding month (October 16 through November 14). Our results indicate that the fraction of locked/crossed quotes actually *declined* on November 15. Specifically, the average fraction of locked (crossed) quotes fell from 0.62 to 0.48% (0.67 to 0.19%). Therefore, November 15 was not characterized by an increase in the fraction of locked or crossed quotes, indicating that market makers had no difficulty in adjusting their quotes to maintain a positive inside spread.

We partition each trading day into 13 equal 30-minute intervals, beginning with the quotes established after 9:30 AM. We then test for differences in average spreads during these 13 intervals with a comparison period that extends from October 16 through

November 14, 1991. The results are contained in table 3. The average inside spread varies between 38.4 and 42.9 cents per share throughout November 15. However, the widest spreads do not coincide with the periods of greatest market stress, nor are these values significantly different from their control period estimates, excluding the 10:00 to 10:30 time interval when the spreads on November 15 are actually *less* than the control period. Therefore, the conclusion that inside spreads were not adversely impacted by the market stress on November 15, 1991 can be extended to a much broader sample of NASDAQ stocks.

Since we are using the same sample as Christie and Schultz (1994), it may be important to separate the issues whose market makers avoid odd-eighth quotes versus the stocks whose market makers routinely quote odd-eighths. Specifically, since the absence of odd-eighth quotes prevents inside spreads from narrowing to less than $0.25, these stocks may be less susceptible to periods of market stress. To examine whether the liquidity of NASDAQ issues was affected by the frequency of odd-eighth avoidance, we computed the average inside spread separately for the 70 issues whose market makers avoided odd-eighth quotes and the 30 issues where odd-eighth quotes were common.

Our results are presented in table 4. Panel A provides the results for the 70 even-eighth stocks and demonstrates that the inside spread did not significantly widen during the three periods of market stress. Panel B, which presents our findings for the mixed-eighth stocks, permits us to draw a similar conclusion.[6] While average spreads do widen among the 30 mixed-eighths stocks during the 10:30 to 11:00 AM interval, this time period does not coincide with our definition of market stress.

Table 3. Intraday dollar spreads for all sample NASDAQ firms during the stress and nonstress periods for the November 15, 1991, market break

Time interval	10/16/91–11/14/91	11/15/91	*t*-statistic
9:30–10:00 AM	40.3	42.1	1.49
10:00–10:30 AM	40.0	39.3	−2.72
10:30–11:00 AM	39.9	41.7	1.15
11:00–11:30 AM	39.4	38.5	−0.45
11:30–12:00 PM	***40.1***	***38.5***	***−1.22***
12:00–12:30 PM	***40.8***	***40.2***	***−0.42***
12:30–1:00 PM	42.0	38.4	−1.93
1:00–1:30 PM	40.4	39.9	−0.30
1:30–2:00 PM	*40.6*	*40.6*	*0.01*
2:00–2:30 PM	*40.3*	*39.6*	*−0.67*
2:30–3:00 PM	40.6	42.9	1.38
3:00–3:30 PM	*40.0*	*41.7*	*1.54*
3:30–4:00 PM	*39.7*	*41.7*	*1.71*

Note: Dollar spreads are measured in cents per share and averaged using all inside quote revisions during each given time interval. The estimates are obtained using the Christie and Schultz (1994) sample of 100 NASDAQ stocks that are selected from the 50 largest market capitalization stocks and 50 randomly selected stocks whose market capitalization exceeds $100 million. The period of market stress is concentrated during the following three intervals, which are highlighted in the table: 11:30 AM to 12:30 PM (−0.52%); 1:30 PM to 2:30 PM (−1.05%); and 3:00 PM to 4:00 PM (−1.63%). The *t*-statistic tests whether the averages across the two periods are significantly different from one another.

Table 4. Intraday dollar spreads during the nonstress and stress periods for NASDAQ stocks based on the frequency of odd-eighth quotes

Time interval	10/16/91–11/14/91	11/15/91	*t*-statistic
Panel A. Results for the 70 firms whose market makers avoid odd-eighth quotes			
9:30–10:00 AM	45.3	44.2	−0.85
10:00–10:30 AM	44.9	39.7	−3.58
10:30–11:00 AM	44.9	42.2	−1.63
11:00–11:30 AM	45.0	43.2	−0.85
11:30–12:00 PM	*45.3*	*45.0*	*−0.23*
12:00–12:30 PM	*45.3*	*44.6*	*−0.45*
12:30–1:00 PM	47.4	43.3	−1.95
1:00–1:30 PM	45.5	46.6	0.60
1:30–2:00 PM	*45.6*	*45.6*	*0.04*
2:00–2:30 PM	*45.4*	*42.9*	*−2.05*
2:30–3:00 PM	46.0	46.0	0.01
3:00–3:30 PM	*44.4*	*46.0*	*1.28*
3:30–4:00 PM	*44.5*	*45.2*	*0.56*
Panel B. Results for the 30 firms whose market makers routinely used odd-eighths			
9:30–10:00 AM	24.1	26.5	1.31
10:00–10:30 AM	23.8	21.6	−1.35
10:30–11:00 AM	22.8	25.0	6.10
11:00–11:30 AM	22.6	23.7	0.55
11:30–12:00 PM	*23.6*	*25.9*	*1.69*
12:00–12:30 PM	*23.7*	*24.5*	*0.58*
12:30–1:00 PM	23.3	22.0	−0.77
1:00–1:30 PM	23.1	22.5	−1.34
1:30–2:00 PM	*23.8*	*25.3*	*0.82*
2:00–2:30 PM	*23.4*	*23.9*	*0.38*
2:30–3:00 PM	23.4	23.9	0.22
3:00–3:30 PM	*24.3*	*22.7*	*−1.33*
3:30–4:00 PM	*23.4*	*22.6*	*−0.49*

Note: Dollar spreads are measured in cents per share and averaged using all inside quote revisions during each given time interval. The period of market stress is concentrated during the following three intervals, which are highlighted in the table: 11:30 AM to 12:30 PM (−0.52%); 1:30 PM to 2:30 PM (−1.05%); and 3:00 PM to 4:00 PM (−1.63%). The *t*-statistic tests whether the averages across the two periods are significantly different from one another.

This evidence suggests that, among a broad sample of NASDAQ stocks, inside spreads were not adversely affected by the abnormally large decline in average stock prices. In contrast to the market crash in 1987, liquidity in the NASDAQ market was quite resilient to the onset of market stress. Since the greatest difference between 1987 and 1991 was the introduction of NASD rules intended to maintain liquidity in "hot markets," our evidence suggests that these rule changes were successful. Alternatively, market makers simply may have become more proficient at updating their quotes during intense periods of price uncertainty. Indeed, the total number of daily quote revisions for the sample of 100 NASDAQ stocks increased from an average of 1,696 between October 16 and November 14 to 3,113 on November 15. The absence of locked or crossed quotes despite an 83%

increase in the total number of quote revisions indicates that market were better equipped to meet the demands of an exceptionally active market. Finally, the lack of a response in quoted spreads may be due to a general widening of spreads in anticipation of losses during periods of stress arising from the affirmative obligations imposed by the SEC following the crash of 1987 or a lack of competition in quotes. Whatever the source, this paper has confirmed that trading costs, as measured by inside spreads, did not increase during an unusually active trading session characterized by steep price declines.

Evidence of market stress among exchange-listed issues

Our inferences regarding the impact of market stress on quoted spreads hinge on the assumption that markets experienced unusual stress on November 15, 1991. This section uses quoted spreads for listed stocks to gauge whether this assumption is appropriate. Specifically, we examine the intraday spreads for the 100 AMEX/NYSE issues used by Christie and Schultz (1994) in their study of the frequency of odd-eighth quotes. We follow the same empirical procedure of assigning spreads to 13 intervals and test for significant differences in average spreads between November 15, 1991, and the preceding month.

The results for the sample of listed stocks appear in table 5. Consistent with the hypothesis that the abnormal price declines were associated with wider inside spreads, table 5 shows that spreads widened significantly during the two episodes of more intense price declines. During the interval between 1:30 and 2:30 PM, when average prices declined by approximately 1.05%, inside spreads widened from a control period average

Table 5. Intraday dollar spreads for NYSE and AMEX firms during the stress and nonstress periods for the November 15, 1991 market break

Time interval	10/16/91–11/14/91	11/15/91	*t*-statistic
9:30–10:00 AM	27.8	28.2	0.55
10:00–10:30 AM	26.5	26.8	0.38
10:30–11:00 AM	26.1	27.3	1.48
11:00–11:30 AM	25.7	25.8	0.22
11:30–12:00 PM	*25.5*	*26.1*	*0.60*
12:00–12:30 PM	*25.7*	*27.4*	*1.68*
12:30–1:00 PM	25.5	25.1	−0.41
1:00–1:30 PM	25.5	26.0	0.57
1:30–2:00 PM	*25.5*	*26.5*	*1.01*
2:00–2:30 PM	*25.5*	*28.9*	*4.19*
2:30–3:00 PM	25.5	26.1	0.72
3:00–3:30 PM	*25.5*	*27.5*	*2.68*
3:30–4:00 PM	*26.1*	*31.6*	*5.54*

Note: Dollar spreads are measured in cents per share and averaged using all inside quote revisions during each given time interval. The estimates are obtained using the Christie and Schultz (1994) sample of 100 stocks that are matched with the NASDAQ sample using average price and end-of-year market values. The period of market stress is concentrated during the following three intervals, which are highlighted in the table: 11:30 AM to 12:30 PM (−0.52%); 1:30 PM to 2:30 PM (−1.05%); and 3:00 PM to 4:00 PM (−1.63%). The *t*-statistic tests whether the averages across the two periods are significantly different from one another.

of 25.5 cents per share to almost 29 cents per share. Indeed, the t-statistic for the 2:00 to 2:30 interval is 4.19. During the final hour, when prices took their steepest plunge, average inside spreads increased to 27.5 cents between 3:00 and 3:30 and to 31.6 cents during the final 30 minutes of trading. Each of these final intervals exceeded the control period average at the 1% level of statistical significance. This evidence supports our belief that this trading day indeed was unique and that our tests of changes in liquidity among both samples of NASDAQ stocks are conducted during a period of unusual market stress.[7]

6. Effective spreads

This section completes our analysis of trading costs by focusing on the prices actually paid by investors, rather than the quotes displayed to the market. The distinction arises since investors, particularly those trading large blocks, may be able to negotiate prices inside the prevailing quotes. The effective spread for a trade is estimated as

$$\text{Effective spread}_t = \left|\text{Price}_t - \left(\frac{\text{Ask}_t + \text{Bid}_t}{2}\right)\right|$$

where Price_t is the transaction price and Bid_t and Ask_t are the respective inside bid and ask quotes posted at the time of the trade. We compute effective spreads for the expanded sample of 100 NASDAQ stocks from Christie and Schultz (1994) over two intervals: (1) October 16, 1991–November 14, 1991, and (2) November 15, 1991. The first period serves as the nonstress interval and allows us to test whether effective spreads are significantly higher on November 15. We use all trades executed between 9:30 AM and 4:00 PM, and align the trade with the inside quote that prevailed immediately preceding the trade report. Finally, we estimate effective spreads separately for stocks as a function of whether the issue is quoted routinely in even-eighth quotes. The absence of odd-eighth quotes may permit greater latitude for price improvement. If the period of market stress reduces this opportunity to trade inside the posted quotes, we might expect to observe a greater increase in effective spreads among the even-eighth stocks.

Panel A of table 6 reports our estimates of effective spreads across our two sample periods.[8] Across all sample stocks, effective spreads increase from 13.3 to 14.2 cents per share, representing an increase of slightly under 7%. This result provides our first indication that trading costs rose on November 15, 1991, but also shows that the increase was quite modest in light of the degree of price pressure that emerged during the day. The likely source of this increase becomes clearer when the stocks are partitioned based on the frequency of odd-eighth quotes. For those stocks quoted solely in even-eighths, effective spreads rise significantly from 14.8 to 15.4 cents per share. In contrast, effective spreads are unaffected among issues quoted in both even and odd-eighths. Therefore, the benefit of narrower inside spreads among the mixed-eighth stocks also appears to translate into a relative insensitivity of effective spreads to market stress.

The main source of the increase in effective spreads can be attributed to trades in excess of 1,000 shares among stocks quoted exclusively in even-eighths. The effective spreads for these trades increased from 11.5 to 13.2 cents per share, or 14.8%. In comparison, the effective spreads for trades of 1,000 shares or less remained virtually constant at close to

Table 6. The efficiency of trade executions: Effective spreads and price improvement

	10/1/91–11/14/91	11/15/91
Panel A. Average effective spreads (cents per share)		
All Sample Stocks (100)	13.3	14.2*
Even-Eighth Stocks (70)	14.8	15.4*
Trades of 1,000 shares or less	15.8	16.0*
Trades in excess of 1,000 shares	11.5	13.2*
Mixed-Eighth Stocks (30)	8.0	8.1
Trades of 1,000 shares or less	8.5	8.5
Trades in excess of 1,000 shares	7.1	7.3
Panel B. Average proportion of trades within the inside quotes (%)		
All Sample Stocks (100)	23.0	20.0*
Even-Eighth Stocks (70)	24.9	20.8*
Trades of 1,000 shares or less	19.4	16.7*
Trades in excess of 1,000 shares	41.9	34.8*
Mixed-Eighth Stocks (30)	15.8	15.7
Trades of 1,000 shares or less	12.6	12.6
Trades in excess of 1,000 shares	22.2	22.4

Note: Panel A of the table provides the average effective spread for the sample of 100 NASDAQ active stocks used by Christie and Schultz (1994). Effective spreads are computed as

$$\text{Effective spread}_t = \text{Price}_t - \left(\frac{\text{Ask}_t + \text{Bid}_t}{2}\right)$$

where Price_t is the transaction price and Bid_t and Ask_t are the respective inside bid and ask quotes posted at the time of the trade. The estimates are averaged across all trades for all 100 stocks and reported in cents per share. Panel B reports the percentage of trade prices that lie within the inside spread. The data also are partitioned by the frequency of odd-eighth use, where 70 issues are traded by market makers who routinely avoid odd-eighth price fractions in their quotations.

*Indicates that the figure for 11/15/91 is significantly different from the period 10/1/91–11/14/91 at the 1% level.

16 cents per share. The major distinction between these two trade categories was that trades of 1,000 shares or less were eligible for execution through SOES. Trades in excess of 1,000 shares were negotiated between dealers. The evidence in table 6 suggests that the opportunity to negotiate price improvement inside the posted quotes declined on November 15, imposing higher trading costs on investors wishing to trade larger lots.

Panel B of table 6 provides estimates of the proportion of trades that were executed within the inside quotes during the two sample periods and across stocks partitioned by the frequency of odd-eighth quotes. The proportion of trades within the inside spread declined across all stocks from 23 to 20%. However, consistent with the results in panel A, this result was driven by a decline in the fraction of trades inside the quotes among stocks quoted solely in even-eighths, particularly for trades in excess of 1,000 shares. Specifically, the fraction of large trades executed at prices better than the posted quotes declined from 41.9% in the prebreak period to 34.8% on November 15. The pattern that emerges from these results is that, although the posted inside quotes were not materially affected during the episode of market stress on November 15, the ability to trade inside those quotes was eroded, especially for large trades in stocks, where the inside spreads already were relatively wide.

7. Conclusions

One of the most important attributes that a financial market can possess is the ability to provide liquidity during periods of large price fluctuations. A vivid example of strain on financial markets occurred on October 19, 1987. This paper provides empirical evidence on the degree to which NASDAQ market makers provided liquidity during periods of extreme price pressure by focusing on the largest postcrash market break through 1996. The objective is to assess whether the performance of NASDAQ market makers improved in the wake of changes imposed by the NASD in response to the collapse of the NASDAQ market's ability to supply liquidity during the October 1987 crash. Our concern lies with the willingness of market makers to continue posting inside bid and ask prices that are not sharply wider than surrounding periods. We also are interested in whether the depth of the market was eroded through the withdrawal of market makers from the inside market or the widening of individual dealer spreads. Finally, we examine whether trading activity, measured by the average number of trades, declined during the periods of market stress and whether effective spreads rose. We examine these issues using data downloaded from the Bridge Quotation System, which consists of both the inside quotes and all of the individual dealer quotes.

The postcrash market break occurred on November 15, 1991, when the NASDAQ index fell over 4%, reflecting one of the most significant one-day declines in the past 20 years. This trading day provides a unique opportunity to judge whether the NASDAQ market maintained its primary responsibility of providing liquidity to investors.

Our evidence is consistent across issues and across our various measures of performance. NASDAQ market makers did not (1) widen the width of the inside spread, (2) widen individual dealer spreads, (3) relinquish the responsibility for establishing an inside market to a small fraction of dealers, (4) post inside quotes only at the inside ask rather than at the inside bid, or (5) fail to continue trading despite the increased price uncertainty. These results are particularly striking, since inside spreads for listed stocks did significantly widen during the periods of greatest price pressure. The only evidence of a concession in trading costs arose among large trades in stocks whose market makers routinely avoided odd-eighth quotes. Trades in excess of 1,000 shares experienced a significant increase in effective spreads and a corresponding decline in the proportion of trades executed within the relatively wide inside spreads. These results suggest that the opportunity for price improvement deteriorated on November 15 for large negotiated trades that might otherwise have been executed at prices superior to those reflected in the posted quotes. However, taken together with the evidence on posted quotes, the liquidity of NASDAQ issues on November 15, 1991, did not appear to have been seriously compromised, which is noteworthy in light of the criticism leveled on the market in the wake of the crash. As the NASDAQ market continues to evolve through the incorporation of limit orders (see Barclay et al., 1998), we might look forward to greater enhancements to liquidity through the participation of the public and other investors in the price discovery process.

Acknowledgments

The authors are grateful for the helpful comments of George Benston, Gene Finn, Margaret Forster, Larry Harris, Erik Sirri, Hans Stoll, and workshop participants at the Ohio State University, the University of North Carolina at Chapel Hill, the University of Texas at Austin, the 1997 Journal of Financial Intermediation Conference on Liquidity at Washington University, and the 1997 Financial Markets Research Center Conference on Volatility at Vanderbilt University. We also are indebted to Jeff Harris and Christoph Schenzler for their excellent research assistance. Christie acknowledges the financial support of the Dean's Fund for Faculty Research at the Owen Graduate School of Management and the Financial Markets Research Center at Vanderbilt University. Schultz acknowledges the financial support from the Dice Center for Financial Research at the Ohio State University. All remaining errors are ours.

Notes

1. The crash of October 1987 is chronicled in a number of academic and government publications, including Blume, MacKinlay, and Terker (1989); Harris (1989); the Report of the Presidential Task Force on Market Mechanisms (1988); and the Report by the Division of Market Regulation of the U.S. Securities and Exchange Commission (1988).
2. See the *Report of the Special Committee of the Regulatory Review Task Force on the Quality of Markets*, which summarizes the NASD's recommendations to improve the liquidity of markets.
3. The performance of the London Stock Market appeared superior to NASDAQ despite the similarities in their market structures (see Schwartz, 1991). One of the main differences was the presence of a "fast market" indicator for market makers in London. When the "fast market" indicator appeared, posted quotes no longer were considered firm and had to be confirmed prior to a trade execution. Therefore, dealers need not fear locked or crossed quotes, abandon the market, or widen their spread given the increased level of price uncertainty. The absence of affirmative obligations among London dealers represented a marked difference relative to the SEC in their respective approaches to adopting regulations that apply during periods of market stress.
4. The combination of the mandatory participation in SOES and the continuation of SOES trading in the presence of locked or crossed quotes contributed to the cottage industry of "SOES bandits" who exploited cross-sectional discrepancies in individual dealer quotes, particularly when dealers were slow to refresh their posted prices.
5. This rule was amended in 1993 to require that market makers set individual spreads that did not exceed 125% of the average of the three dealers posting the narrowest spreads.
6. The difference in average inside spreads across the samples in panels A and B highlight the impact that avoiding odd-eighth quotes has on this measure of trading costs. The average inside spreads for the even-eighth stocks average approximately 45 cents per share, while the average spreads for the mixed-eighth stocks is approximately 23 cents per share. These differences are very similar to the values found by Christie and Schultz (1997) in their study of issues whose market makers alter their use of odd-eighth quotes.
7. Although the spreads of listed stocks widened in the presence of market stress while the inside quotes for NASDAQ issues did not, listed issues continued to be considerably less expensive to trade. At their widest,

inside spreads for listed stocks averaged 31.6 cents per share on November 15. In contrast, the average inside spread for the full sample of 100 NASDAQ issues never fell below 38.4 cents per share during either the nonstress period or November 15.

8. The effective spread estimates include all trades, independent of the location of the trade relative to the inside quotes. The fraction of trades that lie outside the best bid or ask rose from 1.73% in the prestress period to 2.43% on November 15. These trades are included since we wish to estimate the true cost to investors from executing trades during periods of stress. We replicated the analysis excluding these trades, and the results remain qualitatively unaffected.

References

Barclay, M., W. Christie, J. Harris, E. Kandel, and P. Schultz, "NASDAQ Market Reform: New Evidence That Competition from the Public Reduce Lower Costs," 1998, *Journal of Finance*, forthcoming.

Blume, M., C. MacKinlay, and B. Terker, "Order Imbalances and Stock Price Movements on October 19 and 20, 1987," *Journal of Finance* 44 (September 1989), 827–848.

Chan, K.C., W. Christie, and P. Schultz, "Market Structure and the Intraday Pattern of Bid-Ask Spreads for NASDAQ Securities," *Journal of Business* 68 (January 1995), 35–60.

Christie, W., J. Harris, and P. Schultz, "Why Did NASDAQ Market Makers Stop Avoiding Odd-Eighth Quotes?" *Journal of Finance* 49 (December 1994), 1841–1860.

Christie, W., and P. Schultz, "Why Do NASDAQ Market Makers Avoid Odd-Eighth Quotes?" *Journal of Finance* 49 (December 1994), 1813–1840.

Christie, W., and P. Schultz, "The Initiation and Withdrawal of Odd-Eighth Quotes Among NASDAQ Stocks: An Empirical Analysis," 1998, *Journal of Financial Economics*, forthcoming.

Harris, L., "The October 1987 S&P 500 Stock-Futures Basis," *Journal of Finance* 44 (December 1989), 1155–1176.

Huang, R., and H. Stoll, "Dealer versus Auction Markets: A Paired Comparison of Execution Costs on NASDAQ and the NYSE," *Journal of Financial Economics* 41 (July 1996), 313–358.

Report by the Division of Market Regulation of the U.S. Securities and Exchange Commission, U.S. Government Printing Office, Washington, DC: 1988.

Report of the Presidential Task Force on Market Mechanisms, Washington, DC: 1988.

Report of the Special Committee of the Regulatory Review Task Force on the Quality of Market, U.S. Government Printing Office, Washington, DC: National Association of Securities Dealers, 1988.

Schultz, P., and M. Zaman, "Aftermath Support and Underpricing of Initial Public Offerings," *Journal of Financial Economics* 35 (April 1994), 199–219.

Schwartz, Robert, *Reshaping the Equity Markets: A Guide for the 1990s*, New York: Harper Business Books, 1991.

Journal of Financial Services Research 13:3 231–255 (1998)

Margin Requirements, Volatility, and Market Integrity: What Have We Learned Since the Crash?

PAUL H. KUPIEC
Senior Economist, Trading Risk Analysis Section, Division of Research and Statistics, Board of Governors of the Federal Reserve System

Abstract

This study assesses the state of the policy debate that surrounds the federal regulation of margin requirements. A review of the literature finds no undisputed evidence that supports the hypothesis that margin requirements can be used to control stock return volatility and correspondingly little evidence that suggests that margin-related leverage is an important underlying source of "excess" volatility. The evidence does not support the hypothesis that there is a stable inverse relationship between the level of Regulation T margin requirements and stock returns volatility nor does it support the hypothesis that the leverage advantage in equity derivative products is a source of additional returns volatility in the stock market.

1. Introduction and overview

The Securities Exchange Act of 1934 granted the Federal Reserve Board (FRB) power to set initial, maintenance, and short sale margin requirements on all securities traded on a national exchange for purposes of regulating the securities credit extended by exchange members. Pursuant to this authority, the FRB established Regulation T (Reg T), the rules governing the percentage of equity value a broker/dealer was allowed to lend on exchange-traded securities.[1] Although securities markets have a long history of federal margin regulation, not until 1992, when the U.S. Congress extended the FRB's margin-setting authority to include the levels of margin on stock index-futures contracts, was a federal regulation responsible for setting margin levels for futures products.[2]

Initial margin requirements in the equity market determine the maximum loan value of a security. For example, if the initial margin requirement were set at 40%, an investor could post a marginable security as collateral and borrow up to 60% of the security's value. Alternatively, if the investor were to buy the security on margin, the investor would be required to deposit at least 40% of the value of the security in a margin account to complete the margin transaction.

In contrast to Reg T margin requirements, margin requirements in equity derivative markets are collateral requirements designed to ensure contract performance. From an economic perspective, there is no extension of credit in equity derivative markets.[3]

The conclusions herein are those of the authors and do not represent the views of the Federal Reserve Board or any of the Federal Reserve Banks.

Despite differences in their form and function, the margin requirements on equity derivative contracts affect the cost of taking positions and implicitly define the maximum amount of return leverage that can be obtained in such contracts.

The 1934 U.S. Congress established federal margin authority with three apparent objectives: to reduce the use of "excessive" credit in securities transactions, to protect investors from overleveraging, and to reduce the volatility of stock prices.[4] The Congress evidently believed that a federal margin policy could be used to control the amount of credit allocated to "unproductive" investment in the stock market and thereby reduce the effects of destabilizing speculation on stock prices. The view prevailing in Congress held that a fixed pool of credit was available to support investment activities, and any credit used to purchase stocks was unavailable to finance productive investments in new plant and equipment. Moreover, it was widely believed that stock-related credit supported the activities of speculators, whose trading activities allegedly created unnecessary volatility in the stock market.

In apparent sympathy with the views held in the U.S. Congress, the evidence suggests that, until at least the late 1960s, the Federal Reserve Board exercised margin authority in a spirit aligned with the original congressional intent. Indeed, in U.S. Senate testimony in 1955, FRB Chairman Martin summarized the institution's view on margin policy:

> The task of the Board, as I see it, is to formulate regulations with two principal objectives. One is to permit adequate access to credit facilities for securities markets to perform the basic economic functions. The other is to prevent the use of stock market credit from becoming excessive. The latter helps to minimize the danger of pyramiding credit in a rising market and also reduces the danger of forced sales of securities from under-margined accounts in a falling market.[5]

As federal margin authority has yet to be repealed, the U.S. Congress may still hold the view that margin requirements can be effective as a selective credit control and useful as a tool for stabilizing stock prices. Notwithstanding the opinions of those who share the 1934 congressional viewpoint, the majority in the finance profession appear to have abandoned the beliefs that underlie the original margin authority mandate. Few believe that selected credit controls are an efficient way to limit the volume of credit extended, and the majority view is that margin requirements have no predictable effect on stock price volatility. Indeed a 1984 staff study by the FRB, "A Review and Evaluation of Federal Margin Regulations," concluded that margin requirements were ineffective as selective credit controls, inappropriate as rules for investor protection, and unlikely to be useful in controlling stock price volatility.

Prior to the 1987 stock market crash, little evidence suggested that margin policy was effective in accomplishing the goals behind the 1934 authorization.[6] By the early 1980s, the academic research on margin policy had shifted focus from evaluating the effects of changes in Reg T margins to analyzing the procedures appropriate for setting prudential margins in the futures markets.[7] The shift in research focus likely reflected two distinct forces: first, the belief that the most interesting issues surrounding Reg T margin policy were more-or-less settled; second, the expansion of financial futures trading that increased the importance and interest in the largely unregulated margin policies of the futures clearinghouses.

The 1987 stock market crash and the studies that followed rekindled interest in margin policy and spawned a political and academic debate on the efficacy of margin policy for common stocks and their derivative products. Although all the major stock market crash studies discussed margin policy in the context of market integrity, the studies reached significantly different conclusions.

The New York Stock Exchange's report on the crash, the so-called Katzenbach report (1987), concludes (p. 16)

> margin rules provide the Federal Reserve Board with an effective tool for controlling the amount of leverage that may be used in securities transactions and, ultimately, the ease with which speculation may occur. The margin rules thus provide the FRB with a means to prevent and control market fluctuations and help stabilize the economy in general.

Although the Katzenbach report contradicts the findings of the FRB's 1984 margin study, it provides no evidence to justify this difference of opinion. After establishing its position on margin efficacy, the report then observes that the low margins and trading costs associated with stock index futures products create a sizeable leverage advantage compared to the leverage that can be achieved in the cash market. The report concludes that the leverage in index futures products encourages speculation that ultimately leads to greater volatility in the cash markets and recommends raising margin requirements on stock index futures contracts and changing futures settlement procedures to remove the leverage advantage enjoyed by stock index futures products.

In its margin policy recommendations, the Securities and Exchange Commission's report, "The October 1987 Market Break" (1988), largely concurs with the recommendations of the Katzenbach report. The SEC's report recommends (pp. xiv–xv)

> thought should be given to steps to bring the available leverage of derivative products in line with the leverage of stock products.... the margin treatment for stock index futures and options provides significantly higher leverage for users of these products that [sic] can be achieved under stock margin requirements.....the Division [Market Regulation] believes that relatively low margins may contribute to increased concentrated institutional trading and resulting greater price volatility.

In contrast to the aforementioned studies, neither the Brady Commission report or the report of the President's Working Group on Financial Markets explicitly calls for raising derivative product margin requirements. The Brady Commission report (1988), "Report of the Presidential Task Force on Market Mechanisms," concludes that (p. vii), "Margins should be made consistent across marketplaces to control speculation and financial leverage." It is notable perhaps that, although the Brady Commission seems to accept the hypothesis that volatility and leverage are related, it did not recommend increasing margins on equity derivative products to coincide with the 50% initial margin required on stock transactions. Despite recommending equalizing leverage, the Brady Commission was unwilling to suggest the appropriate level at which leverage should be equalized.

The "Interim Report of the Working Group on Financial Markets" (1988), the report jointly authored by the Secretary of the Treasury and the chairpersons of the FRB, SEC, and CFTC, finds that, for prudential purposes, the prevailing margin requirement settings for stocks and stock index futures products were adequate. Indeed, the report concludes that, for prudential purposes, it is appropriate for margin requirements to differ across stock and stock index derivative products. The principals, however, were unable to agree on whether or not margin policy could be effectively used to control stock market volatility. Chairman Ruder of the SEC held the view that raising futures margins would reduce volatility in the cash market. Chairman Greenspan of the FRB, Chairman Gramm of the CFTC, and Secretary Gould of the Treasury did not believe that the evidence supported the view that higher margins discourage volatility, while they did find compelling the evidence that suggests that higher futures margins reduce market liquidity.

Recommendations that margin requirements should be set to coordinate the leverage in stock and stock derivative contracts led some to suggest regulatory changes that would entrust stock and stock derivative margin-setting policy to a single regulator.[8] Ultimately, these recommendations led the U.S. Congress to grant the FRB margin-setting authority for stock index futures contracts in 1992. The FRB exercised this mandate by delegating regulatory authority over stock index futures contracts to the CFTC in 1993.

The margin policy controversy apparent in the official reports that analyzed the 1987 crash generated renewed academic interest in margin policy research. In particular, an influential study by Hardouvelis (1988) concluded that historical evidence supported the proposition that margin requirements could be used to control stock market volatility. The conclusions of the Hardouvelis study were disputed by many subsequent studies and the margin-volatility literature expanded significantly. On balance, the empirical literature that follows the Hardouvelis study supports the precrash academic view: Little direct empirical evidence favors the proposition that margin policy can be an effective tool in controlling stock market volatility. Despite the predominate academic finding, some still hold the view that margin requirements function as the 1934 Congress envisioned. Margin policy advocates support their position by claiming that the lack of strong direct econometric evidence can be easily explained. They claim that the true underlying margin-volatility relationship may be econometrically obscured by the infrequency with which margins have been changed, the substantial noise component in stock price and return data, and the inappropriate measurement techniques used in most margin-volatility studies.[9]

This study assesses the state of the margin policy debate using both the direct and indirect evidence that has accumulated since the 1987 crash. In contrast to earlier literature reviews by France (1991) and Chance (1990), this study not only discusses more recent evidence but also incorporates the findings of the indirect but related literature that investigates the effects of derivative markets on cash market volatility.

The hypothetical relationship between margin requirements and volatility is driven by leverage. While there clearly is a positive relationship between leverage and the return volatility of an individual investor's portfolio, the margin-volatility debate deliberates the claim that the return volatility of unleveraged equity portfolios is determined at least in part by the amount of leverage chosen by individual investors. A necessary condition for the existence of a negative margin-volatility relationship is that, on average, there must be a positive association between the degree of leverage in individual investor portfolios and the volatility in the underlying market. Indeed, the margin recommendations of three of the major postcrash studies are premised on the hypothesis that leverage enables speculators to generate unnecessary volatility.

Derivative contracts offer significant leverage advantages over cash market transactions and facilitate short selling. Therefore, if margin requirements affect volatility by constraining investors' abilities to leverage their portfolios, the introduction of a derivative market should have effects similar to those generated by a reduction in the cash market margin requirement. As a consequence, a negative relationship between the level of margin requirements and volatility, if it exists, should manifest itself in the form of higher volatilities following the introduction of a derivative contract. Moreover, once derivative product trading commences, leverage constraints will be determined by the level of margin in the derivative market as cash market margins no longer will be the binding constraint on speculators. Thus, the results of studies that investigate the relationship between margin requirements and volatility in the futures market become directly relevant to the margin-volatility policy debate.

After examining the academic evidence that investigates the relationship between margin and volatility in both the cash and futures market and considering the results of studies that measure the effects of derivative market introductions, this study concludes that no substantial body of evidence supports the hypothesis that margin requirements can be systematically altered to manage the volatility in stock markets. The empirical evidence shows that, while high Reg T margin requirements may reduce the volume of securities credit lending and high futures margins do appear to reduce the open interest in futures markets, neither of these measurable effects appears to be systematically associated with lower stock return volatility. The evidence to date suggests that, contrary to the leverage arguments advanced by the pyramiding-depyramiding hypothesis and explicitly accepted by many of the official studies of the 1987 stock market crash, little or no empirical evidence supports the hypothesis that tightening leverage constraints in either the cash or equity derivative markets will reduce stock return volatility.

2. Reg T margins, leverage, and volatility: The theory

The view held by the 1934 U.S. Congress and those who continue to believe that high margin requirements attenuate volatility is that low initial margins enable speculators to exert undue influence in stock markets and thereby create excess volatility. It is alleged that speculators force stock prices above their fundamental values through a process known as *pyramiding*. *Pyramiding* refers to the dynamic in which gains in stock prices allow overoptimistic agents to borrow additional funds for equity purchases. These leveraged purchases in turn create additional upward pressures on equity prices and the gains can be used to borrow additional funds for further equity purchases. When the inevitable market correction begins, leveraged investors faced with margin calls are forced to liquidate positions. The "depyramiding" process allegedly causes overshooting of the fundamental equilibrium. As a result, low margin requirements create an additional source of volatility over the volatility attributable to fundamental economic forces.

Despite the intuitive appeal of this pyramiding-depyramiding argument, it is at best incomplete. It identifies only one possible avenue through which margin requirements may affect volatility. Goldberg (1985) develops a theoretical model that suggests a positive relationship between margin requirements and stock price volatility. In Goldberg's model, when investors are constrained by margin requirements, they bid up the prices of more highly leveraged firms and thereby encourage increased corporate leverage. In the resulting general equilibrium, corporate leverage is substituted for private leverage and stock price volatility increases in response to increased corporate leverage.

Kupiec and Sharpe (1991) develop an equilibrium model in which irrational speculators may create excess stock price volatility. In contrast to the pyramiding-depyramiding hypothesis, this model suggests the possibility of a positive relationship between margin requirements and excess stock market volatility. The model demonstrates that high margin requirements may reduce the equity purchases of liquidity-constrained rational investors when a shift in irrational noise trader demands causes a decline in equity prices. Because those who are willing to bear risk are constrained from borrowing to purchase additional shares, equity prices fall below their fundamental values. Thus, higher margin requirements create greater equity price volatility; conversely, low margins reduce stock price volatility. Depending on the characteristics of investors in the model, consistent with the pyramiding-depyramiding hypothesis, it also is possible for margins to reduce volatility in the Kupiec-Sharpe model by constraining the leverage of irrationally optimistic agents. Given the possibility of these two polar cases, the Kupiec-Sharpe model establishes that there is no unique theoretical relationship between margin requirements and asset price volatility; from a theoretical standpoint it is equally plausible that low margin requirements may reduce stock price volatility as increase it. Indeed, over time, the effects of margin requirements may vary as the sources of excess stock price volatility change over time.

3. Margins, leverage, and volatility: Evidence from the stock market

Prior to the late 1980s, virtually all published academic evidence suggested that changes in the Reg T margin requirements had no statistically measurable effect on stock price volatility when volatility was measured by the standard deviation of the returns on a broad stock market index.[10] In summarizing the early literature, it is instructive, and perhaps timely, to revisit the conclusions of Moore (1966):

> Margin requirements add to paper work and to the costs of stock market transactions; ... and, most important, they fail to fulfil their stated objectives. However, they do give the Federal Reserve a way of expressing its concern with movements in the stock market. But statements by the Federal Reserve setting forth its view might be substituted for changes in margin requirements, if the Federal Reserve feels a need to voice its view of stock market activity. (p. 167)

The 1988 study by Hardouvelis disputed Moore's conclusions and the results of earlier academic findings and concluded that, over the 1934–1987 period, monthly stock return volatility is systematically related to the level of Reg T margin requirements. Hardouvelis finds evidence of a statistically significant negative correlation between the level of margins and the volatility of monthly S&P 500 stock returns. He interprets this correlation in a causal way and concludes that Reg T margin requirements can be used to attenuate stock price volatility. Contrary to the existing literature, not only does Hardouvelis find a statistically significant negative margin-volatility relationship, he claims that changes in margins can cause substantial changes in monthly stock returns volatility. According to Hardouvelis (pp. 87–88), a 10 percentage point increase in the Reg T margin requirement, on average, will result in a 8% decline in stock return volatility in the following month and greater reductions in the long run.[11] In an expanded study, Hardouvelis (1990) affirms his 1988 study's findings using a different measure of monthly stock return volatility.

Subsequent (or coincident) to the original Hardouvelis (1988) study and his expanded analysis (1990), a bevy of studies re-examined the margin-volatility issue. Ferris and Chance (1988), Schwert (1989a, 1989b), Salinger (1989), Kupiec (1989), and Hsieh and Miller (1990) all empirically investigated the hypothesis that Reg T margin requirements and stock price volatility are inversely related. Using different econometric techniques to evaluate time series aggregate stock returns data, without exception, these studies find no support for an inverse margin-volatility relationship. The upshot of the results of these studies is that increases in volatility appear to precede increases in margin requirements and increases in margin requirements seem to depress the volume of margin credit extended, but there is no evidence to suggest that the level of margin requirements and stock return volatility are systematically related.

How can the results of the Hardouvelis studies differ so sharply from those of other researchers? Hsieh and Miller (1990) directly investigate this question. The Hardouvelis (1988) study measured monthly return volatility using a 12-month rolling standard deviation estimate. The use of a rolling standard deviation introduces substantial positive autocorrelation in monthly measures of volatility. In this analysis, Hardouvelis regresses overlapping monthly volatility estimates on 12-month moving averages of Reg T margin requirements and, in an expanded regression, includes the moving average of margin credit as well.

Hsieh and Miller show that the moving average constructions used by Hardouvelis induce a spurious correlation between his measures of margin requirements and volatility. If one properly accounts for this correlation, Hsieh and Miller show that there is no statistically significant margin-volatility relationship. Moreover, according to the pyramiding-depyramiding hypothesis, if margins are to have an affect, they must do so by altering the level of margin credit. As a consequence, margin credit should not be included as an an explanatory variable in Hardouvelis's expanded regression if it is attempting to measure the volatility-magnifying effects of leverage. If margin credit is included, the volatility regression measures the effect of margin requirements on volatility, holding constant the level of margin credit. According to the pyramiding-depyramiding hypothesis, there should be no margin effect if margin credit is held fixed; and so the expanded Hardouvelis model is misspecified if it is attempting to measure the effect of margin requirements on stock price volatility. When Hsieh and Miller correct the Hardouvelis (1988) analysis for these problems, they find no evidence of the claimed margin-volatility relationship.

In Hardouvelis (1990), monthly stock return volatility is measured as a multiple of the absolute value of the residuals generated from a regression of monthly returns on lagging 12 month returns and 12 monthly dummy variables. Hardouvelis claims that this volatility estimate is a modification of the volatility estimate proposed in Schwert (1989a, 1989b). Hsieh and Miller (1990) examine this modified Schwert estimator and demonstrate that the Hardouvelis modifications destroy the integrity of the original Schwert volatility estimator. Instead of a close correspondence with more traditional measures of volatility, Hsieh and Miller show that the Hardouvelis measure produces volatility estimates with extremely undesirable sample properties, including a preponderance of extreme volatility estimates in the sample period. Hsieh and Miller conclude that this volatility measure is unsuitable for analysis.

The findings of studies that directly revisit Hardouvelis's analysis are augmented by studies that investigate the margin-volatility hypothesis using different experimental designs. Grube, Joy, and Howe (1987) examine the abnormal return effects generated when nonmarginable OTC securities gain margin eligibility status. They find that these OTC stocks experience a statistically significant abnormal positive price appreciation when they are included in the FRB's margin eligibility list and little price effect if they are subsequently removed from the list of marginable securities. When an OTC security is not marginable, investors must acquire the stock certificate and use it as collateral to obtain credit. This presumably is costly. Once marginable, the security can be left in street name at the broker and included as collateral in a margin account. Grube, Joy, and Howe speculate that a subsequent delisting may not have an effect owing to a grandfather clause in Reg T that prohibits new loans but allows existing lending arrangements to continue. They interpret their findings as consistent with a Fed endorsement effect or a convenience effect.

Seguin (1990) also studies the effects generated when a sample of previously nonmarginable OTC stocks gain margin eligibility. In contrast to Grube and colleagues (1987), Seguin studies the events' effect on volatilities, trading volumes, returns, and return autocorrelations. Seguin finds that, on average, margin eligibility is associated with a 2% decline in return volatility, about a 2% increase in average share value, and about a 30% increase in trading volume where all the aforementioned effects are statistically significant.[12]

Seguin and Jarrell (1993) examine the pyramiding-depyramiding hypothesis by examining the relative return and volume behavior of marginable and nonmarginable stocks during the October 1987 stock market crash. They argue that, since margin credit was at a historical high during October 1987 and there is evidence that the crash precipitated substantial margin call activity, if depyramiding price pressures exist, they should be especially evident in the return profiles of marginable stocks during the crash period. Seguin and Jarrell find that, during the crash, marginable securities experienced higher excess volumes relative to nonmarginable securities (14 to 40% higher) as predicted by the margin-call depyramiding hypothesis.[13] Despite greater excess trading volumes, Seguin and Jarrell find that the price declines recorded by marginable securities were less severe (returns were 0.8% greater) than those recorded by nonmarginable securities.

Aside from the disputed claims of the Hardouvelis studies, the results of the balance of studies that investigate the effects of Reg T margin requirements suggest that, while margin requirements can have effects on the level of margin credit and equity trading volumes, no direct evidence supports the proposition that Reg T margin requirements can be used to control stock return volatility.

4. Derivative markets, leverage, and the margin volatility debate

In the late 1980s, the margin volatility debate moved from Reg T margin requirements to the margin requirements on stock index futures products. Margin requirements in futures markets serve as a performance bond guarantee. In futures markets, margins are designed to protect the futures clearinghouse from the risk generated from a single-day's potential loss in a contract's value. Owing to the institutional differences in futures-style trading and settlement, the margin needed to control a clearinghouse's one-day risk exposure on a futures contract is far smaller than the 50% initial margin requirement that has been set by the FRB to "protect" lenders in security transactions.

The difference in required margin between futures and cash transactions creates a leverage advantage for stock index futures products. Similarly, the leverage available using individual stock options dominates that available in the cash market. Moreover, individual stock options and stock index futures allow traders to circumvent the short-selling rules that prevail in the cash market.[14] If leverage is the source of "excess" volatility in stock markets, the introduction of stock options and stock index futures trading should have had measurable effects on the volatility in the stock market.

Those who associate leverage with speculation and excess volatility have noted the advantages accorded futures products. These views are expressed in the Katzenbach report (p. 28):

> The trivial cost and tremendous leverage available make index futures and options an ideal instrument for speculation in short-term market movements. Speculation is in the index—the market itself—and the futures and options market reacts far more quickly to macroeconomic factors than does the underlying market, precisely because it is an index product.... To quite a substantial extent, the tail is wagging the dog.

Although it is clear that stock index futures products and options transactions have a significant transactions cost and leverage advantage over direct cash market purchases or sales, it is an open question whether or not this leverage advantage is of any consequence for the volatility of returns in the underlying stock market. This question has at least two separable aspects: Does the introduction of a derivatives market affect the return volatility of the underlying instrument, and given the existence of the derivative product, does a change in its margin requirement affect the price volatility of the underlying instrument? The subsequent sections will review the scientific evidence that relates to these logically separable issues.

5. Derivatives and cash market volatility: The theory

Theoretical models can be constructed to examine the effects of introducing a derivative market on the volatility in the underlying cash market. Turnovsky and Campbell (1985) develop an equilibrium model designed to assess the volatility and welfare implications associated with the introduction of a futures market. Because their model is highly nonlinear, they can only simulate equilibria. They find that, in virtually all model calibrations, the introduction of a futures market either stabilizes cash market prices or has no effect on volatility. Weller and Yano (1987) also analyze this question in a two-good, two-agent model with exogenous stochastic output. They find that the introduction of a futures market has two effects: a price arbitrage effect and an wealth transfer effect. The price arbitrage effect unambiguously reduces price volatility in the cash market, but the volatility effects engendered by the wealth transfers that result from futures market trading are ambiguous as they depend on the heterogeneity in the trading populations' utility functions.

Detemple and Selden (1991) model the effects of introducing a call option contract into a incomplete market setting, where assets include only a stock and a risk-free bond. They show that the price and return volatility of the stock in general will be affected by the introduction of the derivative security. For a given set of endowments, when a derivative is introduced into an incomplete market setting with sufficiently diverse agents, the derivative contract will be traded. Derivative trading will facilitate a reallocation of consumption, which will be reflected by a change in the equilibrium price and return characteristics of the underlying security. In a specialized quadratic utility example, Detemple and Seldon show that the introduction of the derivative will increase the price of the security and reduce its return volatility.

Stein (1987) develops a theoretical model in which the introduction of a futures market can destabilize cash market prices. In the Stein model, the presence or absence of a futures market does not affect speculators by altering their leverage constraint. Rather, misinformed speculators are unable to trade in the spot market by assumption. When a futures market is introduced, speculators can trade and their trading may affect the information content of spot market prices. In this setting, Stein establishes the theoretical possibility that the "noise" in speculators' information sets can create spot market price volatility that cannot be distinguished from the underlying "fundamental" volatility by the other traders in this model. The opening of a futures market allows the imperfectly informed speculators to trade, and their trading distorts the information content of market-clearing spot prices. Because spot traders are risk averse and cannot differentiate between price shocks that owe to fundamental supply disturbances and those caused by the demands of imperfectly informed speculators, their inventory holdings are less responsive to price shocks when imperfectly informed speculators are allowed to trade in the futures market. The change in spot traders' inventory holdings leads to additional spot price volatility and reduced social welfare.

Stein interprets his model as a formal counterexample to the conjecture that the addition of speculators to an existing market will add to the depth and liquidity of the market and thereby reduce the price effects created by transitory shocks to demand or supply. Even though agents voluntarily trade with the new futures market speculators, they can be made worse off. Stein's results are a specific example of Hart's (1975) general finding that, when markets are incomplete, opening an additional market may make agents worse off if markets remain incomplete. In both the Hart and Stein models, it is notable that leverage does not play a role in generating the destabilizing price speculation or the loss in social welfare.

6. Does the introduction of a derivative contract create volatility?

Empirical evidence from the futures markets

Powers (1970) investigates the effects of the introduction of a futures market on the volatility in the underlying cash market for pork bellies and live choice-grade cattle. He examines differences in average weekly cash price variation for the four-year periods before and after futures contract trading. By differencing the data, he removes positively autocorrelated price variation components and focuses on the volatility of idiosyncratic price increments. He finds that the idiosyncratic component of cash price volatility falls by a statistically significant amount during the period when futures are trading.

The evidence on the relationship between volatility and futures contract trading for GNMA pass-through certificates is dated and somewhat unclear.[15] Froewiss (1978) investigates the effects of GNMA futures trading on the weekly return volatility of GNMA pass-though certificates. To remove systematic macroeconomic effects, he regresses spot GNMA returns on the return of 10-year Treasury bonds for samples before and after the introduction of the GNMA futures contract. He finds no significant difference in the slope coefficient estimates across the pre- and post-futures trading samples but does find statistically significant evidence that the regression standard error declined after the futures contract introduction.

Figlewski (1981) examines the volatility effects associated with the introduction of GNMA futures trading. In contrast to Froewiss, Figlewski measures GNMA contract price volatility. In apparent contrast to Froewiss's findings, Figlewski concludes that the introduction of GNMA futures trading coincided with an increase in the price volatility in the GNMA pass-through market. He speculates that the additional price volatility likely owes to the trading activities of uninformed GNMA futures traders.

Simpson and Ireland (1982) revist the GNMA futures trading issue. To investigate volatility effects, they regress yields on GNMA pass-though certificates on the 10-year Treasury bond rate and the yields on FNMA securities and dummy variables that allow for parameter shifts during the futures contract period. Simpson and Ireland detect no futures-trading induced changes in their regression slope coefficients. Because they use a dummy variable approach, they assume that the regression error variance is constant and do not test for the idiosyncratic variance reduction found by Froewiss.

Aside from the difficulty in reconciling the aforementioned studies, in part because they consider different volatility measures (return, price, and yield), Edwards (1988) takes issue with their methodologies. All three studies use simple regressions that include the contemporaneous prices or yields on closely related financial instruments to "control" for economywide effects on GNMA pass-through certificate volatility. Edwards concludes that the estimates in these studies are subject to endogenous variable bias as the absence of arbitrage requires that the "control" variables used in the regressions are endogenous and heavily influenced by the introduction of the futures contracts.

Edwards (1988) considers the behavior of cash market volatility in samples surrounding the introduction of four financial futures contracts: S&P 500, Value Line, 90-day Eurodollars, and 90-day T-bill futures contracts. Edwards measures volatility before and after the introduction of each financial futures contract, excluding data during the 1979–1982 period when the Federal Reserve altered its operating procedures. Following the introduction of financial futures contract trading, except for stocks in 1987, volatility was lower in all cash markets in all years after the introduction of a financial futures contract. Although he does recognize the expiration-day volatility effects on S&P 500 stock index returns documented by Stoll and Whaley (1987), because these effects are small and transitory, Edwards concludes that, on balance, the statistical evidence strongly suggests that cash market volatility has been lower subsequent to the introduction of the financial futures contracts considered in his study.

The Edwards study is just one study in a relatively large literature that investigates the affects of the introduction of S&P 500 stock index future contract trading on the underlying return volatilities of the stocks in the composite index. Aside from any change in volatility that may owe to the enhanced leverage opportunities facilitated by the introduction of the stock index futures contract, many nonleverage related institutional factors may alter the returns volatility of the stocks in the futures contract index, such as a change in the frequency with which stocks trade. Other factors that may affect returns volatility are changes in individual stocks' bid-asked spreads that may owe to the introduction of stock index futures trading and changes in the transactions cost of trading on macro-financial information.

Changes in stock values may be attributed to changes in economywide factors that affect firms' values and changes in value that owe to idiosyncratic firm developments. Although true underlying stock values may change continuously as economywide and firm-specific news is disseminated, new share valuations are observed only infrequently when a trade occurs. If investors utilize new information efficiently, true underlying stock price changes will be uncorrelated. As true underlying stock price changes are not observed instantaneously, infrequent trading will cause the returns on a stock index constructed from observed trade prices to be positively autocorrelated and less volatile than the return on the true (but unobserved) stock index value.

The introduction of a stock index futures contract can have significant effects on the volatility of the measured stock index, even if it has no effect on the volatility of the underlying true value of the index. Stock index futures prices and the true underlying prices of individual stocks in a stock index contract are tightly related throuh an absence-of-arbitrage cost of carry condition:

$$F_t = S_t e^{(r-d)(T-t)} \tag{1}$$

where F_t is the futures price at time t, S_t is the true value of the stock index at time t, r is the "cost of carry" rate of interest, d is the continuous dividend yield on the stock index, and T is the contract maturity date.[16] Should eq. (1) fail to hold, an arbitrage profit can be generated by taking appropriate positions in the stock index futures and the underlying stocks in the index. If r and d are approximately constant over short time intervals, eq. (1) implies that the volatility of the rate of return on the true value of the stock index and the volatility of the return on the index futures contract are equal. Owing to transactions costs, eq. (1) will not hold exactly; and when S_t is replaced by the measured index value, the volatility of the returns to the futures contract will exceed the volatility of the returns to the measured stock index, owing to the affects of infrequent trading.

Absent an index futures contact, individual shares trade with a frequency that can for present purposes be taken as exogenous. The introduction of a stock index futures contract may increase the average frequency of trading in individual stocks because, when index arbitrage becomes profitable, investors must trade all shares in the index to profit from the arbitrage.[17] Index arbitrage trades that convey no new information will have no effect on the true underlying share price or return volatility and yet the increased frequency of trading will increase the volatility and reduce the autocorrelation of measured stock index returns. Alternatively, if the introduction of index futures contract trading lowers the transactions cost of trading on new macro-economic information, macro information will be reflected more quickly in index futures prices, and these prices changes will be transferred through index arbitrage activity to the cash market, where they will be reflected as an increase in individual stock return volatility. Again, such an increase in volatility is unrelated to leverage.[18]

Harris (1989) investigates the hypothesis that the introduction of S&P 500 index futures contract increases the volatility of the underlying instruments. Harris uses a regression model to explain the yearly return variance characteristics for stocks included in the S&P 500 index and the yearly return variances for a sample of comparable nonindex stocks. Harris examines volatility differences for each year between 1975 and 1987. Prior to index futures trading, Harris finds no statistically significant difference in return volatility after controlling for each stock's beta, size, price level, and a measure of trade frequency. Subsequent to the introduction of index futures trading, however, Harris finds that the short-horizon returns of S&P 500 stocks are more volatile when compared to comparable non-S&P 500 stocks. The average differences in S&P 500 daily stock return volatility during the futures trading period are very small between 0.03 and 0.14%, and likely insignificant economically when compared to an average daily return standard deviation of about 2% in his sample. Although the estimated daily differences are small, the post-index futures daily return volatility differences, however, are statistically different from zero in 1985, 1986, and 1987.

Jegadeesh and Subrahmanyam (1993) provide some results that may in part explain the Harris (1989) ''excess volatility'' findings as a consequence of competitive market making behavior and not speculative excesses. Jegadeesh and Subrahmanyam test a hypothesis advanced by Subrahmanyam (1991) and Gorton and Penacchi (1993). The hypothesis suggests that, because the adverse selection charges implicit in the average bid-asked spreads of individual stocks are likely to be much larger than the adverse selection component of a stock index future market maker's quote, uninformed traders face incentives to redirect their trades from individual stocks to the index futures contract. The migration of uninformed traders increases the proportion of informed traders faced by the market makers for individual stocks, and individual share bid-ask spreads are predicted to widen accordingly.

To test the uninformed trader migration hypothesis, Jegadeesh and Subrahmanyam (1993) examine month-end bid-asked spreads for a sample of firms included in the S&P 500 index and a random sample of nonindex firms of roughly comparable size in a period that encompasses the introduction of S&P 500 index futures trading. After controlling for the common bid-asked spread explanatory variables, they find that average proportional spreads increased subsequent to the introduction of index future trading. Moreover, they find that bid-asked spreads increased significantly more for S&P 500 stocks, but the increase in the magnitudes of implied trading cost is not economically significant. These changes in bid-asked spreads could, at least in part, explain the finding of Harris (1989), as the wider bid-asked spreads could imply a greater bid-asked spread bounce component in daily stock return volatility estimates.

Hong and Subrahmanyam (1994) use intraday data to assess the impact that may have been imparted by the introduction of the Major Market Index (MMI) index futures contract on the bid-asked spreads and volatilities of the individual stocks in the MMI index. Although the MMI was introduced after the S&P 500, and all MMI stocks are included in the S&P 500 index, no intraday data are available to study the effects of the S&P 500 futures contract introduction. Using intraday data on selected stocks during 1984 (the MMI began trading on July 23, 1984), the authors find that, consistent with the findings of Jegadeesh and Subrahmanyam (1993), subsequent to the introduction of the MMI futures contract, MMI stocks on average experienced a statistically significant increase in their bid-asked spreads after controlling for other common bid-asked spread determinants (size, volatility, price, volume). Although statistically significant, the magnitude of the average change is unimportant economically. When examining intraday volatility, Hong and Subrahmanyam removed the effects of bid-asked spread bounce and find no evidence that the introduction of MMI futures trading altered intraday volatility in the sample period.

Kamara, Miller, and Siegel (1992) study the effects of S&P 500 index futures market trading on the return distribution of the S&P 500 index. Using univariate nonparametric tests to correct for the abnormality in the underlying return distribution, in contrast to Edwards (1988), they find that daily return distributions exhibit higher volatility in the post-index futures sample period. Similar to Harris (1989), they find that longer-horizon return volatility is unaffected by the introduction of stock index futures trading. Despite the measured differences in daily return volatility, the authors conclude that the observed changes in volatility do not owe to the introduction of the stock index futures contract. Rather, they show that, if the pre- and post-index futures sample periods are randomly split, the data show statistically significant evidence of changing daily return variances. They conclude that daily return variances are nonstationary and the nonstationarity is unrelated to the introduction of stock index futures trading.

Kamara and colleagues also examine the number of outlier returns in the pre- and post-index futures trading period. They cannot reject the hypothesis that there are more outliers in the sample period with index futures trading—indeed, the data show that *positive* return outliers are far more prevalent when index futures are trading. If October 1987 is excluded from the sample however, outliers are equally likely with or without index futures. In a multivariate analysis intended to control for macro-economic sources of variation in S&P 500 returns, Kamara and colleagues examine whether the regression's residual volatility differs between the pre- and post-index futures trading samples. If October 1987 is excluded from the sample, the post-index futures residual volatility is significantly smaller than the residual volatility before S&P 500 stock index futures were introduced. Including October 1987, the post-index futures residual variance is almost twice as large as the pre-index futures sample residual variance. They conclude that, unless one believes that the 1987 crash was caused by the futures markets, futures markets do not appear to have increased the S&P 500's "excess volatility."

Bessembinder and Seguin (1992) examine the relationship between the cash volatility of the S&P 500 index, trading volume in both the cash and futures market, and open interest in the futures market over the sample period January 1978 to September 1989. They decompose cash and futures markets volumes into three components that correspond with the long-term trend, a transitory expected component, and an unexpected component. Bessembinder and Seguin find that the unanticipated component of cash trading volume is positively related to volatility in the spot market, and the introduction of futures contract trading attenuates this volatility-volume relationship. They also find that volatility in the cash market is negatively related to the expected component of futures trading volume. Thus, unlike the well-known positive volume-volatility relationship evident in the cash market, increases in the predicable component of futures trading volume are associated with lower, not higher, cash market volatility. As in the cash market, they find that unexpected futures trading volume is positively related to cash market volatility. Bessembinder and Seguin suggest that their results are consistent with the hypothesis that futures markets improve the liquidity and the depth of markets. They find no evidence that supports the hypothesis that futures markets are a conduit for destabilizing speculation.

Although the empirical evidence relating to the introduction of equity index futures contracts suggest that derivative market introductions, on average, have had a stabilizing influence on stock return volatility, some evidence suggests that the existence of derivatives products may have exacerbated transitory spikes in volatility. For example, Stoll and Whaley (1987) found that the introduction of stock index futures led to significantly higher cash market volatility on index futures expiration days, and indeed recognition of these effects led to changes in contract expiration procedures that seem to have attenuated expiration day volatility effects.[19] Another potential example of derivative-related transitory volatility is the behavior of S&P 500 stock returns during the October 1987 crash. Although it is unclear whether the underlying order imbalances owe to the existence of the S&P 500 index futures contract, Blume, MacKinlay, and Terker (1989) find evidence that, during the 1987 crash period, stocks included in the S&P 500 index experienced larger transitory increases in volatility than non-S&P 500 stocks.

Empirical evidence from the options markets

Skinner (1989) examines the effect of option listing on the volatility of underlying stock returns. Using a sample of 304 option listings over the period April 1973 to December 1986, Skinner finds that, on average, an option listing event is associated with a 17% decline in total daily return volatility. Roughly 70% of the firms in Skinner's sample experienced volatility declines. If individual volatility estimates are deflated by the average daily market volatility over each event window, volatility declines by about 10% for the median firm in Skinner's sample. He finds that option listing has no statistically significant effect on firms' systematic risks and, on average, stock trading volume increases about 17% in the six-month period following option listing. After adjusting for changes in overall market trading volume, the average firm experienced an excess volume increase closer to 4%. Trading volume increased the greatest amount for the smallest firms in the sample.

Conrad (1989) examines the stock price and volatility effects associated with the introduction of listed options trading for a sample of 96 stocks that listed options between December 1974 and December 1980. Conrad finds that, on average, individual stocks experience statistically significant positive abnormal returns and reductions in their average total return variance subsequent to the introduction of options trading. Conrad estimates that an equally weighted portfolio of these stocks would experience an option-listing gain of about 2%. Consistent with Skinner, she finds that stocks' market model betas are unaffected by the introduction of options trading, and so reductions in volatility owe to declines in stocks' idiosyncratic variances.

Detemple and Jorion (1990) examine the effects of options listing and delisting on the returns of the underlying stocks. In a sample of 300 options listings over the period April 1973 through December 1976, they find that an option introduction generates cumulative abnormal returns that average 2.8%, and stocks experience on average about a 7% reduction in return variance over the two-week window surrounding the option listing date. The decline in return volatility does not owe to the recorded price increases, as the magnitude of volatility changes is not statistically related to the magnitude of the price changes recorded in the sample. Consistent with other researchers, Detemple and Jorion find that most of the variance increases owes to a decrease in firms' idiosyncratic risks, as market model betas are little changed by the event. In contrast, the authors find that option delisting (32 events) generates negative cumulative abnormal returns (about 2%) and increases (about 9%) in return volatility.

Detemple and Jorion also find evidence of statistically significant marketwide positive abnormal returns associated with option listing events. They estimate that the equally weighted market portfolio experienced a cumulative abnormal return of 1.5% (1.1% for the value-weighted stock) in the two weeks surrounding option listing events. Moreover, for individual stock option listings that followed the introduction of index options in 1982, the price and volatility effects associated with option listing no longer are statistically significant. The authors suggest that these marketwide effects are consistent with theoretical models that predict the introduction of an option into an incomplete market will cause both own and cross-security price effects, whereas the introduction of an option that does little to alter market completeness will have little price impact.

Chamberlain, Cheung, and Kwan (1993) investigate the volume, volatility, and liquidity effects associated with the introduction of options trading on 37 companies listed on the Toronto Stock Exchange over the period November 1979 through January 1987. The authors examine changes in measures of volatility, volume, and the bid-asked spread from a period four months before to four months after the introduction of stock options. Controlling for marketwide volatility, volume, and liquidity effects, they find that, on average, the introduction of options trading was associated with a slight decline in volatility, a slight increase in trading activity, and a slight decrease in the bid-asked spread. None of the estimated changes in their sample, however, is statistically significant.

Damodaran and Lim (1991) study the effects of options introduction on the return generating processes for a sample of 200 stocks in a 500-day window before and after options introduction. They document that, on average, the introduction of options lowers total daily return volatility and the residual volatility of daily market model residuals. Their results suggest that average total daily return volatility declined by about 24% and the sample average excess return volatility declined by 22.5%. Damodaran and Lim also decompose the return variance into two components: an intrinsic value component and a noise component. The noise component can be further decomposed into a bid-asked spread effect and an idiosyncratic noise term. Damodaran and Lim find that the reduction in return volatility on average owes to a reduction in the noise term, which in part owes to a reduction in the average bid-asked spread. If the sample is partitioned into firms that experienced variances increases and decreases, they find that, on average, while variance declines owe to declines in the both intrinsic and the noise components of return variance, the decline in the noise component is more substantial. When firms experience variance increases subsequent to options introduction, the variance increase appears to owe primarily to an increase in the intrinsic return component of volatility. Moreover, stocks that show increases in variance also show evidence of significantly faster spread of adjustments to intrinsic value information shocks whereas stocks that show declining variance show no significant changes in their speed of adjustment parameters. Therefore, the data are consistent with the hypothesis that option introduction increase the efficiency of underlying stock prices by speeding up the price adjustment process and, on average, reducing the "noise" component in daily returns.

7. Margins and volatility in the futures markets

Theoretical results

Many theoretical models relate futures margin requirements to trading activity and price volatility in the futures contract. A substantial literature investigates both the theory of prudential margin requirements and theories that attempt to relate margin requirement changes to changes in the speculative behavior of agents.

In futures markets, margin requirements set the counterparty collateral rules that help ensure contract performance.[20] This so-called prudential function generally is associated with margin requirements on clearinghouse-guaranteed derivative contracts, although, given settlement procedures, a stock purchase actually is a forward contract subject to default risk. For example, if the price of a clearinghouse-guaranteed derivative contract moves against a clearinghouse counterparty or if an option is exercised against it, the clearinghouse counterparty may have an incentive to default on the contract obligation. To minimize a counterparty's incentive to default, the clearinghouse requires that the counterparty post collateral or an initial margin amount with the clearinghouse. A significant literature discusses the optimal approach for setting prudential margin requirements.[21] A uniform implication of the prudential margin literature is that, other things equal, margin requirements should be set so that they are positively related to expected futures contract price volatility. Therefore, if futures clearinghouses follow efficient prudential margin setting procedures, one should observe a positive relationship between futures margin requirements and futures contract price volatility, regardless of any effect that margin may have on the activities of speculators.

In the literature that relates margin requirements to the behavior of futures traders, most models follow Telser (1981) and assume that margin requirements impose a liquidity cost on futures market participants. Telser argues that all agents have a precautionary demand for liquid asset holdings like Treasury bills. Treasury bills also can be posted to satisfy futures margin requirements. Even though the Treasury bill owner still accrues interest, T-bills posted as margin deposits no longer satisfy an agent's demand for precautionary balances. Other things equal, a higher margin requirement will induce a contraction in an agent's futures positions so that an agent's overall endowment can support both the futures position margin requirement and the precautionary demand for liquid balances.

Hartzmark (1986) considers the effects of altering margin requirements on the price volatility and level of trading activity in futures markets. He develops a theoretical framework that includes groups of traders that differ in their price expectations, risk aversions, optimal cash holdings, and their perception of the covariance between spot and futures price changes. In his model, a uniform change in the margin requirement imposes differential changes in liquidity costs across agents, owing to differences in agent's characteristics and overall expectations profiles. Because of these unobservable differences in liquidity costs, the margin requirement is not a tool that can be used effectively to encourage the selective exit of those agents causing the unwarranted price volatility in the Hartzmark model. Because a margin change will cause an unpredictable shift in the composition of the trading population, it will have unpredictable effects on price volatility.

Pliska and Shalen (1991) formulate a theoretical model designed to investigate the effects of margin requirements and position limits on futures trading activity and price volatility. Their model incorporates an exogenous hedger demand and multiple speculators with heterogeneous expectations. Margin requirements are assumed to impose a cost in proportion to the absolute value of a futures position. Speculators transact in the futures market by maximizing a mean-variance utility function based on a noisy expectation of the spot price. Pliska and Shalen show that margin costs induce a bid-asked spread discontinuity into individual speculator's demand functions. As margins are increased, each speculator's bid-asked spread widens, and in aggregate, speculators' trading demands fall and open interest declines. Although Pliska and Shalen are unable to analytically establish the implications of a change in margin requirements, they investigate volatility effects in a numerical simulation exercise. They find that, once margin requirements are increased beyond a threshold level, increases in margin requirements increase volatility.

There is another potential channel through which futures margin requirements may affect the underlying instrument's cash price volatility. The ability to default on a clearinghouse-guaranteed derivative contract may be valuable to a clearinghouse counterparty. It can be formally demonstrated that the value of this implicit default option is equal to the value of a put option written on the instrument that underlies the contract. This implicit option is granted to the counterparty by the clearinghouse.[22] The strike price on this implicit put option, in part, is determined by the contract's prudential margin requirement.[23] Since it does not explicitly charge for this default put option, the clearinghouse should adjust margins so that the option is valueless to all its counterparties. Otherwise, agents may demand contracts and take positions simply to profit from a mispriced clearinghouse guarantee. Therefore if a contract's margin requirement is set inappropriately low from a prudential standpoint, contract demand could be stimulated. Such a situation could result in solvency problems for the clearinghouse, with associated effects on market volatility.

Empirical evidence. Fishe, Goldberg, Gosnell, and Sinha (1990) study the relationship between initial margin requirements and price volatility using data on 10 futures contracts traded on the Chicago Board of Trade (CBOT) over the 1972–1988 sample period. They find that, consistent with theories of prudential margin management, the CBOT clearinghouse's initial margin requirement is higher the higher is a contract's price or the higher is the average intraday price volatility and is lower the smaller is the contract open interest. Examining the effects of all initial margin changes on 10 CBOT contracts from 1972–1988 shows mixed evidence concerning volatility effects across contracts. Some contracts show volatility increases, some decreases, and some show no evidence of change. The authors conclude that their evidence does not support the hypothesis that changes in margins have systematic effect on futures price volatility.

Fishe and Goldberg (1986) investigate the relationship between margin changes, volume, and open interest on all futures contracts traded on the CBOT between 1972 and 1978. They find a 10% increase in initial margin requirements reduces open interest by between 0.33 and 0.50% on nearby contracts; for intermediate and longer-term contracts, higher margins reduce open interest but not by a statistically significant magnitude. They also find that trading volume is weakly positively associated with margin changes. This evidence is consistent with their open-interest finding because intraday volume is not margined.

Kupiec (1993) studies the relationship between margin requirements on the S&P 500 futures contract and the intraday volatility of S&P 500 stock index returns. The study measures futures margin requirements as the hedge initial margin requirement divided by the contract value on the nearest term quarterly S&P 500 futures contract. This measure of futures margin requirements is a measure of the leverage available in an S&P 500 index futures contract. S&P 500 intraday return volatility is estimated using the range estimator suggested by Parkinson (1980) over the sample period July 1987 through July 1989 and thus includes the 1987 crash period. The results of the analysis suggest that, consistent with expected clearinghouse behavior, high margin rates in the futures market tend to be associated with periods of high intraday S&P 500 stock index return volatility. Kupiec finds no evidence to support the hypothesis that low margin rates in the futures market are associated with above average volatility in the cash market.

Moser (1992) analyzes the relationship between futures return volatility and changes in margin requirements for the S&P 500 stock index futures contract and for the deutsche mark futures contract. Moser finds strong evidence that margins and volatility are related. Consistent with the prudential management of margins, he finds that changes in return volatility lead changes in futures margin requirements and no evidence that changes in margin requirements cause changes in volatility.

Hardouvelis and Kim (1995) examine metals futures contracts. They exclude silver contracts during the Hunt brothers squeeze period, arguing that the special circumstances of the period would contaminate their sample. Hardouvelis and Kim find strong evidence that high metals futures margins reduce contract open interest but no evidence that higher margins attenuate contract price volatility. Indeed, their evidence suggests that any empirical margin-volatility relationship in the data owes to the prudential activities of the futures clearinghouses. Higher volatility leads the clearinghouse to increase margins, but the increase in margin has no measurable effect on contract price volatility subsequently. Hardouvelis and Kim (1996) examine the same data and model volatility including a jump process. This embellishment uncovers no new compelling evidence. They conclude that their empirical evidence suggests that futures clearinghouses react to higher volatility by raising futures margin requirements.

Day and Lewis (1997a) consider the relationship between margin requirements and expected volatility in the crude oil futures market. They use the price of options on oil futures contracts and a stochastic volatility options pricing model to extract estimates of the term structure of implied volatility in the crude oil futures market. They examine the reaction of their forward volatility estimates to changes in the margin requirements on crude oil futures contracts. They find that, consistent with the prudential risk management functions of margins, the clearinghouse appears to raise (lower) margins following an increase (decrease) in implied volatility. Although clearinghouses may alter margins on observing changes in volatility conditions, Day and Lewis's statistical evidence does not support the hypothesis that clearinghouse margin changes affect the magnitudes of their forward volatility estimates. Their results clearly suggest that return volatility changes in the crude oil market cause futures margin changes, but futures margin changes do not cause any systematic change in return volatility.

As discussed earlier, it is theoretically possible that futures clearinghouses may create the potential for excess volatility by undermargining clearinghouse-guaranteed derivative contracts. Although possible, little evidence suggests that this is likely to be a widespread problem. Craine (1992) attempts to estimate the value of the implicit put option created by an undermargined clearinghouse guarantee. Using data on S&P 500 futures contract margins over alternative sample periods, Craine finds that these implicit options are valueless in most instances. The week of the October 1987 market crash, however, is an exception. Craine estimates that, during this week, the default put option associated with an S&P 500 futures clearinghouse guarantee had a positive value. According to his estimates, the put was valuable for only a brief period as, by the week's end, the clearinghouse posted a significant increase in margin requirements that eradicated any default put option value.

In a more recent study, Day and Lewis (1997b) also model the clearinghouse guarantee as a default put option owned by the clearinghouse counterparty. In contrast to Craine, Day and Lewis model the guarantee as a barrier option and estimate its value for NYMEX oil contracts over the period November 1986 to March 1991, a period that includes the oil price volatility associated with Iraq's invasion of Kuwait. Similar to Craine's findings, Day and Lewis find that, on average, the clearinghouse sets maintenance margins sufficiently high that the implict default option on crude oil futures contracts is valueless. Day and Lewis, however, do detect transitory periods of heightened oil price volatility in which margins were set sufficiently low that the implicit guarantee default option could have had a positive value. In both the Craine and Day and Lewis studies, the default option value is calculated ignoring the performance incentive-enhancing effects created by clearinghouse exchange standards, membership capital requirements, and financial condition monitoring. Although the default option value calculations are informative, whether or not the calculations imply that the exchanges were truly undermargining contracts is an open question.

8. Conclusion

After examining the academic evidence that investigates the relationship between margin and volatility in both the cash and futures markets and considering the results of studies that measure the effects of derivative market introductions, this study concludes that no substantial body of scientific evidence supports the hypothesis that margin requirements can be systematically altered to manage the volatility in stock markets. The empirical evidence shows that, while high Reg T margin requirements may reduce the volume of securities credit lending and high futures margins do appear to reduce the open interest in futures contracts, neither of these measurable effects appears to be systematically associated with lower stock return volatility. The evidence to date suggests that, contrary to the leverage arguments advanced by the pyramiding-depyramiding hypothesis and explicitly accepted by many of the official studies of the 1987 stock market crash, no scientific evidence supports the hypothesis that tightening leverage constraints in either the cash or equity derivative markets will reduce stock return volatility.

Acknowledgments

I am grateful to Pat White, Pat Parkinson, Greg Duffee, and Katherine Allen for helpful discussions.

Notes

1. Reg T was subsequently followed by Regulation U, the rules that extend Reg T margin requirements to bank security lending; Regulation G, the rules that govern securities lending by all other domestic lenders; and Regulation X, the guidelines for the extension of securities credit by foreign lenders. Until the introduction of exchange-traded equity options in 1973, the FRB did not exercise its authority to establish uniform margin requirements for stock options.
2. The Commodities Futures Trading Commission (CFTC) always has had regulatory authority to approve futures clearinghouse margining systems (17CFR Section 1.31). Although the CFTC had the authority to approve the margining systems, Sections 5(a)(12) and 8(a)(7) of the Commodity Exchange Act (CEA) expressly precluded the CFTC from exercising authority over the level of margins for futures transactions. An exception is granted under Section 8(a)(9) of the CEA, where the CFTC is granted authority under its emergency powers clause to set temporary margin levels in order to maintain or restore orderly trading in the futures markets.

3. The legal profession may have a difference of opinion. Historically, Reg T required that long options be paid for in full (a 100% margin requirement). Under recently adopted Reg T rule changes, long options will be eligible to receive collateral value but not until the NYSE modifies its rules to accommodate this change. So, historically, it was legally impossible to obtain a loan using options as collateral. However, from a legal point of view, options apparently are viewed as an extension of credit. As near as I can tell, the legal argument is as follows: The writer of the option is extended credit by the option purchaser because the purchaser is subject to the risk of contract performance. The legal interpretation that performance risk is an extension of credit to the option writer apparently was the argument used to assert legal jurisdiction over equity option margin requirements under Sections 7 and 8 of the 1934 Securities and Exchange Act (please consult your own securities attorney before acting on this historical interpretation). Regardless of the legalities, from an economic standpoint, the margin requirements on written options satisfy a prudential function and are not related to any economic extension of credit. See Kahl, Rutz, and Sinquefield (1985) for a comparison of the role margin requirements on stocks and futures contracts.
4. Moore (1966) summarizes the discussion that transpired in the congressional hearings on margin authority. Alternatively, see the discussion in France (1991).
5. Chairman Martin's testimony before the U.S. Senate Committee on Banking and Currency, 84th Congress, 1955, as quoted in Moore (1966, p. 163).
6. See, for example, Moore (1966); Officer (1973); Largay and West (1973); or Grube, Joy, and Panton (1979).
7. See, for example, Telser (1981), Figlewski (1984), or Edwards (1983).
8. See, for example the NYSE's (1990) study, "Market Volatility and Investor Confidence," Recommendation 8.
9. See, for example the discussion in Hardouvelis (1989).
10. See the references in note 6.
11. His estimates suggest that the long-run effect for small stocks would be about a 15% reduction in monthly return volatility.
12. Seguin finds no statistically significant changes in return autocorrelation patterns.
13. Seguin and Jarrell present evidence that suggests that the higher excess volume likely owes in part to forced margin-call sales.
14. For a discussion, see Cox and Rubinstein (1985) or Manaster and Rendleman (1982).
15. The contract terminated trading in the late 1980s.
16. This relationship assumes interest rates are constant over the life of the contract.
17. This is clearly simplified. Index arbitrage is often conducted as an "approximate" arbitrage, where only a portion of shares in the index are traded.
18. Stoll and Whaley (1990) estimate that the bid-asked component of the transactions cost is approximately 10 basis points for a stock index futures transaction and 150 basis points for an individual share purchase.
19. See, for example, Stoll and Whaley (1991) or Chen and Williams (1994).
20. See Telser (1981) for an extensive discussion.
21. A partial list of references includes, Telser (1981); Tomek (1985); Figlewski (1984); Edwards (1983); Gay, Hunter, and Kolb (1986); Fishe and Goldberg (1986); Craine (1992); Fenn and Kupiec (1993); Moser (1992); Kupiec (1994); Kupiec and White (1996); and Day and Lewis (1997b).
22. See for example, Fishe and Goldberg (1986); Craine (1992); and Day and Lewis (1997b).
23. The strike price also is implicitly set by the rigor of clearinghouse membership standards and the ease with which clearinghouse default losses can be recovered in the courts in the event of default.

References

Bessembinder, Hendrik, and Paul Seguin, "Futures Trading Activity and Stock Price Volatility," *Journal of Finance* 47, no. 5 (1992), 2015–2034.

Blume, M., A. MacKinlay, and B. Terker, "Order Imbalances and Stock Price Movements on October 19 and 20, 1987," *Journal of Finance* 44, no. 4 (1989), 827–848.

Chatrath, Arjun, Sanjay Ramchander, and Frank Song, "Does Options Trading Lead to Greater Cash Market Volatility," *Journal of Futures Markets* 15, no. 7 (1995), 785–803.

Chamberlain, Trevor, C. Sherman Cheung, and Clarence Kwan, "Option Listing, Market Liquidity and Stock Behavior: Some Canadian Evidence," *Journal of Business, Finance and Accounting* 20, no. 5 (1993), 687–698.

Chance, Don, *The Effects of Margins on Volatility and Derivative Markets: A Review of the Evidence*, Monograph Series in Finance and Economics, No. 1990-2. New York: New York University Solomon Center, 1990.

Chen, Chao, and James Williams, "Triple-Witching Hour, the Change in Expiration Timing, and Stock Market Reaction," *Journal of Futures Markets* 14, no. 3 (1994), 275–292.

Conrad, Jennifer, "The Price Effect of Option Introduction," *Journal of Finance* 44, no. 2 (1989), 487–498.

Cox, Charles, "Futures Trading and Market Information," *Journal of Political Economy* 84, no. 6 (1976), 1215–1237.

Cox, John, and Mark Rubinstein, *Options Markets*, Englewood Cliffs, NJ: Prentice-Hall, 1985.

Craine, Roger, "Are Futures Margins Adequate?" University of California, Berkeley working paper No. 92-192, April 1992.

Damodaran, Aswath, and Joseph Lim, "The Effects of Option Listing on the Underlying Stock's Return Processes," *Journal of Banking and Finance* 15, no. 3 (1991), 647–664.

Darrat, Ali, and Shafiqur Rahman, "Has Futures Trading Caused Stock Price Volatility?" *Journal of Futures Markets* 15, no. 5 (1995), 537–557.

Day, Theodore, and Craig Lewis, "Initial Margin Policy and Stochastic Volatility in the Crude Oil Futures Markets," *Review of Financial Studies* 10, no. 2 (1997a), 303–332.

Day, Theodore, and Craig Lewis, "Margin Adequacy in Futures Markets," Memo, Owen Graduate School of Management, Vanderbilt University, 1997b.

Detemple, Jerome, and Philippe Jorion, "Option LIsting and Stock Returns," First Boston working paper, No. 89-13, Columbia University, 1990.

Detemple, Jerome, and Philippe Jorion, "Option Listing and Stock Returns," *Journal of Banking and Finance* 14, no. 4 (1990), 781–801.

Detemple, Jerome, and Larry Seldon, "A General Equilibrium Analysis of Option and Stock Market Interactions," *International Economic Review* 32, no. 2 (1991), 279–303.

Edwards, Franklin, "The Clearing Association in Futures Markets: Guarantor and Regulator," *Journal of Futures Markets* 3, no. 4 (1983), 369–392.

Edwards, Franklin, "Futures Trading and Cash Market Volatility: Stock Index and Interest Rate Futures," *Journal of Futures Markets* 8, no. 4 (1988), 421–439.

Federal Reserve Board, "A Review and Evaluation of Federal Margin Regulations," Washington, DC: Board of Governors of the Federal Reserve System, December 1984.

Fenn, G., and P. Kupiec, "Prudential Margin Policy in a Futures-Style Settlement System," *Journal of Futures Markets* 13, no. 4, 389–408.

Ferris, Stephen, and Don Chance, "Margin Requirements and Stock Market Volatility," *Economic Letters* 28, no. 3 (1988), 251–254.

Figlewski, Stephen, "Futures Trading and Volatility in the GNMA Market," *Journal of Finance* 36, no. 2 (1981), 445–456.

Figlewski, Stephen, "Margins and Market Integrity: Setting Margins for Stock Index Futures and Options, Association in Futures Markets: Guarantor and Regulator," *Journal of Futures Markets* 4, no. 3 (1984), 385–416.

Fishe, Raymond, and Lawrence Goldberg, "The Effects of Margins on Trading in Futures Markets," *Journal of Futures Markets* 6, no. 2 (1986), 261–271.

Fishe, R., L. Goldberg, T. Gosnell, and S. Sinha, "Margin Requirements in Futures Markets: Their Relationship to Price Volatility," *Journal of Futures Markets* 10, no. 5 (1990), 541–554.

France, Virginia, "The Regulation of Margin Requirements," In: Lester Telser (ed.), *Margins and Market Integrity*, Chicago: Mid America Institute, Probus Publishing Company, 1991.

Froewiss, Kenneth, "GNMA Futures: Stabilizing or Destabilizing?" *Federal Reserve Bank of San Francisco, Economic Review* (Spring 1978), 20–29.

Goldberg, Michael, "The Relevance of Margin Regulation," *Journal of Money, Credit, and Banking* 17, no. 1 (1985), 521–527.

Gordon, G., and G. Pennacchi, "Security Baskets and Index-Linked Securities," *Journal of Business* 66, no. 1 (1993), 1–28.

Grube, R.C., O.M. Joy, and J.S. Howe, "Some Empirical Evidence on Stock Returns and Security Credit Regulation in the OTC Equity Market," *Journal of Banking and Finance* 11, no. 1 (1987), 17–31.

Grube, R.C., O.M. Joy, and D. Panton, "Market Responses to Federal Reserve Changes in the Initial Margin Requirement," *Journal of Finance* 34, no. 3 (1979), 659–674.

Gay, G., W. Hunter, and R. Kolb, "A Comparative Analysis of Futures Contract Margins," *Journal of Futures Markets* 6, no. 2 (1986), 307–324.

Hardouvelis, Gikas, "Margin Requirements and Stock Market Volatility," *FRBNY Quarterly Review* (Summer 1988).

Hardouvelis, Gikas, "Commentary: Stock Market Margin Requirements and Volatility," *Journal of Financial Services Research* 3, nos. 2–3 (1989), 139–151.

Hardouvelis, Gikas, "Margin Requirements, Volatility, and the Transitory Component of Stock Prices," *American Economic Review* 80, no. 4 (1990), 736–763.

Hardouvelis, Gikas, and Dongcheol Kim, "Margin Requirements, Price Fluctuations, and Market Participation in Metal Futures," *Journal of Money, Credit, and Banking* 27, no. 3 (1995), 659–671.

Hardouvelis, Gikas, and Dongcheol Kim, "Price Volatility and Futures Markets," *Journal of Futures Markets* 16, no. 1 (1996), 81–111.

Harris, Lawrence, "S&P500 Cash Stock Price Volatilities," *Journal of Finance* 44, no. 5 (1989), 1155–1176.

Hart, Oliver, "On the Optimality of Equilibrium When the Market Structure Is Incomplete," *Journal of Economic Theory* 11, no. 3 (1975), 418–443.

Hartzmark, Michael, "The Effects of Changing Margin Levels on Futures Market Activity, the Composition of Traders in the Market, and Price Performance," *Journal of Business* 59, no. 2 (1986), S147–S180.

Hayes, S., and M. Tennenbaum, "The Impact of Listed Options on the Underlying Shares," *Financial Management* (1979), 72–76.

Hong, Choi, and Avavidhar Subrahmanyam, "Using Intraday Data to Test for Effects of Index Futures on the Underlying Stock Markets," *Journal of Futures Markets* 14, no. 3 (1994), 293–322.

Hsieh, D., and M. Miller, "Margin Regulation and Stock Market Volatility," *Journal of Finance* 45, no. 1 (1990), 3–30.

Jegadeesh, Narasimhan, and Avanidhar Subrahmanyam, "Liquidity Effects on the Introduction of the S&P 500 Index Futures Contract on Underlying Stocks," *Journal of Business* 66, no. 2 (1993), 171–187.

Kahl, Kandice, Roger Rutz, and Jeanne Sinquefield, "The Economics of Performance Margins in Futures Markets," *Journal of Futures Markets* 5, no. 1 (1985), 103–112.

Kalavathi, L., and Latha Shanker, "Margin Requirements and the Demand for for Futures Contracts," *Journal of Futures Markets* 11, no. 2 (1991), 213–237.

Kamara, Avraham, Thomas Miller Jr., and Andrew Siegel, "The Effect of Futures Trading on the Stability of Standard and Poor 500 Returns," *Journal of Futures Markets* 12, no. 5 (1992), 645–658.

Katzenbach, N., "An Overview of Program Trading and its Impact on Current Market Practices." A study commissioned by the New York Stock Exchange. New York: Dec. 1987.

Kupiec, Paul, "Initial Margin Requirements and Stock Returns Volatility: Another Look," *Journal of Financial Services Research* 3, nos. 2–3 (1989), 189–202.

Kupiec, Paul, "Futures Margins and Stock Price Volatility: Is There Any Link?" *Journal of Futures Markets* 13, no. 6 (1993), 677–691.

Kupiec, Paul, and Steve Sharpe, "Animal Spirits, Margin Requirements and Stock Price Volatility," *Journal of Finance* 46, no. 2 (1991), 717–732.

Kupiec, Paul, "The Performance of S&P 500 Futures Product Margins Under the SPAN Margining System," *Journal of Futures Markets* 14, no. 7 (1994), 789–812.

Kupiec, Paul, and A. Pat White, "Regulatory Competition and the Efficiency of Alternative Derivative Product Margining Systems," *Journal of Futures Markets* 16, no. 8 (1996), 943–968.

Largay, James, "100 Percent Margins: Combating Speculation in Individual Security Issues," *Journal of Finance* 28, no. 4 (1973), 973–986.

Largay, James, and Richard West, "Margin Changes and Stock Price Behavior," *Journal of Political Economy* 81, no. 2 (1973), 328–339.

"Market Volatility and Investor Confidence." A report commissioned by the New York Stock Exchange. New York, 1990.

Manaster, Steven, and Richard Rendleman, Jr., "Options Prices as Predictors of Equilibrium Stock Prices," *Journal of Finance* 37, no. 4 (1982), 1043–1057.

Moore, Thomas, "Stock Market Margin Requirements," *Journal of Political Economy* 74, no. 2 (1966), 158–167.

Moser, J., "Determining Margin for Futures Contracts: The Role of Private Interests and the Relevance of Excess Volatility," *Federal Reserve Bank of Chicago Economic Perspectives* (March–April 1992), 2–18.

Officer R., "The Variability of the Market Factor of the New York Stock Exchange," *Journal of Business* 46 (July 1973), 434–453.

Parkinson, Michael, "The extreme Value Method for Estimating the Variance of the Rate of Return," *Journal of Business* 53, no. 1 (1980), 61–65.

Pliska, Stanley, and Catherine Shalen, "The Effects of Regulations on Trading Activity and Return Volatility in Futures Markets," *Journal of Futures Markets* 11, no. 2 (1991), 135–151.

Powers, Mark, "Does Futures Trading Reduce Price Fluctuations in the Cash Markets," *American Economic Review* 60, no. 5 (1970), 460–464.

Presidential Task Force on Market Mechanisms. "Report of the Presidential Task Force on Market Mechanisms," Washington D.C., U.S. Government Printing Office, 1988.

Salinger, M., "Stock Market Margin Requirements and Volatility: Implications for Regulation of Stock Index Futures," *Journal of Financial Services Research* 3, nos. 2–3 (1989), 121–138.

Schwert, G.W., "Why Does Stock Market Volatility Change over Time?" *Journal of Finance* 44, no. 5 (1989a), 1115–1154.

Schwert, G.W., "Margin Requirements and Stock Volatility," *Journal of Financial Services Research* 3, nos. 2–3 (1989b), 153–164.

Seguin, Paul, "Stock Volatility and Margin Trading," *Journal of Monetary Economics* 26, no. 1 (1990), 101–121.

Seguin, Paul, and Gregg Jarrell, "The Irrelevance of Margin: Evidence from the Crash of '87," *Journal of Finance* 48, no. 4 (1993), 1457–1473.

Simpson, Gary, and Timothy Ireland, "The Effects of Futures Trading on the Price Volatility of GNMA Securities," *Journal of Futures Markets* 2, no. 4 (1982), 357–366.

Skinner, Douglas J., "Options Markets and Stock Return Volatility," *Journal of Financial Economics* 23, no. 1 (1989), 61–78.

Stein, Jeremy, "Information Externalities and Welfare-Reducing Speculation," *Journal of Political Economy* 95, no. 6 (1987), 1123–1145.

Stoll, H., and R. Whaley, "Expiration Day Effects of Index Options and Futures," *Financial Analysts Journal* 43 (1987), 16–28.

Stoll, H., and R. Whaley, "The Dynamics of Stock Index and Stock Index Futures Returns," *Journal of Financial and Quantitative Analysis* 25, no. 4 (1990), 441–467.

Stoll, H., and R. Whaley, "Expiration Day Effects: What Has Changed?" *Financial Analysts Journal* 58 (1991), 58–72.

Subrahmanyam, Avavidhar, "A Theory of Trading in Stock Index Futures," *Review of Financial Studies* 4, no. 1 (1991), 17–51.

Tesler, L., "Margins and Futures Contracts," *Journal of Futures Markets* 1, 255–285.

Tomek, William, "Margin on Futures Contracts: Their Economic Roles and Regulation," In: Anne Peck (ed.), *Futures Markets: Regulatory Issues*, American Enterprise Institute, 1985.

Turnovsky, Stephen, and Robert Campbell, "The Stabilizing and Welfare Properties of Futures Markets: A Simulation Approach," *International Economic Review* 26, no. 2 (1985), 277–303.

U.S. Securities and Exchange Commission. "The October 1987 Market Break." A report by the Division of Market Regulation, Feb. 1988.

Weller, Paul, and Makoto Yano, "Forward Exchange, Futures Trading and Spot Price Variability: A General Equilibrium Approach," *Econometrica* 55, no. 6 (1987), 1433–1450.

Working Group on Financial Markets. "Interim Report of the Working Group on Financial Markets," Washington D.C., U.S. Government Printing Office, May 1988.

Journal of Financial Services Research 13:3 257–282 (1998)

Mutual Funds and Stock and Bond Market Stability

FRANKLIN R. EDWARDS
Graduate School of Business, Columbia University, New York

XIN ZHANG
The World Bank, Washington, DC

Abstract

The unprecedented growth of mutual funds has raised questions about the impact of mutual fund flows on stock and bond prices. Many believe that the equity bull market of the 1990s is attributable to the huge flows of funds into equity mutual funds during this period and that a withdrawal of those funds could send stock prices plummeting. This article investigates the relationship between aggregate monthly mutual fund flows (sales, redemptions, and net sales) and stock and bond monthly returns during a 30-year period beginning January 1961 utilizing Granger causality and instrumental variables analysis. With one exception, flows into stock and bond funds have not affected either stock and bond returns. The exception is 1971–1981, when widespread redemptions from equity mutual funds significantly depressed stock returns. In contrast, the magnitude of flows into both stock and bond funds are affected significantly by stock and bond returns.

1. Introduction

From 1990 through 1996, the S&P 500 stock index soared by more than 120% (from 329 on January 1, 1990, to 725 by early 1997), sending financial analysts in search of explanations for this unprecedented bull market. By 1996, conventional stock market yardsticks provided little comfort to investors: price-earnings ratios (of more than 20) approached the lofty levels seen right before the 1987 stock market crash and dividend-to-price ratios (of less than 2%) were at historical lows. The market to book ratio for the S&P 500 companies, another closely watched stock market indicator, also rose from about 1 in the early 1990s to over 1.4 by 1996, a level not seen since right before the bear market of the 1970s.

Despite these signs of an overvalued stock market, mutual fund investors continued to pour money into stock mutual funds at an unprecedented pace. The assets of equity mutual funds went from $249 billion in January 1990 to over $1.7 trillion by year-end 1996, an increase of nearly 600%. During the entire 1984–1996 bull market, stock prices and equity mutual fund net sales also exhibited a strong positive correlation[1] (see figures 1 and 2). It is hardly surprising, therefore, that financial analysts and the financial press have pointed to equity mutual funds as the driving force behind the sustained run-up of stock prices (see Wyatt, 1996; McGough, 1997). Their argument is simple and deceptively appealing: Equity mutual fund growth manifests a greater demand by individuals to hold stock, and this ''price pressure'' must surely result in higher stock prices as more investors chase a

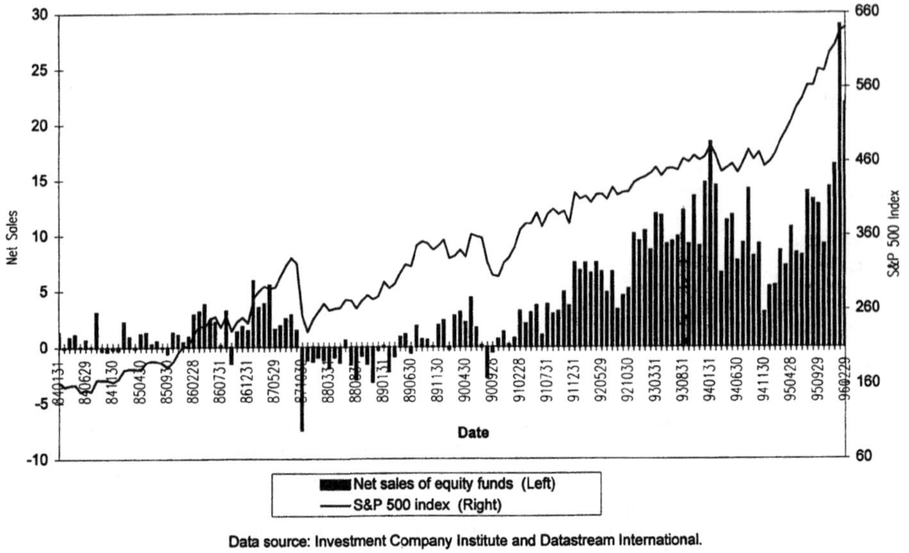

Figure 1. Net sales of equity mutual funds (in billions of dollars) and S&P 500 index (month-end data, Jan. 1984–Feb. 1996). Data source: Investment Company Institute and Datastream International.

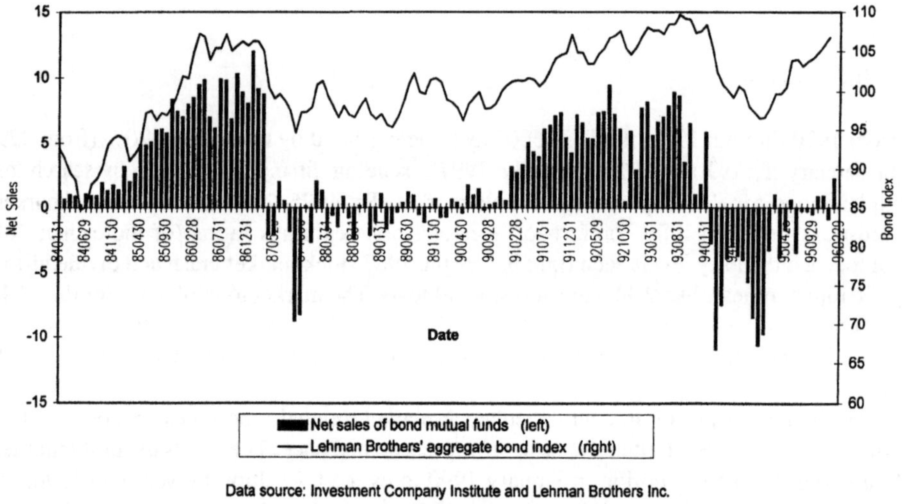

Figure 2. Net sales of bond mutual funds (in billions of dollars) and Lehman Brothers' aggregate bond index (month-end data, Jan. 1984–Feb. 1996). Data source: Investment Company Institute and Lehman Brothers Inc.

relatively fixed supply of corporate equity. Indeed, from 1990 through 1996, corporate buyback programs actually reduced the amount of equity outstanding.

The flip side of this view, which analysts also have recognized, is that a change-of-heart by investors could result in widespread mutual fund redemptions, sending stock prices plummeting (see Wyatt, 1997; Kinsella, 1996). Each month analysts scrutinize mutual fund redemptions for signs that the stock market boom may be reaching its end.

Notwithstanding these perceptions and fears, we know very little about the effect of mutual fund flows on either stock or bond prices, markets in which mutual funds have become increasingly important. Despite the obvious correlation between mutual fund net sales and both stock and bond prices, this relationship is not sufficient to infer causality between mutual fund flows and asset prices. A positive correlation between fund flows and asset prices could exist for a number of reasons: Increased equity mutual fund flows in fact could increase stock prices, an increase in stock prices could cause more people to buy equity mutual funds, or a two-way causality between fund flows and asset prices may exist. Alternatively, both fund flows and asset prices could be caused by (or be positively associated with) other economic factors. For example, higher expected corporate profits could result in both higher stock prices and increased equity mutual funds sales, as investors shift assets into equity mutual funds to obtain higher returns.

This paper investigates the causal relationships between mutual fund flows and stock and bond prices. Specifically, we analyze the relationship between aggregate monthly mutual fund flows into stock and bond mutual funds and monthly stock and bond prices utilizing different econometric procedures designed to identify causal relationships. Equity mutual fund flows (sales, redemptions, and net sales) are examined for the 30-year period from January 1961 through February 1996, and bond mutual fund flows are examined for the 20-year period from January 1976 through February 1996.

2. Why should mutual fund flows affect asset returns? Alternative theories

In an efficient market, changes in stock prices (and returns) should reflect fundamental economic factors, such as changes in expected corporate profits or in interest rate levels (or the discount factor). Similarly, changes in bond prices (and returns) should reflect changes in expected interest rate levels. While stock and bond prices may stray from fundamental equilibrium values for short periods of time, such deviations can be expected to be random and short-lived, given the breadth and depth of U.S. financial markets. Therefore, flows into or out of mutual funds, no matter how large, arguably should have no effect on equilibrium asset prices or returns independent of changes in market fundamentals.

Suppose, for example, that a certain small segment of investors—say, those buying mutual funds—decides to buy more equity (possibly for irrational reasons), even though there is no change in market fundamentals, but other segments of the investor population do not change their views about the fundamentals (or about expected corporate earnings and the appropriate risk premium). While we would expect to observe an increased flow of funds into stock mutual funds, this increased demand for stock quickly should be met by a willingness to sell on the part of other stockholders (such as pension funds) who did not change their view of the fundamentals, thereby preventing a rise in stock prices.

Mutual funds, after all, are only a small segment of the stock and bond markets: As of year-end 1994 mutual funds held 12.2% of total outstanding corporate equity and about 14% of total U.S. government and corporate bonds.[2] Pension funds are a much bigger player in both stock and bond markets than mutual funds: At year-end 1994 pension fund assets constituted nearly 28% of household financial assets, compared to about 7% for mutual funds.[3] Finally, individuals still *directly* hold a substantial amount of stocks and bonds, and foreign financial institutions probably now hold a considerable amount as well.[4] So, as big as they have become, stock and bond mutual funds are not the only game in town. In the absence of changes in economic fundamentals, therefore, it is reasonable to think that buying or selling by mutual fund investors will not affect stock and bond prices because such demands quickly will be met by selling or buying on the part of other more informed investors.

It is notable that, in the 15 years from 1982 through 1996, individuals holding stock directly (as opposed to through mutual funds) were net sellers of corporate equity in every year but one, 1992, and since 1990 net flows into equity mutual funds have been mirrored by reductions in the direct holdings of stock by individuals[5] (see figure 3). Therefore, in the aggregate, individuals have increasingly chosen to hold stock indirectly through mutual funds. This trend may reflect a belief that higher returns and greater liquidity can be obtained by entrusting money to mutual funds or, alternatively, the shift towards defined-contribution pension plans and the associated increased use of mutual funds as an investment option in such retirement plans. These stock flows, of course, are ex post accounting identities and tell us nothing about whether equity mutual fund flows have affected stock prices or vice versa.

A view that increased flows into equity mutual funds have not affected stock prices is perfectly consistent with the existence of a positive correlation between equity mutual fund net sales and either equity prices or returns.[6] For example, if new, favorable, information about future corporate earnings were to occur, we would expect to observe an increase in both stock prices and net flows into equity mutual funds. Mutual fund investors could be expected to buy equity mutual fund shares in anticipation of higher stock returns

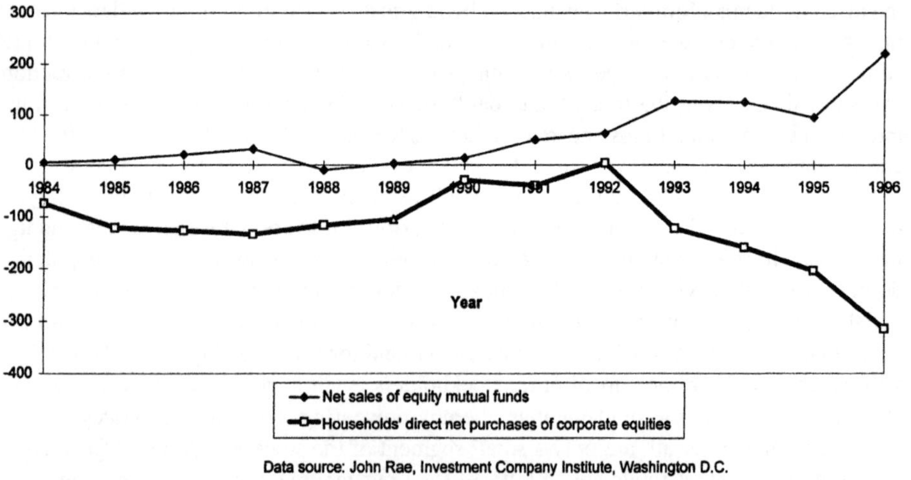

Figure 3. Net sales of equity mutual funds and households' direct net purchases of corporate equities (yearly data, 1984–1996, in billions of dollars). Data source: John Rae, Investment Company Institute, Washington DC.

or, alternatively, in response to higher stock returns as stock prices rose. Similarly, a rise in expected interest rates could be expected to result in both decreased stock prices and decreased flows into equity mutual funds (or a rise in fund redemptions). Both stock returns and mutual fund net flows, therefore, could be affected by a common third factor, such as changes in expected corporate earnings or interest rates, that results in a positive correlation between mutual fund net sales and returns. Therefore, a positive correlation is insufficient to infer causality.

Those who believe that equity mutual fund flows have affected stock prices have a different view of markets. Finance theory provides two possibilities. The first might be labeled the *informed trader theory*. In particular, if mutual fund investors can be viewed as being especially astute or well-informed investors, their purchases and sales might be seen as revealing information about economic fundamentals (or about future equilibrium stock prices) to less-informed investors, who in turn then trade in the same direction as mutual funds investors. Thus, increased purchases (sales) by equity mutual fund investors may signal that current stock prices are below (above) fundamental values, resulting in all investors trading in the same direction as equity mutual fund investors and causing stock prices to rise (fall). This behavior also would result in a positive correlation between net equity mutual fund flows and stock returns.

This view is hard to accept. Mutual fund investors tend to be relatively small and inexperienced investors compared to many other participants in financial markets. The median mutual fund account is $18,000, and mutual fund investors have a median annual household income of $60,000 and median total financial assets of $50,000. About 36% of today's mutual fund holders had no mutual fund account prior to 1991 (Investment Company Institute, 1996). Compared to wealthy individuals or institutional investors such as pension funds, it seems implausible that the market would view mutual fund shareholders as particularly well-informed or astute.

Another theory of why mutual fund flows might affect stock or bond prices is the noise trader theory of De Long, Shleifer, Summers, and Waldmann (DSSW, 1990). The nub of this theory is the existence of a significant body of "noise" traders (or investors) who are largely uninformed and behave "irrationally." Noise traders are characterized as investors who falsely believe that they have special information about future stock prices and as a consequence buy and sell in unpredictable ways. For example, they may overestimate expected stock returns (or underestimate ex ante risk) and demand more stock or underestimate expected stock returns (or overestimate ex ante risk) and demand less stock, causing stock prices to rise or fall in a random or unpredictable way. The contribution of the noise trader theory is to provide a framework to explain why, in the face of such irrational buying or selling, arbitrage by informed investors may fail to keep asset prices from being affected by the actions of noise traders. Why do not the actions of noise traders create profitable trading opportunities for informed traders to trade against the irrational noise traders, thereby preventing prices from straying very far from fundamental values?

An essential element of the noise trader theory is that the unpredictability of noise traders' beliefs and actions itself creates another price risk (in additional to fundamental price risk) that deters rational investors from betting too heavily against them. For example, if noise traders overestimate returns or underestimate the risk of holding stock, they will drive stock prices above fundamental values. However, informed investors still may not bet heavily against them by selling stock, fearing that noise traders will continue to drive prices even higher, imposing losses on them. Because the behavior of noise traders is irrational and unpredictable, there is no assurance that this will not happen. Therefore, stock prices can diverge significantly from fundamental values before informed investors become willing to bet aggressively against noise traders or a market shock reverses noise trader expectations. Indeed, it even can become an inticing trading strategy for informed traders to try to predict the behavior of noise traders in order to trade with them, at times creating a ''bandwagon'' effect on asset prices.

The noise trading theory is premised on a number of critical assumptions: that informed traders are risk averse and focus on short horizons, that the supply of the asset in question (say, stocks or bonds) is fixed or inelastic, that the behavior of irrational traders is unpredictable, that noise traders constitute a not insignificant part of the investor population, and that in the long run noise traders are not driven from the market. DSSW (1990) argue that in today's financial markets none of these assumptions is unrealistic.

Do mutual investors behave like noise traders, at times irrationally and unpredictably overestimating expected returns (or underestimating risk) and at other times underestimating expected returns (or overestimating risk), driving asset prices too high or too low? The findings of a poll of mutual fund investors taken in 1996 by Liberty Financial suggests that such irrational behavior may exist. Mutual fund investors were asked about their views about stock prices in the future (Norris, 1997). Despite stock prices (the Dow Jones Index) having risen an unprecedented 14.2% a year over the last 15 years, most of those surveyed thought that the next decade would bring about the same returns as in the last decade. Only about one in seven thought that stock prices would fail to continue rising as quickly through the next 10 years, and many more thought that prices would rise even faster. Such expectations seem excessively optimistic, given the history of stock returns in the United States. Therefore, if mutual fund investors can be viewed as acting like noise traders, it is possible that their excessively optimistic or pessimistic beliefs could cause stock and bond prices to rise or fall in ways inconsistent with an efficient markets view of asset prices.

3. Identifying causality

Economic theory provides no clear answer to the question of whether changes in mutual fund flows can cause changes in asset prices. While an efficient markets view of markets suggests that mutual fund flows should not affect asset prices, a noise trader view suggests that some price effects are possible. Further, the causality well may run in the opposite direction: Changes in asset prices (or returns) may cause changes in mutual fund flows. In particular, higher stock returns may cause investors to raise their expectations of future stock returns and, as a consequence, increase their holdings of equity mutual funds. To determine whether a causal relationship exists, and if it does in which direction, we must turn to empiricism.

We employ two statistical procedures to identify a causal relationship: Granger causality analysis and the instrumental variables method. Granger causality analysis attempts to identify a causal relationship between two variables by examining the ''lead-lag'' relationships between those variables. If a variable is found to statistically predict (or lead) another variable, it is considered to ''cause'' that variable. Therefore, if Granger tests were to show that monthly mutual fund net sales statistically predict (or lead) monthly stock or bond returns, we would conclude that those flows Granger–cause asset returns. (Granger causality analysis is discussed more fully in section 5.) Such a finding would be consistent with a noise trader view of markets as well as with the popular ''street'' view that mutual fund sales have been a major factor in the bull market of the 1980s and 1990s. Alternatively, if asset returns are found to statistically predict (or lead) mutual fund net sales, we conclude that asset returns Granger–cause fund sales.

The second procedure, instrumental variables, utilizes additional economic factors (or instruments) that affect mutual fund flows and asset returns as part of the statistical procedure for identifying the causal relationship between mutual fund flows and asset returns. (The instrumental variables method is discussed in section 6.) This procedure has more economic content than Granger causality analysis and, unlike Granger analysis, utilizes contemporaneous data to identify causal relationships. However, the procedure may be sensitive to the choice of the instruments used in the analysis.

4. Data and variables

We examine aggregate monthly flows of U.S. equity mutual funds from January 1961 through February 1996 and aggregate monthly flows of U.S. bond mutual funds from January 1976 through February 1996.[7] The net sales of funds is defined as sales minus redemptions, where sales are new sales plus sales through exchanges from other funds within the same family of mutual funds, and where redemptions include those made through exchanges into other funds within the same fund family.[8] Therefore, when redemptions exceed sales, net sales is negative.

For equity and bond returns we use monthly excess returns. Specifically, excess equity returns are annualized monthly returns on the value-weighted New Stock Exchange Composite Index minus the annualized one-month T-bill return, and excess bond returns are annualized monthly returns on the Lehman Brothers' aggregate bond index minus the annualized one-month T-bill return. Monthly stock returns are measured as the percentage change in monthly stock prices plus the monthly dividend yield, and monthly bond returns are measured as the percentage change in monthly bond prices plus the monthly bond yield. Not surprisingly, most of the monthly variation in these returns is due to price changes.

In addition, we employ a number of economic factors as instruments in the instrumental variables analysis. These variables are discussed in section 6 and defined in table 1.

5. Granger causality analysis

Granger causality analysis identifies ''causality'' by examining the prediction error (see Granger, 1969). If past information contained in variable x improves forecasts of another variable, y, variable x is said to cause variable y. Alternatively, if past information contained in y helps to forecast x, y is said to cause x. Thus, mutual fund flows can be said

Table 1. Glossary and definitions of variables

Symbol	Variable	Definition
Basic data series		
Net sales	Mutual fund net sales	Monthly net sales of equity or bond mutual funds (sales less redemptions)
Redemptions	Mutual fund redemptions	Monthly redemptions of equity or bond mutual funds
Sales	Mutual fund total sales	Monthly sales of equity or bond mutual funds
Eqret	Equity market return	Monthly returns on the value-weighted NYSE stock index (annualized)
Bdret	Bond market return	Monthly returns on the Lehman Brothers' aggregate bond index (annualized)
TBL1m	One-month Treasury-bill rate	Monthly rates on one-month T-bills (annualized)
TBL3m	Three-month Treasury-bill rate	Monthly rates on three-month T-bills (annualized)
LGB	Long-term government bond yield	Average monthly returns on 10-year government bonds (annualized)
Baa	Low-grade bond yield	Average monthly returns on bonds rated Baa or under (annualized)
Aaa	High-grade bond yield	Average monthly returns on bonds rated Aaa (annualized)
IP	Industrial production	Monthly Industrial Production Index
Savings	Savings	Monthly aggregate household savings
DEM	Demographics	Population 35 years and older as a percentage of those 16 years and older (monthly data interpolated from yearly data)
Derived series		
Unetsales(t)	Unexpected net sales	The unexpected net sales of equity or bond funds obtained from an AR(4) process
Eqreturn(t)	Excess equity return	Eqret(t) – TBL1m(t)
Bdreturn(t)	Excess bond return	Bdret(t) – TBL1m(t)
MIP(t)	Monthly growth of industrial production	Log [IP(t)/IP(t – 1)]
MDEM(t)	First difference of DEM	DEM(t) – DEM(t – 1)
Msaving(t)	Monthly growth rate of savings	Log [saving(t)/saving(t – 1)]
Riskprem(t)	Risk premium	Baa(t) – LGB(t)
Termstrt(t)	Term structure premium	LGB(t) – TBL1m(t – 1)

to Granger–cause asset returns if returns are better predicted by using both past returns and past fund flows than by using only past returns; alternatively, asset returns can be said to Granger-cause mutual fund flows if fund flows are better predicted by using both past fund flows and returns than by using only past fund flows. In this procedure, mutual fund flows and asset returns are treated symmetrically. Therefore, to determine whether mutual fund flows Granger–cause asset returns, or vice versa, the following system of equations is estimated:

$$\text{Return}_t = a_1 + \sum_{i=1}^{4} b_{1i}\text{Fundflow}_{t-i} + \sum_{i=1}^{4} c_{1i}\text{Return}_{t-i} + \epsilon_{1t} \tag{1a}$$

$$\text{Fundflow}_t = a_2 + \sum_{i=1}^{4} b_{2i}\text{Fundflow}_{t-i} + \sum_{i=1}^{4} c_{2i}\text{Return}_{t-i} + \epsilon_{2t} \tag{1b}$$

where Return represents either equity or bond excess monthly returns and Fundflow is either equity or bond mutual fund monthly flows. Both returns and fund flows are assumed to be stationary variables, and the two disturbance terms in eqs. (1a) and (1b) are assumed to have zero means, constant variances, and be individually serially uncorrelated.

The respective causality hypotheses are that Fundflow does not Granger–cause Return if and only if all of the coefficients of the lagged Fundflow variables are 0, or

$$\text{H}_0: \quad \text{b}_{11} = \text{b}_{12} = \text{b}_{13} = \text{b}_{14} = 0 \tag{2}$$

and Return does not Granger–cause Fundflow if and only if all of the coefficients of the lagged Return variables are 0, or

$$\text{H}_0: \quad \text{c}_{21} = \text{c}_{22} = \text{c}_{23} = \text{c}_{24} = 0 \tag{3}$$

The system of equations represented by (1a) and (1b) can be estimated with simple ordinary least squares (OLS) methods because the equations have identical independent variables. OLS methods are used to estimate the two equations separately, and the null hypotheses are tested with simple F-tests.

Because estimation of these equations requires that the variables be stationary, we use two measures of mutual fund flows that meet the stationarity requirement: first differences of monthly flows, and percentage monthly flows, defined as monthly flows divided by total fund assets at the end of the preceding month (which we call *normalized flows*).[9] Of these variables, normalized flows are preferable because the variance of the first difference variable is not constant over the entire sample period. In addition, the equations are estimated using different lag structures of up to 13 monthly lags to capture possible delayed responses in the relationship between mutual fund flows and asset returns. Results for only four monthly lags for each variable are reported because the results do not change when more than four lags are used.

Tables 2 and 3 show the results of the Granger causality tests for equity and bond funds. Equations (1a) and (1b) are estimated for three equity and bond mutual fund flow variables, Netsales (monthly net sales), Sales, and Redemptions; and for two return variables, Eqreturn (excess equity returns) and Bdreturn (excess bond returns). Definitions of these variables can be found in table 1. In addition, estimates are provided for the entire time period studied as well as for several subperiods to determine if structural changes have occurred over the period.

Equity funds

Panel 1 in tables 2 and 3 shows the results for equity mutual funds. For the entire period January 1961 through February 1996, the null hypothesis that mutual fund net sales do not

Table 2. Granger causality tests (F-statistics and significance levels)

	Jan. 1961–Feb. 1996 (1)	Jan. 1961–Dec. 1983 (2)	Jan. 1984–Feb. 1996 (3)	Jan. 1990–Feb. 1996 (4)	Jan. 1971–Dec. 1981 (5)
Panel 1. Equity fund flows					
Net sales					
Normalized flow	1.09	1.39	0.90	1.22	2.30
	(0.35)	(0.23)	(0.46)	(0.30)	(0.06)**
First difference	0.47	1.35	0.14	0.11	1.38
	(0.75)	(0.25)	(0.96)	(0.96)	(0.25)
Redemptions					
Normalized flow	1.98	1.28	1.07	1.09	2.35
	(0.09)	(0.27)	(0.36)	(0.37)	(0.058)**
First difference	1.20	1.47	0.10	1.04	1.50
	(0.31)	(0.21)	(0.98)	(0.39)	(0.20)
Sales					
Normalized flow	1.03	0.91	1.40	1.87	1.39
	(0.38)	(0.45)	(0.23)	(0.12)	(0.23)
First difference	0.61	0.73	0.67	0.80	0.58
	(0.65)	(0.56)	(0.60)	(0.52)	(0.67)

	Jan. 1976–July 1996 (1)	Jan. 1976–Sept. 1987 (2)	Nov. 1987–July 1996 (3)	Jan. 1990–July 1996 (4)
Panel 2. Bond fund flows				
Net sales				
Normalized flow	0.56	0.93	0.53	1.42
	(0.68)	(0.44)	(0.71)	(0.23)
First difference	0.70	0.33	1.19	2.23
	(0.58)	(0.85)	(0.32)	(0.075)**
Redemptions				
Normalized flow	0.30	0.32	1.33	2.84
	(0.87)	(0.86)	(0.26)	(0.03)*
First difference	0.17	0.36	1.26	2.18
	(0.95)	(0.83)	(0.29)	(0.08)**
Sales				
Normalized flow	0.59	0.75	0.65	0.78
	(0.66)	(0.56)	(0.62)	(0.53)
First difference	0.67	0.54	0.82	0.68
	(0.61)	(0.70)	(0.51)	(0.60)

Notes:
Null hypothesis: Fund flows do not Granger cause returns:

$$H_0: \quad b_{11} = b_{12} = b_{13} = b_{14} = 0$$

Regression:

$$\text{Return}_t = a_1 + \sum_{i=1}^{4} b_{1i}\text{Fundflow}_{t-i} + \sum_{i=1}^{4} c_{1i}\text{Return}_{t-i} + \epsilon_{1t}$$

where Return is, alternatively, value-weighted NYSE stock index returns in excess of one-month T-bill returns (Eqreturn) and Lehman Brothers' aggregate bond index returns in excess of one-month T-bill returns (Bdreturn); and Fundflow denotes, alternatively, equity and bond mutual fund net sales, redemptions and sales.

cause stock returns cannot be rejected (panel 1 in table 2, regression 1). However, in the 1971–1981 period, the null is rejected at the 10% level of significance (panel 1 in table 2, regression 5). In contrast, for the entire period, the null hypothesis that stock returns do not cause equity mutual fund net sales is rejected at the 5% level of significance (panel 1 in table 3, regression 1). Further, redemptions are responsive to returns in all periods, while sales are responsive to returns only in the 1961–1983 period, a result due largely to the strong statistical relationship between redemptions and returns in the shorter 1971–1981 period (panel 1 in table 3).

Why is 1971–1981 different? First, it is a period of low stock market returns. During 1971–1981 equity returns averaged 8.4% annually, and excess returns averaged less than 1% annually. In contrast, annual returns for the entire sample excluding the 1971–1981 period averaged 15.2%, and excess stock returns averaged 9.1%. Second, no doubt because of the low stock returns during 1971–1981, equity fund redemptions outpaced sales, resulting in negative net sales. From January 1971 through December 1981, the average monthly net sales normalized by asset values at the end of the previous month is negative 0.38%, compared to positive 0.83% for the entire period excluding 1971–1981. The 1971–1981 period, therefore, differs markedly from the other periods studied in that excess stock returns were low and mutual fund redemptions were exceptionally high. So, while our results generally support the view that equity mutual fund flows do not affect equity returns, during periods of lackluster stock returns and high fund redemptions, equity fund flows may affect stock returns.[10]

With respect to asset returns causing mutual fund flows, a difference also is found between estimates for the period January 1984 through February 1996 and for the entire sample period. In 1984–1996, stock returns do not appear to cause either equity mutual fund sales or net sales, while for the entire period (1961–1996) they do (panel 1 in table 3, regression 3 versus regression 1). Even in the 1984–1996 period, however, fund redemptions are responsive to stock returns. A possible reason for the unresponsive of equity mutual fund net sales to stock returns in 1984–1990 is that this period was one of only growth, with equity mutual fund sales far exceeding redemptions. Further, during this period, the growth of household savings, demographic trends, changes in mutual fund technology, and the growth of self-directed defined-contribution retirement plans may have swamped the effect of higher stock returns on fund flows. Stated another way, in 1984–1996 equity mutual fund net sales seem to have been driven by factors unrelated

---

Numbers in parentheses are the significance levels. Asterisks indicate that the null is rejected at the 5% (*) or 10% (**) significance level.

The reported F-statistics are for equations using four lags (of independent variables). We also tested lag structures as long as 12 months. The results were unchanged.

The normalized flow equations are estimated using the monthly fund flows normalized by the fund asset at the end of previous month. The first-difference equations are estimated using the first differences of monthly net sales and the first differences of the natural logarithms of monthly redemptions and sales.

From 1976 through 1983, bond funds include bond and municipal bond funds; and from 1984 through 1996, they include income bond, government, GNMA, high-yield bond, state municipal bond, long-term municipal bond, corporate bond, and global bond funds.

Table 3. Granger causality tests (*F*-statistics and significance levels)

	Jan. 1961– Feb. 1996 (1)	Jan. 1961– Dec. 1983 (2)	Jan. 1984– Feb. 1996 (3)	Jan. 1990– Feb. 1996 (4)	Jan. 1971– Dec. 1981 (5)
Panel 1. Equity fund flows					
Net sales					
Normalized flow	5.37	14.99	1.86	1.09	9.34
	(0.0003)*	(0.0000)*	(0.11)	(0.36)	(0.0000)*
First difference	1.59	10.12	2.05	0.40	10.23
	(0.17)	(0.0000)*	(0.08)**	(0.80)	(0.0000)*
Redemptions					
Normalized flow	14.39	12.75	7.49	2.03	11.5
	(0.00000)*	(0.00000)*	(0.0000)*	(0.10)**	(0.00000)*
First difference	44.41	31.24	4.11	6.41	21.34
	(0.00000)*	(0.00000)*	(0.003)*	(0.0002)*	(0.00000)*
Sales					
Normalized flow	2.23	4.06	1.54	1.10	3.38
	(0.06)**	(0.003)*	(0.19)	(0.36)	(0.011)*
First difference	1.57	1.12	1.52	0.63	0.63
	(0.17)	(0.34)	(0.20)	(0.63)	(0.41)

	Jan. 1976– July 1996 (1)	Jan. 1976– Sept. 1987 (2)	Nov. 1987– July 1996 (3)	Jan. 1990– July 1996 (4)
Panel 2. Bond fund flows				
Net sales				
Normalized flow	2.85	1.89	1.08	1.03
	(0.02)*	(0.13)	(0.37)	(0.39)
First difference	0.73	0.43	0.68	0.92
	(0.56)	(0.78)	(0.60)	(0.45)
Redemptions				
Normalized flow	0.92	0.57	1.37	1.20
	(0.45)	(0.67)	(0.25)	(0.31)
First difference	5.37	4.04	4.20	3.49
	(0.0003)*	(0.04)*	(0.003)*	(0.012)*
Sales				
Normalized flow	5.52	3.71	1.67	2.77
	(0.0002)*	(0.007)*	(0.16)	(0.035)*
First difference	7.43	4.48	2.40	3.39
	(0.0000)*	(0.002)*	(0.056)**	(0.014)*

Notes:

Null hypothesis: Returns do not Granger cause fund flows:

$$H_0: \quad c_{21} = c_{22} = c_{23} = c_{24} = 0$$

Regression:

$$\text{Fundflow}_t = a_2 + \sum_{i=1}^{4} b_{2i}\text{Fundflow}_{t-i} + \sum_{i=1}^{4} c_{2i}\text{Return}_{t-i} + \epsilon_{2t}$$

where Return is, alternatively, value-weighted NYSE stock index returns in excess of one-month T-bill returns (Eqreturn) and Lehman Brothers' aggregate bond index returns in excess of one-month T-bill returns (Bdreturn); and Fundflow denotes, alternatively, equity and bond mutual fund net sales, redemptions and sales.

to stock returns, even though fund redemptions continued to be closely tied to stock returns.

Finally, some observers argue that the 1990s represent an entirely new stock market environment, so that results based on prior historical periods may not be applicable to the future. In particular, during the 1990s, equity mutual fund net sales accelerated sharply: Average monthly net sales went from $774.20 million in the 1980s to $8485.78 million in the 1990s, and as a percentage of prior-month fund assets, they went from a monthly average of 0.67% to a monthly average of 1.33%. Nevertheless, estimates for the 1990–1996 period are no different from those for the 1984–1996 period (see panel 1 in table 2, regression 4, and panel 1 in table 3, regression 4).

Bond funds

Panel 2 in tables 2 and 3 shows the results for bond funds. For the entire sample period January 1976 through February 1996, as well as for all subperiods, the null that bond flows do not cause bond returns cannot be rejected (panel 2 in table 2). In contrast, for the entire sample period, the null that bond returns do not cause fund flows is rejected at the 5% level of significance (panel 2 in table 3). The latter finding, however, is not sustained when the sample is divided into two equal 10-year periods (panel 2 in table 3, regressions 2 and 3). We are unable to explain this discrepancy, other than to note that the shorter periods have fewer observations. In general, the results support the view that bond mutual fund net sales have not affected bond returns.

Summary

The Granger causality tests generally support the conclusion that neither equity nor bond mutual fund net sales have had a significant effect on asset returns. In only one period, January 1971 through December 1981, did the net sales of equity funds appear to have a significant effect on equity returns. In contrast, the results strongly support the conclusion that asset returns have affected net mutual fund sales, although the results for equity mutual funds are not particularly robust in the 1984–1996 period.

One possibility is that Granger causality analysis may fail to find stronger causal

---

Numbers in parentheses are the significance levels. Asterisks indicate that the null is rejected at the 5% (*) or 10% (**) significance level.

The reported F-statistics are for equations using four lags (of independent variables). We also tested lag structures as long as 12 months. The results were unchanged.

The normalized flow equations are estimated using the monthly fund flows normalized by the fund asset at the end of previous month. The first-difference equations are estimated using the first differences of monthly net sales and the first differences of the natural logarithms of monthly redemptions and sales.

From 1976 through 1983, bond funds include bond and municipal bond funds; and from 1984 through 1996, they include income bond, government, GNMA, high-yield bond, state municipal bond, long-term municipal bond, corporate bond, and global bond funds.

relationships (from flows to returns) because the appropriate time interval over which to investigate causality may be shorter than a month. If investors respond more quickly to mutual fund flows and asset returns, it may not be possible to observe Granger causality using monthly data.[11] It is notable, however, that we *do* find evidence of Granger causality using monthly data (from returns to fund flows), which suggests that a monthly time interval may not be inappropriate.[12]

6. Instrumental variables analysis

A criticism of Granger causality analysis is that it does not utilize the information contained in contemporaneous data to identify causality. Strictly speaking, variable x can be said not to cause variable y only if y is exogenous to x. A necessary condition for such exogeneity is that *both* current and past values of x do not affect y. Granger causality tests, however, satisfy a weaker condition of exogeneity: that only past values of x, in addition to past values of y, do not affect y.

This potential deficiency is not present in the instrumental variables methodology. This methodology uses all exogenous variables in a structural model as instrumental variables to predict mutual fund flows and asset returns, and then uses the predicted flow and return variables to test for causality between flows and asset returns. This procedure purges both mutual fund flows and asset returns of the simultaneity that may exist between them. Thus, unlike Granger causality analysis, the instrumental variables method is able to utilize the information contained in contemporaneous data to test for causality.

In this analysis we use only the unexpected components of mutual fund flows and asset returns because only the unexpected components of these variables should have an effect. If, for example, market participants correctly anticipate mutual fund flows in the next month, there should be no effect on asset returns when those flows are realized. In addition, in this analysis we investigate only the relationship between mutual fund net sales and returns (and not between redemptions or sales and returns).

Before discussing the results of the instrumental variables analysis, we first discuss how the unexpected component of mutual fund net sales is estimated as well as the economic factors used in the instrumental variables analysis to predict asset returns and mutual fund net sales.[13]

Generating unexpected net sales of mutual funds

To generate unexpected normalized mutual fund net sales (Unetsale), the following AR(4) process is estimated:

$$\text{Netsales}_t = a + b_1\text{Netsales}_{t-1} + b_2\text{Netsales}_{t-2} + b_3\text{Netsales}_{t-3} + b_4\text{Netsales}_{t-4} + \epsilon_t \tag{4}$$

where Netsales denotes, alternatively, the monthly net sales of equity or bond mutual funds (sales less redemptions) normalized by the respective fund assets at the end of the previous month.

The variable Unetsale, unexpected normalized net sales, is estimated as the residual from the preceding fitted equation. This procedure eliminates the predictable (or trend) component of mutual fund net sales.

Table 4 shows the estimates for regression 4 for both equity and bond fund net sales. The normalized mutual fund net sales of both equity and bond funds exhibit significant serial correlation. For bond fund net sales, an AR(2) process works as well as an AR(4) process.

Stock and bond returns and economic factors

Chen, Roll, and Ross (CRR, 1986) argue that asset prices and returns should be determined only by undiversifiable or systematic risk factors (or by "systematic state variables"). After investigating alternative proxies for systematic risk, they conclude that the following variables best explain asset returns: industrial production, the credit risk premium, the term structure premium, and the T-bill return.[14] These findings are supported in a later study of asset returns using quarterly data by Chen (1991). Following CRR (1986) and Chen (1991), we use the same four state variables as instruments to predict stock and bond returns.[15] (This procedure, as well as those of CRR, 1986, and Chen, 1991, assumes that the macro-state variables are exogenous to stock and bond market returns.)

Industrial production. The monthly growth rate of U.S. industrial production, MIP_t, is used to capture real systematic production risk in the economy:

Table 4. Serial correlation of mutual fund net sales

	Equity funds, Jan. 1961–Feb. 1996 (1)	Bond funds, Jan. 1976–July 1996 (2)
Constant	0.00075	0.0014
	(0.00035)*	(0.0010)
Lag 1	0.27	0.61
	(0.05)*	(0.07)*
Lag 2	0.287	0.14
	(0.05)*	(0.076)**
Lag 3	0.198	0.11
	(0.05)*	(0.07)
Lag 4	0.102	0.04
	(0.04)*	(0.07)

Notes:
Regression:

$$\text{Netsales}_t = a + b_1\text{Netsales}_{t-1} + b_2\text{Netsales}_{t-2} + b_3\text{Netsales}_{t-3} + b_4\text{Netsales}_{t-4} + \epsilon_t$$

where Netsales denotes the normalized net sales of stock and bond mutual funds, respectively.

Numbers in parentheses are the standard errors. Asterisks indicate that the null is rejected at the 5% (*) or 10% (**) significance level.

$$\text{MIP}_t = \log[\text{IP}_t/\text{IP}_{t-1}]$$

where IP_t is the U.S. monthly industrial production index (obtained from *Datastream International*). The MIP_t process displays little serial correlation and is noisy enough to be treated as an innovation. In addition, because IP_t is a flow variable that represents industrial production during month t, MIP_t reflects the change of industrial production lagged by a partial month. Therefore, consistent with CRR (1986), we lead this variable by one month to make it consistent with the timing of the other variables.

Risk premia. The aggregate risk premium is the "default" spread between the long-term corporate bond yield and the long-term government bond yield. Riskprem_t is defined as

$$\text{Riskprem}_t = \text{Baa}_t - \text{LGB}_t$$

where Baa_t is the average yield on long-term corporate bonds rated Baa or lower at the end of month t (obtained from Ibbotson & Associates), and LGB_t is the average yield on 10-year government bonds at the end of month t (obtained from Citibase).

Term structure premia. The term structure premium, Termstrt_t, is defined as

$$\text{Termstrt}_t = \text{LGB}_t - \text{TB1m}_{t-1}$$

where TB1m_{t-1} is the one-month T-bill rate at the end of month $_{t-1}$ and LGB_t is as defined previously.

Interest rates. To capture changes in interest rate levels, which fluctuate with the business cycle (see Fama and French, 1990), we use TB3m_t, the monthly discount yield on three-month T-bills at the beginning of month t.[16] Definitions of these variables can be found in table 1.

Table 5 contains simple OLS estimates of the relationship between asset returns and the foregoing economic factors. Regressions 2 and 5 in the table show estimates that are consistent with those of CRR (1986) and Chen (1991): Except for MIP, the factors are significantly related to returns from both stocks and bonds. When Unetsales is included in the estimating equations, a significant relationship is found between contemporaneous unexpected mutual fund net sales and both stock and bond returns (see regressions 3 and 6).

Mutual fund flows and economic factors

Economic factors other than asset returns may determine the net sales of mutual funds. Two such factors could be aggregate household savings and demographic changes. In the instrumental variables analysis, therefore, these variables are used as economic factors to explain mutual fund net sales.

Savings. To the extent that households do not spend all of their income, they generate savings used to acquire financial assets. An increase in aggregate household savings, therefore, increases the demand for financial assets generally and, at least to some

Table 5. Asset returns and economic factors: OLS estimators

Independent variable	Equity funds, Jan. 1961–Feb. 1996			Bond funds, Jan. 1976–July 1996		
	(1)	(2)	(3)	(4)	(5)	(6)
Constant	0.058	0.017	0.035	0.024	0.093	0.1
	(0.021)*	(0.075)	(0.069)	(0.013)**	(0.051)**	(0.043)*
Unetsales	34.76		32.43	11.58		8.23
	(3.42)*		(3.32)*	(0.98)*		(0.84)*
MIP		3.44	3.46		−1.92	−0.28
		(2.95)	(2.71)		(1.75)	(1.53)
Riskprem		23.38	18.91		22.50	17.50
		(3.87)*	(3.56)*		(2.05)*	(1.88)*
Termstrt		−2.08	−1.92		−3.75	−2.91
		(1.51)	(1.39)		(0.83)*	(0.72)*
TBL3m		−4.87	−4.12		−5.10	−4.30
		(0.96)*	(0.88)*		(0.50)*	(0.45)*
R^2	0.20	0.11	0.27	0.38	0.44	0.61

Notes:
Regression:

$$\text{Return} = c_0 + c_1\text{Unetsales}_t + c_2\text{MIP}_t + c_3\text{Riskprem}_t + c_4\text{Termstrt}_t + c_5\text{TBL3m}_t + \eta_t$$

where Return denotes, alternatively, value-weighted NYSE stock index returns in excess of one-month T-bill returns and Lehman Brothers' aggregate bond index returns in excess of one-month T-bill returns; Unetsales denotes, alternatively, unexpected equity and bond mutual fund net sales; MIP is the growth rate of monthly industrial production index; Riskprem is the difference between Baa bond yields and average 10-year government bond yields; Termstrt is the difference between average 10-year government bond yields and one-month T-bill yields; and TBL3m is three-month T-bill rates.

Numbers in parentheses are the standard errors. Asterisks indicate that the null is rejected at the 5% (*) or 10% (**) significance level.

R^2 is the uncentered R^2.

extent, for equity and bond mutual fund shares as well (see Kennickell, Starr-McCluer, and Sunden, 1997; Reid, 1997). Therefore, we use the monthly growth rate of aggregate household savings, or Msaving (defined in table 1), to explain mutual fund net sales in our analysis.[17]

Demographics. Significant demographic changes occurred in the late-1960s and 1970s as post-World War II "baby boomers" entered the labor force, creating a population bulge in the 20–35 year-old age group. Initially, this group invested heavily in housing and consumer durables and very little in financial assets, but by the early 1980s, when the "baby boomers" were reaching their late thirties and forties, they began to hold more financial assets. In particular, the demand for the shares of equity and bond mutual funds grew rapidly. Surveys of mutual fund ownership show that the greatest percentage of mutual fund shares are owned by households headed by persons aged 35 to 54. In 1996, for example, 28% of households headed by someone aged 35–44 held stock funds and 19% held bond funds (Norris, 1997). In comparison, only 20% of households headed by someone below 35 years of age held stock funds and only

13% held bond funds; and less than 20% of households headed by someone over 55 years of age held either stock of bond funds. Thus, changing demographics had the effect of changing investors' aggregate "taste" for mutual funds: An increase in "middle-aged" investors resulted in a greater demand for stock and bond mutual fund shares.

To capture this demographic effect, we use the percentage of the population 16 years and older accounted for by persons 35 years and older. Figure 4 shows the close relationship between equity mutual fund net sales (normalized) and this demographic variable over the past 35 years. During the 1960s and 1970s, the percentage of population aged 35 and over was in a steady decline, as were equity mutual fund net sales. In the early 1980s, however, the percentage of the population aged 35 and over began rising and is still rising today; during this time, equity mutual fund net sales also increased sharply.[18] Therefore, in our statistical analysis the first difference of the foregoing demographic variable is used as an instrument to explain mutual fund net sales (see MDEM in table 1).[19]

Table 6 shows simple OLS estimates of the relationship between unexpected mutual fund net sales and the foregoing economic factors. Regressions 2 and 5, in particular, show that these factors generally are statistically significant. In addition, when returns are included as an explanatory variable in the estimating equations, a statistically significant relationship is found between contemporaneous returns and unexpected mutual fund net sales, for both equity and bond funds (see regressions 3 and 6).

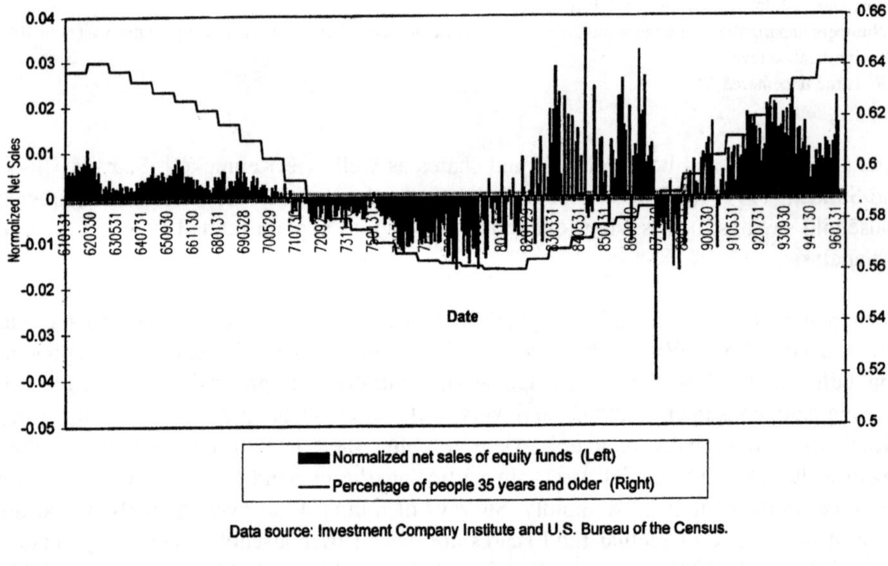

Data source: Investment Company Institute and U.S. Bureau of the Census.

Figure 4. Normalized net sales of equity mutual funds and population 35 years and older as a percentage of the population 16 years and older (month-end data, Jan. 1961–Feb. 1996). Data source: Investment Company Institute and U.S. Bureau of the Census.

Table 6. Unexpected mutual fund net sales and economic factors: OLS estimates

Independent Variable variable	Equity funds, Jan. 1961–Feb. 1996			Bond funds, Jan. 1976–July 1996		
	(1)	(2)	(3)	(4)	(5)	(6)
Constant	– 0.0003	– 0.00002	0.0003	– 0.0008	0.00036	0.0004
	(0.0003)	(0.0003)	(0.0003)	(0.0007)	(0.0011)	(0.0009)
Return	0.0058		0.0056	0.033		0.033
	(0.0005)*		(0.0006)*	(0.003)*		(0.003)*
Msaving		1.94	1.50		1.27	4.09
		(0.69)*	(0.62)*		(2.64)	(2.12)**
MDEM		0.0044	0.0048		0.008	0.006
		(0.0025)**	(0.0027)**		(0.004)*	(0.003)*
R^2	0.19	0.03	0.21	0.37	0.02	0.40

Notes:
Regression:

$$\text{Unetsales}_t = a + b_1\text{Return}_t + b_2\text{MSaving}_t + b_3\text{MDEM}_t + \epsilon_t$$

where Return denotes, alternatively, value-weighted NYSE stock index returns in excess of one-month T-bill returns (Eqreturn) and Lehman Brothers' aggregate bond index returns in excess of one-month T-bill returns (Bdreturn); MDEM is the number of people 35 years and older as a percentage of those 16 years and older; Msaving is the growth rate of aggregate household savings; and Unetsales denotes, alternatively, unexpected equity and bond mutual fund net sales.

Numbers in parentheses are the standard errors. Asterisks indicate that the null is rejected at the 5% (*) or 10% (**) significance level.

R^2 is the uncentered R^2.

The instrumental variable method: Statistical results

To determine whether a causal relationship exists between mutual fund net sales and asset returns the following two-equation structural model is estimated:

$$\text{Return}_t = b_0 + b_1\text{Unetsales}_t + b_2\text{MIP}_t + b_3\text{Riskprem}_t + b_4\text{Termstrt}_t + b_5\text{TBL3m}_t + \eta_t \tag{5a}$$

$$\text{Unetsales}_t = c_0 + c_1\text{Return}_t + c_2\text{MSavings}_t + c_3\text{MDEM}_t + \epsilon_t \tag{5b}$$

where Return and Unetsales are assumed to be endogenous and all other variables are assumed to be exogenous or predetermined. To determine whether there is causality between returns and mutual fund net sales two null hypotheses are tested: First, that mutual fund net sales do not cause returns:

$$b_1 = 0 \tag{6}$$

Second, that returns do not cause mutual fund net sales:

$$c_1 = 0 \tag{7}$$

Because both Return and Unetsales are endogenous in the structural system, Return is correlated with the disturbance term ε_t in eq. (5b), and Unetsales is correlated with the disturbance term η_t in eq. (5a). As a consequence, simple OLS estimators will be biased and inconsistent. Therefore, the results shown in tables 5 and 6, where simple OLS methods are used and significant contemporaneous relationships are found, are unreliable.[20]

To correct for this simultaneity problem, we use two-stage least squares (2SLS), which is equivalent to the instrumental variables method.[21] To estimate eqs. (5a) and (5b), the 2SLS technique replaces the two endogenous independent variables in eqs. (5a) and (5b), Return and Unetsales, with instrumental variables Return(fitted) and Unetsales(fitted). More specifically, both the Return(fitted) and Unetsales(fitted) variables are computed in the first stage by regressing the six exogenous structural variables in system (5a) and (5b), alternatively, on the variables Return and Unetsales, and then using the estimated equations to compute, respectively, Return(fitted) and Unetsales(fitted). In the second stage, OLS regressions are estimated using Return(fitted) and Unetsales(fitted) as independent variables in eqs. (5a) and (5b) in place of Return and Unetsales, respectively. Null hypotheses (6) and (7) then are tested.[22]

Do mutual fund flows cause asset returns? Table 7 shows the instrumental variable estimates for eq. (5a) for equity and bond funds, respectively. Panel 1 in table 7 shows that the null hypothesis that equity mutual fund net sales do not cause stock returns is rejected at the 10% significance level for the entire period January 1961 through February 1996: The estimator of b_1 is statistically significant at the 10% confidence level (regression 1 in panel 1). However, when separate estimates are generated for different subperiods, it becomes clear that this result is driven by the results for the subperiod January 1971 to December 1981 (regression 5). If the 1971–1981 period is excluded from the sample, b_1 no longer is statistically significant. These results are consistent with those of the Granger causality analysis, where we also find that equity mutual fund net sales do not cause stock returns except during 1971–1981, when stock returns were low and equity fund net sales generally were negative (as redemptions exceeded sales). Therefore, although the instrumental variables method incorporates the contemporaneous relationship between fund flows and asset returns, which is absent in the Granger causality analysis, there still is little support for the view that fund flows affect returns.

Panel 2 in table 7 shows similar results for bond funds: Bond mutual fund net sales do not cause bond returns. The estimator of b_1 always is insignificant at the 5% level, although b_1 is significant at the 10% level in subperiod 1976–1987. These results also are consistent with those of the Granger causality analysis, where we find no evidence of causality.

It is notable that the estimates using the instrumental variables method shown in table 7 differ significantly from those in table 5, where simple OLS methods are used. When instrumental variables is used, the causality findings in table 5 generally disappear.

Do asset returns cause mutual fund flows? Panels 1 and 2 of table 8 show the instrumental variable estimates for eq. (5b) for equity and bond funds, respectively. In both panels and all equations, the estimator of c_1 is statistically significant at the 5% level.

Table 7. Instrumental variables method

	Jan. 1961– Feb. 1996 (1)	Jan. 1961– Dec. 1983 (2)	Jan. 1984– Feb. 1996 (3)	Jan. 1990– Feb. 1996 (4)	Jan. 1971– Dec. 1981 (5)	Jan. 1961– Dec. 1970 (6)
Panel 1. Equity fund flows						
Constant	0.052	0.044	−0.12	−0.25	−0.24	0.94
	(0.076)	(0.086)	(0.21)	(0.49)	(0.23)	(0.45)
Unetsales	67.15	84.62	88.08	51.88	261.44	49.86
	(35.60)**	(41.9)*	(50.12)	(32.16)	(123.90)*	(39.56)
MIP	3.39	4.73	−12.43	−6.32	4.74	−0.31
	(2.96)	(3.72)	(7.07)**	(9.96)	(4.88)	(14.42)
Riskprem	14.48	14.8	−3.6	32.55	49.83	41.69
	(4.47)*	(6.28)*	(23.7)	(22.19)	(15.54)*	(12.11)*
Termstrt	−1.33	−0.98	0.41	−3.13	−16.67	−42.74
	(1.55)	(2.91)	(3.37)	(5.86)	(6.57)*	(21.49)*
TBL3m	−3.39	−4.08	5.17	0.12	−6.14	−24.78
	(1.03)*	(1.25)*	(5.18)	(7.23)	(1.65)*	(8.04)*
R^2	0.14	0.14	0.20	0.18	0.14	0.18

	Jan. 1976– July 1996 (1)	Jan. 1976– Sept. 1987 (2)	Nov. 1987– July 1996 (3)	Jan. 1990– July 1996 (4)
Panel 2. Bond fund flows				
Constant	0.10	0.055	−0.013	0.14
	(0.052)**	(0.083)	(0.15)	(0.28)
Unetsales	9.20	10.8	−7.13	13.26
	(6.4)	(5.68)**	(22.03)	(22.85)
MIP	−0.17	0.46	−2.67	0.76
	(1.98)	(2.52)	(3.16)	(3.43)
Riskprem	16.87	16.15	30.067	15.83
	(4.76)*	(4.59)*	(16.11)**	(17.95)
Termstrt	−2.81	−2.17	−4.31	−4.04
	(1.14)*	(1.36)	(1.84)*	(1.94)*
TBL3m	−4.20	−3.66	−4.71	−4.17
	(0.89)*	(1.16)*	(1.73)*	(1.46)*
R^2	0.45	0.49	0.36	0.38

Notes:

Null hypothesis: Unexpected fund net sales do not cause returns:

H_0: $b_1 = 0$

Regression:

$$\text{Return}_t = b_0 + b_1\text{Unetsales}_t + b_2\text{MIP}_t + b_3\text{Riskprem}_t + b_4\text{Termstrt}_t + b_3\text{TBL3m}_t + \eta_t$$

where Return is, alternatively, value-weighted NYSE stock index returns in excess of one-month T-bill returns (Eqreturn) and Lehman Brothers' aggregate bond index returns in excess of one-month T-bill returns (Bdreturn); Unetsales is, alternatively, the unexpected normalized net sales of equity and bond mutual funds; MIP is the growth rate of monthly industrial production index; Riskprem is the difference between Baa bond yields and average 10-year government bond yields; Termstrt is the difference between average 10-year government bond yields and one-month T-bill yields; and TBL3m is three-month T-bill rates.

Numbers in parentheses are the standard errors. Asterisks indicate that the null is rejected at the 5% (*) or 10% (**) significance level.

R^2 is the uncentered R^2.

Table 8. Instrumental variables method

	Jan. 1961– Feb. 1996 (1)	Jan. 1961– Dec. 1983 (2)	Jan. 1984– Feb. 1996 (3)	Jan. 1990– Feb. 1996 (4)	Jan. 1971– Dec. 1981 (5)	Jan. 1961– Dec. 1970 (6)
Panel 1. Equity fund flows						
Constant	– 0.00041	0.00019	– 0.003	– 0.0052	– 0.00028	0.00012
	(0.00032)	(0.0003)	(0.003)	(0.01)	(0.00057)	(0.00021)
Eqreturn	0.0066	0.0045	0.011	0.0086	0.0019	0.0008
	(0.0018)*	(0.0014)*	(0.004)*	(0.0034)*	(0.0005)*	(0.0003)*
Msaving	0.0012	0.0027	– 0.0005	0.0048	0.0016	– 0.0008
	(0.0019)	(0.003)	(0.003)	(0.0026)**	(0.0036)	(0.0016)
MDEM	1.39	1.34	3.43	7.44	– 0.75	0.38
	(0.70)*	(0.78)**	(5.69)	(18)	(1.41)	(0.56)
R^2	0.06	0.05	0.05	0.11	0.03	0.01

	Jan. 1976– July 1996 (1)	Jan. 1976– Sept. 1987 (2)	Nov. 1987– July 1996 (3)	Jan. 1990– July 1996 (4)
Panel 2. Bond fund flows				
Constant	0.00067	– 0.0002	– 0.0054	– 0.011
	(0.001)	(0.0013)	(0.0056)	(0.011)
Bdreturn	0.031	0.032	0.020	0.018
	(0.004)*	(0.0065)*	(0.0059)*	(0.0073)*
Msaving	0.0068	0.11	– 0.0023	– 0.0031
	(0.0039)**	(0.06)**	(0.0027)	(0.0030)
MDEM	4.43	– 1.59	8.00	16.43
	(3.12)	(4.99)	(10.03)	(17.47)
R^2	0.16	0.19	0.14	0.12

Notes:

Null hypothesis: Returns do not cause unexpected fund net sales:

$$H_0: \quad c_1 = 0$$

Regression:

$$\text{Unetsales}_t = c_0 + c_1\text{Return}_t + c_2\text{MSaving}_t + c_3\text{MDEM}_t + \epsilon_t$$

where Unetsales denotes, alternatively, unexpected equity and bond mutual fund net sales; Return is, alternatively, value-weighted NYSE stock index returns in excess of one-month T-bill returns (Eqreturn) and Lehman Brothers' aggregate bond index returns in excess of one-month T-bill returns (Bdreturn); Msaving is the growth rate of household savings; and MDEM is the number of people 35 years and older as a percentage of those 16 years and older.

Numbers in parentheses are the standard errors. Asterisks indicate that the null is rejected at the 5% significance level.

R^2 is the uncentered R^2.

Therefore, the null hypothesis that asset returns do not cause mutual fund net sales is rejected for both equity and bond funds.

These findings are consistent with those of the Granger causality analysis, although they are even more supportive of a finding of causality. In the Granger analysis, for the entire sample period, we find that returns cause both equity and bond mutual fund net sales.

However, estimates for subperiods, where there were fewer observations, often fail to support such a finding. In contrast, the instrumental variables estimates, which incorporate contemporaneous effects, support a finding of causality in all periods. Last, the instrumental variables estimates in table 8 are consistent with those in table 6, where simple OLS methods are used (in contrast to the instrumental variable estimates in table 7 versus the OLS estimates in table 5).

7. Conclusions

This paper investigates the causal relationships between equity and bond mutual fund flows and stock and bond returns. In particular, it examines the relationships between aggregate monthly mutual fund flows into stock and bond mutual funds (sales, redemptions, and net sales) and monthly stock and bond returns utilizing econometric procedures designed to identify causal relationships: Granger causality analysis and instrumental variables analysis. Equity mutual fund flows are examined for the 30-year period from January 1961 through February 1996, and bond mutual fund flows are examined for the 20-year period from January 1976 through February 1996.

The results of the Granger causality analysis generally support the conclusion that neither equity nor bond mutual fund net sales significantly affect asset returns. In only one period, January 1971 through December 1981, did the net sales of equity funds significantly affect equity returns. During this period equity returns were quite low and equity mutual fund redemptions were exceptionally high, so that the monthly net sales of equity mutual funds typically were negative. In contrast, the Granger causality results support the conclusion that causality runs in the opposite direction: from asset returns to equity and bond mutual fund flows. Higher (lower) returns cause larger (smaller) equity and bond fund flows. Further, redemptions from stock mutual funds are particularly sensitive to changes in stock returns.

The results of the instrumental variables analysis are similar but more robust. Except for the 1971–1981 period, mutual fund net sales do not cause either equity or bond returns. In the 1971 through 1981 period, the net sales of equity mutual funds significantly affect equity returns, just as we find in the Granger causality analysis. In addition, in all time periods and for both equity and bond funds, the null hypothesis that asset returns do not cause mutual fund net sales is rejected. Therefore, the instrumental variables method, by incorporating contemporaneous relationships in the analysis, strengthens the findings of the Granger causality analysis.

Taken together, these findings suggest, first, that the recent run-up in stock prices cannot be attributed to the rapid growth of equity mutual funds during the 1980s and 1990s; and second, that the possibility of a mutual fund induced downward price spiral in stock prices cannot be ruled out. The results for the 1971–1981 period suggest that in a ''down'' stock market, when stock returns are low and mutual fund redemptions are high, outflows of funds from mutual funds could put downward pressure on stock prices. This is consistent with a noise trader view of markets. It should be recognized, however, that current mutual fund investors are different from those during 1971–1981. Today, more than half of stock and bond mutual fund assets owned by households are held in some type of retirement plan. Therefore, current mutual fund investors may have different investment objectives and longer investment horizons than those in 1971–1981 and may behave differently in a market downturn.

Acknowledgments

We wish to thank members of the "Free Lunch" Finance Group at the Columbia Business School, participants in the Economics Workshop at the Graduate School of the City University of New York, and especially George Benston, Hans Stoll, and John Rae for helpful comments. The Investment Company Institute graciously provided mutual fund data.

Notes

Franklin R. Edwards is the Arthur F. Burns Professor of Free and Competitive Enterprise at the Graduate School of Business of Columbia University. Xin Zhang is a financial policy analyst in the Financial Policy and Risk Management Department of the World Bank.

1. During this period, bond mutual funds also grew substantially, and there was a positive correlation between the net sales of bond mutual funds and bond prices (see figure 2).
2. Franklin R. Edwards (1996), Chapter 5, Table 5-2, p. 79.
3. Ibid., Chapter 3, Table 3-3, pp. 22–23.
4. Ibid., Chapter 3, Chart 3-7, p. 19.
5. Federal Reserve Board (1996). "Net sales of stock by households" is net sales of stock held directly by households plus net sales of stock held in closed-end funds, which is quite small.
6. For the period January 1961 through February 1996, the simple correlation between the aggregate monthly net sales of equity mutual funds and stock prices is 0.82; and for the period January 1976 to February 1996, the simple correlation between the aggregate net sales of bond funds and bond prices is 0.41.
7. From 1976 through 1983, bond funds include bond funds and municipal bond funds. From 1984 to the present, bond funds include income bond funds, government and GNMA bond funds, high-yield bond funds, state and municipal bond funds, long-term municipal bond funds, and corporate bond funds, and global bond funds. Our data do not include the U.S. stock and bond holdings of foreign-based mutual funds, which are quite small relative to U.S. mutual funds. Our mutual fund data were provided by the Investment Company Institute, Washington, DC.
8. Reinvested dividends are included in sales and therefore in net sales. If reinvested dividends are excluded from sales, our results do not change. Exchange sales and redemptions capture shifts of money from one fund to another within a particular mutual fund complex, such as the Fidelity Funds.
9. Specifically, the first-differences equations are estimated using first differences of monthly net sales and first differences of the natural logarithms of monthly redemptions and sales. Because monthly net sales can be a negative number, logarithms of first differences cannot be used.
10. The 1970s also was a period of financial scandals involving mutual funds, which may have shaken investors' confidence in both the mutual fund industry and the stock market and caused investors to overreact. See Barberis, Shleifer, and Vishny (1997) for the development of such an overreaction theory.
11. Preliminary estimates of monthly mutual fund flow statistics are made available by the Investment Company Institute in the second week of the following month. Final estimates are not made available until the end of the following month.
12. We generally find the same results using estimates of weekly aggregate mutual fund flows and weekly returns supplied to us by Bob Adler, president of AMG Corporation. These data are available only for the last four years. There is evidence that investors respond with a substantial lag to new information; see, for example, Bernard (1992).

13. *Returns* already is a stochastic and unpredictable. Therefore, no procedure is necessary to obtain an unpredictable component for asset returns.
14. They also investigated the predictive power of inflation, market indexes, consumption, and oil prices but found those variables to be insignificant.
15. Chen (1991) also finds that the Gross National Product is significantly related to asset returns. We do not use this variable because it is available only quarterly. In addition, Chen typically finds *R*-square statistics of about 0.17, consistent with our results.
16. In some previous work, the one-month T-bill rate is used instead of the three-month rate to capture this effect, but see Brennan, Schwartz, and Lagnado (1996).
17. Growth rates in aggregate savings are not serially correlated and can be used as innovations.
18. It is notable that the pattern of aggregate household savings is very different from that of the demographic variable: The simple correlation between Msavings and MDEM is -0.02.
19. Demographics also may affect asset prices or returns because it may affect investors' willingness to take risk in the aggregate; see, for example, Bakshi and Chen (1994). In our analysis of returns, however, we explicitly incorporate risk factors to explain returns. Further, to the extent that demographic factors are related to returns, there will be a bias toward finding that mutual fund flows cause returns, which is not what we generally find. Nevertheless, to examine the sensitivity of our results, we estimated eq. (5a) excluding MDEM. The results were unchanged.
20. In a previous study of mutual fund flows, Warther (1995) uses simple OLS methods and concludes that a causal relationship exists between mutual fund flows and returns.
21. We do not use the indirect least squares method because both eqs. (5a) and (5b) are overidentified. In addition, we do not use full-information maximum likelihood methods because these methods are superior to 2SLS only if the complete model is correctly specified, a formidable requirement (see Johnston, 1984, Chapter 11).
22. Note that the covariance matrix of 2SLS estimates are calculated using the actual independent variables, Return and Unetsales, rather than the fitted values, Return(fitted) and Unetsales(fitted) (see Hamilton, 1994, Chapter 9).

References

Barberis, Nicholas, Andrei Shleifer, and Robet Vishny, "A Model of Investor Sentiment," Working paper, Harvard University, January 1997.

Bakshi, Gurdip S., and Zhiwu Chen, "Baby Boom, Population Aging, and Capital Markets," *Journal of Business* 67 (April 1994), 165–202.

Bernard, V., "Stock Price Reactions to Earnings Announcements," In R. Thaler (ed.), *Advances in Behavioral Finance*, New York: Russell Sage Foundation, 1992.

Box, George, and Gwilym Jenkins, *Time Series Analysis, Forecasting, and Control*, San Francisco: Holden Day, 1976.

Brennan, Michael J., Eduardo Schwartz, and Ron Lagnado, "Strategic Asset Allocation," Working paper, UCLA, 1996.

Chen, Nai-fu, "Financial Investment Opportunities and the Macroeconomy," *Journal of Finance* (June 1991), 529–554.

Chen, Nai-fu, Richard Roll, and Stephen Ross, "Economic Forces and the Stock Market," *Journal of Business* 59 (July 1986), 383–403.

De Long, J. Bradford, Andrei Shleifer, Lawrence Summers, and Waldman, "Noise Trader Risk in Financial Markets," *Journal of Political Economy* 98 (August 1990), 703–738.

De Long, J. Bradford, Andrei Shleifer, Lawrence Summers, et al., "The Survival of Noise Traders," *Journal of Business* 64 (January 1991), 1–19.

Dickey, David, and Wayne Fuller, "Distribution of the Estimates of Autoregressive Time Series with a Unit Root," *Journal of the American Statistical Association* 74 (June 1979), 427–431.

Dickey, David, and Wayne Fuller, "Likelihood Ratio Statistics for Autoregressive Time Series with Unit Root," *Econometrica* 49 (July 1981), 1057–1072.

Doan, Thomas, *RATS User's Manual*, Evanston, IL: Estima, 1992.

Ederington, Louis, and Jae Ha Lee, "How Markets Process Information: News Release and Volatility," *Journal of Finance* (September 1993), 1161–1191.

Edwards, Franklin R., *The New Finance: Regulation and Financial Stability*, Washington DC: AEI Press, 1996.

Enders, Walter, *Applied Econometric Time Series*, New York: John Wiley & Sons, 1995.

Engle, R., "Autoregressive Conditional Heteroskedasticity with Estimates of the Variance of U.K. Inflation," *Econometrica* 50 (July 1982), 987–1008.

Fama, E., and K. French, "Business Conditions and Expected Returns on Stocks and Bonds," *Journal of Financial Economics* 25 (November 1989), 23–49.

Federal Reserve Board, "Flow of Funds," *Federal Reserve Bulletin* (September 1996). 16. Table F.100.

Granger, Clive, "Investigating Causal Relations by Econometric Models and Cross Spectral Methods," *Econometrica* 37 (April 1969), 424–438.

Granger, Clive, and P. Newbold, "Spurious Regressions in Econometrics," *Journal of Econometrics* 2 (January 1974), 111–120.

Hale, David, "The Economic Consequences of America's Mutual Fund Boom," *International Economy* (March–April 1994), 24–64.

Hamilton, James, *Time Series Analysis*, Princeton, NJ: Princeton University Press, 1994.

Investment Company Institute, *Report of June 27, 1996*, Washington, DC: Author, 1996.

Jonston, J., *Econometric Methods*, New York: McGraw-Hill Book Company, 1984.

Judge, George, Carter Hill, William Griffiths, et al., *Introduction to the Theory and Practice of Econometrics*, 2nd ed., New York: John Wiley & Sons, 1984.

Kennickell, Arthur B., Martha Starr-McCluer, and Annike E. Sunden, "Family Finances in the U.S.: Recent Evidence from the Survey of Consumer Finances," *Federal Reserve Bulletin* (January 1997), 1–24.

Kinsella, Eileen, "Debate Rages: Would Mutual-Fund Holders Jump?" *Wall Street Journal* (December 11, 1996), p. c1, col. 3.

Lee, Charles, Andrei Shleifer, and Richard Thaler, "Investor Sentiment and the Closed-End Fund Puzzle," *Journal of Finance* 46 (March 1991), 75–109.

McGough, Robert, "Money Pours Into Mutual Funds at Frantic Pace So Far in January," *Wall Street Journal* (January 14, 1997), p. c1, col. 2.

Morgan, Donald P., "Will the Shift to Stocks and Bonds by Households Be Destabilizing?" *Economic Review*, Federal Reserve of Kansas City (Second Quarter 1994), 31–44.

Nelson, D., "Conditional Heteroskedasticity in Asset Returns: A New Approach," *Econometrica* 59 (April 1991), 347–370.

Norris, Floyd, "Growing Nervousness About Market Climate," *New York Times* (January 2, 1997), part II, p. c21, col 5.

Phillips, P.C.B., "Time Series Regression with a Unit Root," *Econometrica* 55 (March 1987), 277–310.

Reid, Brian K., "Mutual Fund Developments," *Perspective*, Investment Company Institute (March 1997), 1–12.

Romolona, Eli, Paul Kleiman, and Debbie Gruenstein, "Mutual Fund Flows and Market Returns," Working Paper, Federal Reserve Bank of New York, 1996.

Ross, S., "The Arbitrage Theory of Capital Asset Pricing," *Journal of Economic Theory* 13 (March 1976), 341–360.

Shliefer, Andrei, "Do Demand Curves for Stocks Slope Down?" *Journal of Finance* 41 (July 1986), 579–590.

Taylor, S., *Modeling Financial Time Series*, New York: John Wiley & Sons, 1986.

Sims, Christopher, "Macroeconomics and Reality," *Econometrica* 48 (January 1980), 1–49.

Wang, Yiwen, "Mutual Fund Flows and Some Economic Factors," Working Paper, Vanderbilt University, 1996.

Warther, Vincent, "Aggregate Mutual Fund Flows and Security Returns," *Journal of Financial Economics* 39 (October–November 1995), 209–235.

Wyatt, Edward, "Some Worries About the Rush Into Mutual Funds," *New York Times* (December 27, 1996), p. a1, col. 3.

Wyatt, Edward, "The Aging Bull's Fate May Be Wrapped in Stock Mutual Funds," *New York Times* (January 2, 1997), part II, p. c21, col. 1.

Journal of Financial Services Research 13:3 283–314 (1998)

Ten Years After: Regulatory Developments in the Securities Markets Since the 1987 Market Break

RICHARD R. LINDSEY
*Director, Division of Market Regulation, U.S. Securities and Exchange Commission**

ANTHONY P. PECORA
*Attorney-Adviser, Division of Market Regulation, U.S. Securities and Exchange Commission**

Abstract

It has been approximately 10 years since uncertainty, panic, and confusion wrested control from the forces of supply and demand and sent the U.S. securities markets plummeting. After much review, discussion, and analysis, it is widely agreed that certain aspects of the financial system contributed to that event. Since October 1987, many reforms have been implemented to address the weaknesses in the system highlighted by the 1987 market break. They include, among others, the implementation of circuit breakers, the approval of the Order Execution Rules, the reduction of the standard settlement time frame to $T+3$, the conversion to a same-day funds settlement system, the initiation of programs that regularly test the capacity of the market's automated systems, the augmentation of firms' capital levels, and improved coordination with regulators in other countries. The market has improved significantly because these changes have reduced or eliminated risk by improving coordination, increasing efficiency, sharing information, or ensuring sufficient system or capital capacity exists. Nevertheless, every market event is unique. Therefore, it remains important to identify and address new issues before they become problems.

It has been approximately ten years since uncertainty, panic, and confusion wrested control from the forces of supply and demand and sent the U.S. securities markets plummeting. After much review, discussion, and analysis, it is widely agreed that certain aspects of the financial system contributed to that event. Many reforms have been implemented since 1987 to address the weaknesses in the system that were highlighted at that time. This article notes some of the shortcomings of the system in 1987 and discusses how those shortcomings have been, and are continuing to be, addressed. It begins with a general review of the 1987 market break. The second section identifies some of the most significant regulatory developments in the U.S. markets since the 1987 market break. It also explains how those developments are responsive to the recommendations contained in the leading reports. The article concludes that the industry has adjusted to the issues brought to the forefront in October 1987 and that the markets are operationally more efficient than they were ten years ago. Nevertheless, each market crisis is unique. Therefore, regulators and market participants must remain committed to continually

* The Securities and Exchange Commission, as a matter of policy, disclaims reponsibility for any private publications by any of its employees. The views expressed herein are those of the authors and do not necessarily reflect the views of the commission or the authors' colleagues on the staff of the commission.

improving the markets by identifying potential problems and resolving them before they inhibit the smooth operation and functioning of the securities markets.

1. Background

In October 1987, the U.S. securities markets experienced an extraordinary surge in volume and price volatility. The Dow Jones Industrial Average (DJIA) declined 394.25 points in the two weeks prior to Black Monday. On Black Monday, October 19, 1987, the DJIA declined an additional 508.32 points. At its low point midday on October 20, 1987, it had declined over 1,000 points (37%) below its August 25, 1987, high of 2746.65. This decline was not limited to the DJIA. Broader indexes also declined. For example, during October 1987, the Standard & Poor's index of 500 stocks (S&P 500) declined 21.8%, and the composite indexes for the American Stock Exchange (AMEX), the New York Stock Exchange (NYSE), and the Nasdaq stock market declined 21.9, 27, and 27.2%, respectively. In terms of sheer size, this decline is comparable only to the 34% drop that occurred over six days in October 1929. What made this market break extraordinary, however, was the speed with which prices fell, the unprecedented volume of trading, and the consequent threat to the financial system.

In the wake of this decline, numerous studies were conducted to determine what happened, why it happened, and what, if anything, could be done to avoid a recurrence. Chief among the studies were those of the Presidential Task Force on Market Mechanisms (Brady report),[1] the Securities and Exchange Commission's Division of Market Regulation (Market Break report),[2] and the presidential Working Group on Financial Markets (Working Group report)[3].

In addition to making general findings, the reports analyzed a number of topics at length and presented various recommendations to improve the financial system. The subjects include trading halts, information systems, market professionals, the clearance and settlement system, dealer capital, future coordination among federal agencies, and international issues.

Trading halts

Both the Brady report and the Working Group report called for the implementation of coordinated, marketwide trading halts and reopenings. The reports reasoned that circuit breakers were necessary to protect markets and investors from large, rapid market declines that might damage the market's infrastructure and create panic conditions. Accordingly, the Working Group report recommended that all U.S. markets for equity and equity-related products should halt trading for one hour if the DJIA declined 250 points from its previous close and for two hours if it declined 400 points below its previous day's closing level. In addition, to help ensure that the circuit breakers did not unnecessarily disrupt trading, the Working Group report stated that the 250 and 400 point triggers should be reviewed at least quarterly to determine if changes in the index levels necessitate changes to these triggers to maintain percentages approximately equivalent to 12 and 20% of the DJIA.

Information systems

The Market Break report detailed the operational performance of the markets' information systems. It found that these systems were not prepared to accommodate the volume experienced on October 19 and 20, 1987. The report noted that some order routing and execution systems caused significant delays in executing trades. One system suffered a complete overload, losing both orders and trade reports.

Among other things, the Market Break report recommended that the SEC include a review of operational capacity as part of the commission's oversight examinations. The report also emphasized the need for improved coordination among the markets, especially when systems are down.

Market professionals

Both the Brady report and the Market Break report questioned the performance of some market professionals during the market break. In fact, the Brady report described the performance of some specialists as "poor by any standard." Similarly, the Market Break report noted a general decline in market maker participation in both the OTC market and the options market.

To address these concerns, the Market Break report recommended the implementation of objective performance standards for specialists. In addition, the report suggested that the NASD consider additional steps to ensure market makers could execute electronically against other marker makers' quotations during high volume periods.

Clearance and settlement system

All the leading reports noted that the clearance and settlement system needed to be improved. The Brady report suggested that a single mechanism should be developed for clearing stocks, stock index futures, and stock options. This, the report reasoned, would facilitate the smooth settlement of intermarket transactions, would allow intermarket exposure to be assessed accurately, and would remove inhibitions on the collateralization of intermarket positions.

Both the Working Group report and the Market Break report expanded on the Brady report's idea. The Working Group report recommended the implementation of several initiatives to reduce cash transfers and simplify settlement systems (e.g., netting of cash flows on a contractual basis, shortening the five-day settlement process for securities transactions, and integrated clearing). The Market Break report suggested that the clearing agencies enhance their member monitoring systems to enable them to obtain better and more timely information about their members' financial strength, activity in other markets, and customer activity. In addition, in light of the record price fluctuations, the report also recommended that the self-regulatory organizations (SROs) reassess their basic volatility assumptions and margin formulas.

Dealer capital

The Market Break report examined the adequacy of the capital required for specialists, options market makers, and broker/dealers. The report found that the rules governing the required capital of these parties did not reflect the actual capital needed to ensure the maintenance of fair and orderly markets in different types of securities. Therefore, it recommended that the markets consider revising the minimum financial requirements imposed on these parties.

Coordination

Both the Brady report and the Working group report suggested that coordination among the regulators needed to be improved. To this end, the Working Group report advocated for the development of contingency plans. The report contended that contingency planning should help ensure that the regulatory agencies and the SROs have systems in place that would allow them to react appropriately in the event of a market crisis.

International issues

The Market Break report found that the major world markets responded quickly and dramatically to movements in other major markets. Accordingly, the Market Break report recommended that regulators work together to develop trading and clearance and settlement links, international trade and quote reporting mechanisms, adequate financial oversight systems, and effective enforcement and surveillance arrangements.

2. Development of the market

A number of regulatory developments have been designed to address the systemic stress experienced during the 1987 market break. These developments typically sought to reduce or eliminate risk by bolstering the effectiveness of the financial system's infrastructure. They have been applied to many different segments, including the structure of the market, automation, the clearance and settlement process, required capital levels, and international coordination. This section highlights the most significant enhancements. A more complete itemization is contained in the appendix.

Market structure

It is widely accepted that the structure of the financial system in 1987 contributed to the confusion and attendant rapid decline in the equities, futures, and options markets. A prime example was the lack of coordination among the different markets. Although trading strategies and products that linked these markets were commonplace, the regulatory framework had not changed to properly accommodate them. Therefore, when the system was placed under extreme stress due to unanticipated, heavy selling pressure, chaos resulted when the system prevented the efficient use of the new products and strategies. Since that time, the structure of the market has changed significantly to address the vulnerabilities highlighted by the 1987 market break. The most significant of these changes has been the marked improvement in interagency and intermarket coordination, the implementation of market controls, including cross-market trading halts, and the increased transparency provided by the Order Execution Rules.

Improved coordination. Coordination among federal agencies and among the various markets has improved considerably since the 1987 market break. In terms of interagency coordination, the Working Group on Financial Markets was established on March 18, 1988, to help coordinate financial policy. The principals of the Working Group, which meets regularly every few months, are the Secretary of the Treasury and the chairpersons of the Federal Reserve Board, the SEC, and the CFTC. In addition, the head of the president's National Economic Council, the chairperson of the Council of Economic Advisers, the Comptroller of the Currency, and the president of the New York Federal Reserve Bank frequently attend Working Group sessions. The Working Group provides a framework for coordinating consideration, resolution, recommendation, and action regarding complex issues facing the U.S. financial system. Among other matters, the Working Group has developed coordinated contingency plans in the event of a financial crisis.

Coordination among the different markets also has improved. Shortly after the 1987 market break, the Intermarket Communications Group, which is composed of representatives from the equity and options markets and from several of the futures exchanges, created a communication system called the *Information Network for Futures, Options, and Equities* (INFOE). This "hoot and holler" system uses dedicated voice transmission lines to link together the SEC, the CFTC, and the SROs for the major securities and futures markets. It is used during periods of market stress to simultaneously disseminate among the equity, options, and futures markets the latest information available concerning the approach, implementation, or suspension of circuit breaker mechanisms; securities experiencing delayed openings or trading halts; order imbalances in NYSE securities; and operational problems concerning the Consolidated Quotation System (CQS), the Options Price Reporting Authority (OPRA), ITS, exchange order routing or order execution systems, or other exchange systems. In 1994, a similar teleconferencing system was implemented to link the chairperson of the SEC to the leaders of the nation's securities markets and clearing organizations. This improved interagency and intermarket coordination should help minimize uncertainty and improve communication during a sudden, sharp market decline.

Market controls. *Circuit breakers.* Circuit breakers are designed to substitute the unplanned, ad hoc trading halts that occurred in 1987 with halts that are planned and coordinated but not to increase the overall frequency of such disruptions in trading. Marketwide circuit breakers are intended to provide three benefits. First, they cushion the impact of market movements that would otherwise damage the market's infrastructure. Second, they limit credit risk by providing a brief respite amid frenetic trading. This allows parties to ensure that everyone is solvent. Third, they facilitate price discovery by providing a time-out to publicize order imbalances, which, in turn, should attract value traders.

There are some disadvantages associated with circuit breakers. They may hinder certain trading and hedging strategies. In addition, they lock investors into a position and prevent them from exiting the market for a certain period of time.

In one way or another, however, circuit breakers are inevitable in a tumultuous market because the financial system has limits. For example, there are limits on the amount of liquidity available and the capacity of the automated systems. When these limits are exceeded, ad hoc circuit breakers will be created. In 1987, they took the form of clogged order processing systems; ad hoc trading halts in individual stocks, options, and stock index futures; jammed communications systems; and some less than responsive specialists and market makers.

The Brady report detailed some of the damage caused by such unanticipated trading halts. For example, when the NYSE's DOT system was rendered ineffective by an overwhelming surge in volume, index arbitrageurs, wanting to avoid this source of risk, withdrew from the market. Their withdrawal deprived the index futures market of an important source of buying power. While this appeared to briefly benefit the equities market, it contributed to the development of a large futures discount that, in turn, placed additional downward pressure on stock prices. Therefore, it may be preferable to have orderly, coordinated circuit breakers that provide the markets and their participants with a time-out whenever a large, rapid decline threatens to overwhelm the market.

Although various trading halts occurred prior to 1987, none were coordinated cross-market trading halts. Hence, the leading reports called for the implementation of trading halts and reopenings coordinated across the markets for stocks, stock index futures, and options. The markets implemented such circuit breakers in October 1988.

The markets amended these rules in July 1996 and January 1997. Originally, trading would halt in all securities markets for one hour if the DJIA declined by 250 points from its previous day's closing level; and if the DJIA declined 400 points from its previous day's close on that same day, trading would halt for an additional two hours. Now, if the DJIA declines by 350 points from its previous day's close, a 30-minute marketwide trading halt is imposed by the markets. If the DJIA declines 550 points that day, an additional one-hour circuit breaker is triggered. Similar provisions exist in the futures market, except the circuit breakers in that market are based on the price level of the SPX futures contract.

Emergency authority. The Market Reform Act of 1990 provided the SEC with additional authority to issue rules on an emergency basis. For example, under extreme conditions, the commission can order marketwide trading suspensions, as long as the president does not object. This authority allows the commission to move quickly and decisively to contend with sudden, severe market conditions.

Other volatility-dampening procedures. Other procedures designed to reduce volatility in the markets have been instituted since 1987. The NYSE has implemented procedures to address program trading during sharp market swings. If the DJIA moves up or down 50 points from the previous day's closing value, NYSE Rule 80A(c) (Collar Rule) requires that program orders to buy or sell stocks as part of an index arbitrage strategy must be entered with directions to have the orders executed in a manner that stabilizes prices. In addition, if the S&P 500 futures contract declines 12 points (roughly equivalent to 100 points in the DJIA), the NYSE implements its "sidecar" procedures to temporarily route program orders to separate electronic files. This procedure facilitates the assessment of possible order imbalances.

Similarly, the stock index futures markets have adopted intraday and daily price limits designed to show a severe decline. For example, three different point price limits on trading in the SPX futures contract will occur before the first circuit breaker is triggered (down 7 points, down 15 points, and down 30 points).

Order Execution Rules. The approval of the Order Execution Rules in August 1996 may represent the most significant change in the structure of the market since the 1987 market break. In general, these rules require that market makers and specialists display customer limit orders that improve quotes by OTC market makers and specialists or add to the size associated with such quotes. In addition, they require OTC market makers and specialists that account for more than 1% of the volume in any listed security to publish their quotations for that security. Furthermore, these parties are prohibited from quoting one price publicly and a different price privately in an electronic communications network (ECN).

These changes reduce systemic risk primarily by enhancing transparency. In both 1987 and 1989, uncertainty caused some market participants to become reluctant to participate in the market or, in some cases, to withdraw entirely as the market moved downward. Their ability to determine the levels of supply and demand were limited. The Order Execution Rules help reduce this uncertainty by improving the ability of all market participants to determine the levels of supply and demand that exist. Moreover, the uniform display of customer limit orders encourages tighter, deeper, and more efficient markets. Indeed, the most current data from the NASD concerning the NASDAQ stocks indicates that the market and investors are benefiting from this structural change—spreads have declined by 30%, intraday volatility has declined, and both the average aggregate quote size and the average number of market makers per stock has increased.

Degree of automation

The markets' increased reliance on automated systems requires that the systems operate properly. Trading volume has increased steadily and dramatically since the early 1960s. This increase accelerated after 1981 and exploded in recent years. For example, the average daily volume of trading on the NYSE has grown from 161 million shares in 1990 to 412 million shares in 1996. The increase in trading volume in the Nasdaq market has been just as dramatic. The average daily trading volume in 1990 was 132 million shares, and in 1996, it ballooned to 544 million shares per day. To accommodate this growth in trading activity, the markets have replaced manually intensive order routing and execution procedures with automated systems that permit electronic routing and execution of certain orders. In addition, the markets have implemented automated systems to enhance the dissemination of transaction and quotation information and the comparison of trades prior to settlement. These automated systems have successfully increased the capacity of U.S. securities markets and improved the efficiency and timeliness with which transactions are executed.

This increased reliance on automated systems, however, makes it imperative that they function effectively. The magnitude of disruption in the market that can occur when systems fail to operate smoothly was evident during the market break of 1987. To help maintain the proper focus of these systems, the SEC issued two automation review policy statements (ARP I and ARP II).

ARP I, released in November 1989, set forth the SEC's view that the SROs, on a voluntary basis, should establish comprehensive planning and assessment programs to determine their systems' capacity and potential vulnerabilities. The SEC emphasized that the SRO programs should have three objectives: (1) each SRO should establish current and future capacity estimates; (2) each SRO should periodically conduct capacity stress tests; and (3) each SRO should obtain an annual independent assessment of whether the affected systems can perform adequately in light of estimated capacity levels and possible threats to the systems.

On May 9, 1991, the SEC published ARP II. This release further refined some of the issues raised in ARP I. In particular, ARP II provided detailed guidance concerning the nature and form that independent reviews should take, and it set forth a standardized methodology for advising commission staff of new systems developments and outages.

In connection with the issuance of these policy statements, the commission implemented its own ARP program. This program requires commission staff members to meet with the SROs on a regular basis to review various aspects of their computer operations. In addition, the commission has conducted spot checks of capacity at major broker/dealers.

This oversight has improved the markets by helping ensure they are ready for volatile trading days. Most exchanges now have excess capacity of approximately three times that needed for an average trading session. The NYSE, which is now averaging 505 million shares per day, reported that its systems could process up to 2.5 billion shares, or five times average capacity. The Chicago Board Options Exchange, which is averaging 733,000 contracts per day, has stated that it has the capacity to handle 2 million contracts, or almost three times average capacity. While Nasdaq, whose volume averages approximately 622 million shares per day, has indicated that it has the capacity to trade 1 billion shares without affecting normal system operation.

Likewise, the major broker/dealers' computerized trading systems should be able to withstand turbulent trading days. Major broker/dealers have around two times average capacity. In addition, these systems have on-line performance monitoring that can identify potential bottlenecks and provide the means to reroute message traffic to alleviate queuing. Moreover, the major broker/dealers utilize capacity modeling and verification models to ensure that their systems remain ahead of projected transaction message growth rates. Ensuring a sufficient capacity in the financial system's order routing and execution systems reduces a major source of systemic risk.

Clearance and settlement

The performance of the clearance and settlement system during the 1987 market break was called into question by all of the leading reports, as well as by some of the financial industry's regulators. Former Treasury Secretary Nicholas F. Brady stated that the clearance and settlement system was the weakest link in the nation's financial system.[4] Alan Greenspan, chairman of the Board of Governors of the Federal Reserve System, noted

> This area was identified by the Brady Commission and others after the market break last year as a potential point of vulnerability in the U.S. financial system. The overloading of the ... clearing systems last October induced breakdowns that dramatically increased uncertainty among investors and likely contributed to additional downward pressures on prices.[5]

Gerald Corrigan, then-president of the Federal Reserve Bank of New York, went so far as to say that "[T]he greatest threat to the stability of the financial system as a whole [during the 1987 market break] was the danger of a major default in one of these clearing and settlement systems."[6]

Many reforms designed to address the systemic risk that existed in the clearance and settlement system in 1987 have been implemented. The most significant developments include the reduction of the standard settlement time for broker/dealer trades from five business days to three business days, the adoption of same-day funds settlement, the execution of cross-margining and cross-guarantee agreements among the major securities and futures clearing agencies, a significant strengthening of the clearing funds since 1987, and the establishment of systems to assist clearing agencies to better monitor participants' risks and share critical information with other securities and futures clearing organizations if problems are detected.

T + 3 settlement. Although the U.S. clearance and settlement system was among the safest in the world in 1987, the record volume and volatility during October 1987 demonstrated that this area needed further attention. At the behest of then-SEC chairman Richard C. Breeden, the U.S. Steering Committee of the Group of Thirty formed a task force, chaired by John W. Bachmann, managing principal, Edward D. Jones & Co., to identify what changes to the clearance and settlement system were necessary and to recommend practical solutions. This task force, known as the *Bachmann task force*, set forth its findings in May 1992. The task force's primary conclusion was that *time = risk*. Therefore, several of the recommendations cited areas where processing time could be reduced. For example, the task force recommended the implementation of an interactive ID process for institutional trades; the settlement of all transactions among financial intermediaries and between financial intermediaries and their institutional clients in book-entry form only and payment for them in same-day funds; and that all new securities be required to be depository eligible. The Bachmann task force's primary recommendation, however, was that the settlement cycle for corporate and municipal securities be reduced to $T + 3$. In support of this recommendation, the task force found that $T+3$ settlement would result in a 58% reduction in risk to the National Securities Clearing Corporation (NSCC) as compared with the $T+5$ settlement that existed at the time.

Subsequently, the SEC proposed a rule that would establish three business days as the standard settlement time frame for broker/dealer trades. After reviewing over 1,900 comment letters, the commission approved the proposal on October 6, 1993. It became effective on June 7, 1995.

Changing to a $T+3$ time frame increased the safety and soundness of the clearance and settlement system by reducing settlement exposure. First, fewer unsettled trades now are subject to credit and market risk because there is less time between the normal trade execution date and the settlement date. Thus, there is less time for the value of trades to deteriorate pending settlement. Second, $T+3$ reduced the liquidity risk among the derivative and cash markets as well as reduced financing costs, by allowing investors that participate in both markets to obtain the proceeds of their securities transactions sooner. Finally, the shorter settlement time frame encouraged the operations of the clearing agencies and broker/dealers to become more efficient.

Same-day funds settlement system. On February 22, 1996, the industry took a major step in addressing the finality of payments in the clearance and settlement system and the liquidity requirements of clearing members by converting to a same-day funds settlement (SDFS) system. Prior to this conversion, the money settlements for securities transactions were processed in either the next-day funds settlement (NDFS) system or the SDFS system, depending on the type of security involved.[7] Payment for transactions processed by the NDFS system occurred on $T+3$ and was by means of a certified check for value on the following day. Payment for transactions processed by the SDFS system also occur on $T+3$, but the funds are immediately available at the time of settlement.

Requiring all securities transactions to be processed by the SDFS system reduced risk in the clearance and settlement process by eliminating overnight credit risk. The proceeds of a sale are now available on $T+3$, instead of $T+4$. In addition, converting to the SDFS system harmonized the payment methods used in the equities, corporate debt, and municipal debt markets with those in the derivatives and government securities markets.

Cross-margining agreements. Cross-margining programs are designed to increase liquidity and depth to the markets by eliminating duplicative margin requirements. The advent of options and futures contracts on stock indexes, foreign currencies, and debt instruments increased intermarket hedging opportunities.

Intermarket hedging involves the establishment of a position in one market and an offsetting position in another market on the same or similar underlying interest so that a decrease in value of one leg of the hedged position is offset, to some extent, by a corresponding increase in value of the other leg of the hedged position. Prior to cross-margining programs, market participants were required to deposit a margin for each leg of an intermarket hedge position, regardless of the net value of the position. For example, original margin requirements on some futures positions increased by more than 100%

during the week of October 19, 1987. Notwithstanding that some institutions were fully hedged across markets, they still were required to meet the continually higher margin requirements. This unnecessarily drained liquidity from the market during the 1987 market break, a time when the need for liquidity was great.

Cross-margining looks to the substance, rather than the form, of an entity's positions. It calculates participants' risk by utilizing the participants' end-of-day positions to determine overall combined daily margin requirements.

By incorporating the effects of intermarket hedging, clearing organizations have been able to reduce the amount of required margin deposit on hedged positions without endangering the clearing organizations' safeguards. In addition, cross-margining reduces risk to the clearing organizations from member defaults. By centralizing control of an intermarket, hedged portfolio, they provide a means whereby individual clearing organizations need not independently manage the risk associated with some components of a clearing member's total portfolio.

Furthermore, cross-margining reduces market exposure to clearing organizations from open positions in clearing member accounts. Cross-margining substitutes cash margin deposits from clearing members (assets that cannot appreciate in value) with assets whose value varies inversely with that of the open positions (assets that can appreciate in value and, thus, reduce the cost of liquidating an open short position). Finally, cross-margining helps prevent financial gridlock by reducing clearing member cash flows.

Since 1987, OCC has established several cross-margining programs. Currently, OCC participates in cross-margining programs with the Intermarket Clearing Corporation (ICC), the Chicago Mercantile Exchange (CME), the Board of Trade Clearing Corporation, the Comex Clearing Corporation, and the Kansas City Board of Trade Clearing Corporation.

Cross-guarantee agreements. Cross-guarantee agreements enhance the ability of clearing agencies to satisfy the obligations of a failed participant by increasing coordination across the various market segments. These agreements between clearing agencies generally provide that in the event of a default of a participant common to both clearing agencies, any resources remaining after the failed participant's obligations to one clearing agency have been satisfied will be made available to the other clearing agency. The guarantee generally is limited in that each party guarantees funds to the other only if it liquidates the assets in its control to a net gain and only up to the amount of the net gain. Cross-guarantee agreements reduce the systemic risk posed by a common member's default because that member may have positions spread across markets in such a manner that its net asset position at one clearing agency is positive, even though its net asset position at another clearing agency is negative.

To date, NSCC has executed cross-guarantee agreements with the Depository Trust Corporation (DTC), OCC, the MBS Clearing Corporation (MBSCC), the Government Securities Clearing Corporation (GSCC), and the International Securities Clearing Corporation (ISCC). In addition, the clearing agencies have amended their rules to allow them to enter into cross-guarantee agreements with other clearing agencies, including futures clearing organizations.

Liquidity improvements. Another prophylactic measure instituted by the clearing agencies since 1987 has been the significant improvement of their liquidity. OCC has increased its total clearing fund deposit to $555 million (up from $454 million in 1987) and increased its minimum clearing fund deposit for equities to $75,000 (up from $10,000 in 1987). Total margin deposits have increased to approximately $8.5 billion (up from $3 billion in 1987). The initial net capital requirement for membership has been increased from $150,000 in 1987 to $1 million, and the minimum net capital requirement was increased from $75,000 in 1987 to $750,000. In 1987, OCC had only $10 million in unsecured lines of credit. Currently, OCC has secured lines of credit of $150 million and unsecured lines of credit of $20 million.

Similar improvements have been adopted at the DTC and NSCC. The DTC has increased its total participants fund to over $658 million (up from $227 million in 1987), and its total lines of credit have increased from $60 million in 1987 to $700 million committed today. The NSCC has increased its total clearing fund deposit to over $764 million (up from $330 million in 1987). In 1987, the NSCC had no lines of credit. At present, the NSCC has total committed lines of credit of $400 million.

Risk control improvements. The clearing organizations have developed and implemented a number of other major systems enhancements to reduce risk in the clearance and settlement system. At OCC, for example, they include the theoretical intermarket margin system, a sophisticated, risk-based methodology for calculating margin; the options automated settlement instructions system, an electronic notification and approval system for settlement processes; and the risk management system, a sophisticated risk analysis system designed to help OCC clearing members and exchanges manage the risk of their customers and members in the same manner that OCC manages its risk.

In 1995, NSCC developed the collateral management system (CMS). The system allows the NSCC to collect and disseminate information regarding a participant's clearing fund, margin, and deposits at participating clearing entities to participants and other clearing entities. The CMS enhances the ability of clearing agencies and their participants to monitor clearing fund, margin, and other deposits that protect a clearing agency against loss should a member default on its obligations to the clearing agency. The DTC, the Philadelphia Stock Clearing Corporation (SCCP), the Philadelphia Trust Company (Philadep), GSCC, MBSCC, the Participants Trust Company (PTC), and OCC have all received SEC approval to participate in the CMS service.

The Securities Clearing Group and the Unified Clearing Group. There have been a number of initiatives since 1987 to improve cooperation and information sharing among the securities and futures clearing organizations. As part of this effort, the major U.S. securities clearing organizations formed the Securities Clearing Group (SCG) in 1989. In 1995, the SCG joined with the futures clearing organizations to create the Unified Clearing Group.

The SCG promotes coordinated action among clearing agencies and fosters their ability to identify, address, and minimize the risks and problems common to more than one clearing agency. The key methods utilized are the sharing of appropriate financial, operational, and clearing information with other clearing agencies in an atmosphere of cooperation and the development of uniform procedures for use among clearing agencies.

Capital levels

While it is unrealistic to expect any one group of market participants to have or commit sufficient capital to offset extraordinary selling pressure, it is critically important that the level of capital in the system be sufficient to absorb the volatility experienced during normal trading situations. Accordingly, all the leading reports concluded that the minimum capital requirements for specialists and market makers needed to be re-evaluated. Many changes have been instituted to respond to those comments. The most significant developments are increased capital in the system, the SEC's enhanced ability to monitor the financial condition of broker/dealers, and improved customer protection in the event of a broker/dealer's financial failure.

Increased capital. As a result of efforts by both broker/dealers and regulators, more capital is available to the financial system today than in 1987. Broker/dealers have improved the financial system by increasing their capitalization and expanding their liquidity. Since 1987, the 15 largest broker/dealers have increased total ownership equity by 24%, total net capital by 64%, and excess net capital by 65%. At the same time, these firms have decreased their exposure to a severe market decline by reducing the market value of their equity positions from around 5% of their total assets in 1987 to approximately 2% today.

Furthermore, reliance on banks to provide short-term funding for operations has been reduced since 1987. In 1987, broker/dealers relied heavily on banks to provide short-term funds to carry or clear securities transactions, to deposit unusual amounts of margin before collections from customers, or to close out stock loan activities. Today, the firms have expanded their sources of funding. For example, broker/dealers have become active participants in the commercial paper market. Five of the top NYSE firms have reported that funds provided by commercial paper issuances represented almost half of their total short-term borrowings. In addition, the major firms have developed contingency plans to provide liquidity in the event of a funding crisis, principally through balance sheet reductions or standby credit facilities with banks or other lending institutions. As a result of these actions, the major firms have greatly enhanced their ability to withstand substantial losses associated with a severe market drop.

Exchange initiatives also have added capital to the system. For example, the NYSE increased the minimum capital required of specialists to the greater of $1 million or 25% of the trading position requirements. In addition, the NYSE increased the trading unit position requirements to theee times their prior levels.

Another initiative taken by the NYSE to add capital to its specialist system involved the removal of a provision in its rules that unnecessarily inhibited large firms from entering the specialist business. The NYSE and the SEC recognized that the increasing institutionalization of the market combined with increased trading volatility would require specialists to commit much greater capital and assume more market risk to accommodate the larger orders and minimize short-term price fluctuations. To address this trend, the exchange identified the large, diversified NYSE members as a significant source of potential capital because they had the resources to expand their businesses and reasonably could be expected to provide the assets necessary to strengthen the capital base of the NYSE's specialist system.

To make it more attractive for these firms to acquire or associate with specialists, the NYSE deleted the provision in its rules that prohibited an approved person of an NYSE specialist from acting as a managing underwriter for a distribution of any security in which an associated specialist was registered. This prohibition originally was intended to dispel any possible perception of a potential conflict of interest between a managing underwriter and its associated specialist acting as a market maker for the same security. The highly volatile nature of the markets in October 1987 and the concomitant financial strain experienced by some specialist firms, however, made it apparent that the managing underwriter prohibition imposed a significant barrier on the ability of integrated broker/dealers to enter the specialist business. Therefore, it was decided that the potential reduction in risk of abuse resulting from the prohibition was outweighed by the benefits that an infusion of additional capital into the specialist system would provide.

The expansion of firm capitalization and sources of funding, the increase in the minimum capital requirements for specialists, and the removal of unnecessary regulatory burdens all have reduced systemic risk by helping to ensure that a sufficient amount of resources are committed to the markets.

Enhanced monitoring. In addition to setting prudent capital levels, the SEC enhanced its ability to monitor broker/dealers' capital. It implemented the Risk Assessment Program and modified the Net Capital Rule.

The commission recognized that, to accurately assess the capital of a broker/dealer, it was important to identify those factors that may affect a broker/dealer's financial position. Accordingly, the SEC implemented the Risk Assessment Program on September 30, 1992. This program requires broker/dealers to designate persons associated with them whose business activities are reasonably likely to have a material impact on their financial and operational condition as "material associated persons." In addition, broker/dealers are required to maintain certain information concerning material associated persons and to file quarterly reports concerning material associated persons with the commission.

There are two broad categories of information concerning material associated persons that broker/dealers must maintain. The first category is the holding company's organization and risk management policies. The second category is the financial condition of the associated person. This includes financial statements together with specialized categories of financial and securities related data, such as information concerning interest rate swaps, financial instruments, and real estate ventures.

The Risk Assessment Program is important for two reasons. First, it enhances the commission's ability to monitor the financial condition of key broker/dealers and their affiliates. Second, the assembly of this information requires broker/dealers to regularly review their financial condition, thereby facilitating their ability to identify potential weaknesses.

Another regulatory development that improved the monitoring of capital levels was the amendment of the Net Capital Rule in 1991. The commission amended the Net Capital Rule to require any broker/dealer that intends to disburse more than a specified percentage of its capital to its parents, shareholders, or related entities to give prior written notice to the commission and the appropriate SRO.

These "ring-fencing" amendments should help alert the commission to situations when capital may be withdrawn rapidly. Moreover, they should provide the commission with the opportunity to take measures in response to a potential, sudden withdrawal of capital from a major firm.

Increased customer protection. Greater protections exist today for customers of failed broker/dealers. The Securities Investor Protection Corporation (SIPC), which was created by the Securities Investor Protection Act of 1970, protects the customers of failed securities broker/dealers against loss of cash and securities up to certain defined limits. SIPC has taken action to further enhance the protection it provides customers and the financial system in general by increasing the size of its fund. In 1987, the SIPC fund totaled approximately $379 million. As of February 15, 1997, the SIPC fund had a balance of approximately $1.1 billion (an increase of 190% since 1987). In addition, SIPC now has access to a $1 billion line of credit established with a consortium of banks and statutory authority to borrow up to an additional $1 billion from the U.S. Department of the Treasury. By increasing this fund, SIPC has dramatically improved its ability to protect customers of broker/dealers that may fail as a result of a sharp market downturn, further promoting confidence in the U.S. securities markets.

International coordination

As the 1987 market break demonstrated, failure to recognize the interdependence of markets can produce catastrophic results. Therefore, with the interaction among the global markets steadily increasing, the SEC continuously has sought to coordinate its regulatory efforts with those of regulators in other countries. To facilitate these efforts, the commission has been, and continues to be, active in several international groups whose goal is to increase such coordination. Such groups include the U.S.–Russia Capital Markets Forum, the Group of Thirty, the International Organization of Securities Comissions (IOSCO), the Council of Securities Regulators of the Americas (COSRA), the Wilton Park Group, the Joint Forum, and the Quadrilateral.

In addition, the SEC has established both formal and informal relationships with foreign regulators to facilitate cooperation in enforcement investigations. In particular, the commission has developed mechanisms for information gathering designed to reduce the use of international borders to escape detection and prosecution. A formal information-sharing arrangement, known as a memorandum of understanding (MOU), has become the standard means for enforcement cooperation among securities and futures authorities. The commission has established formal relationships with the European Community, the Inter-American Development Bank, the United Nations Economic Commission for Latin America and the Caribbean, and 26 countries, including France, Germany, Hong Kong, Japan, and the United Kingdom.

In addition to MOUs, the commission uses other formal and informal information gathering mechanisms, including U.S. mutual legal assistance treaties (MLATs) with foreign criminal authorities. In fact, the MLAT between the United States and Switzerland has been a particularly useful mechanism for the SEC to obtain information located in Switzerland, including detailed bank account information.

3. Conclusion

U.S. securities markets are widely regarded as the deepest, most liquid, and fairest markets in the world. The robustness and stability of the markets have allowed investors throughout the world to participate confidently in trading in the U.S. markets. Investor confidence has been critical to the phenomenal growth and success experienced by the markets. In the past 12 months, the DJIA has broken the 5,000, the 6,000, and the 7,000 point levels. For the first time in history, assets in mutual funds have surpassed those on deposit at commercial banks. More investors than ever before have put their faith and their future in the securities markets.

Reforms have been instituted to address the weaknesses in the system uncovered by the 1987 market break. Risk, however, will remain in the system, regardless of innovations in technology or products. It would be prohibitively expensive and overly burdensome to remove all risk—even assuming it could be done. In some cases, the question may be whether or not regulation is necessary. In others, it may be a matter of degree: Costs must be balanced between being underprepared, appropriately prepared, and overprepared.

Risk always will exist because every market event is different. The underlying structure of the market system changes through time, and consequently the "weak links" also change. Therefore, it remains important to continuously identify and address new issues before they become problems.

Appendix

Market structure

Trading halts among stock, option, and futures markets should be coordinated to avoid instances in which options are trading, but prices in the underlying stock market or related futures market are unknown or uncertain.

- As originally implemented, the coordinated circuit breaker procedures halted trading for one hour if DJIA declined 250 points from its previous close: two hours if it declined 400 points below its previous day's closing level. In addition, trading following a halt would resume using procedures similar to those used to open trading on "Expiration Fridays." [Release Nos. 34-26198 (10/19/88), 53 FR 41637 (10/24/88); 34-26218 (10/26/88), 53 FR 44137 (11/1/88).]
- The commission approved SRO rule changes that reduced the circuit breaker time frames from one hour and two hours to 30 minutes and one hour. [Release Nos. 34-

37457 (7/19/96), 61 FR 39176 (7/26/96) (NYSE); 34-37458 (7/19/96), 61 FR 39167 (7/26/96) (AMEX); 34-37459 (7/19/96), 61 FR 39172 (7/26/96) (BSE, CBOE, CHX, and Phix).]

- The commission approved amendments to the SROs' rules to raise the DJIA limits to 350 points and 550 points. [Release No. 34-38221 (1/31/97), 62 FR 5871 (2/7/97) (NYSE, AMEX, CBOE, CHX, BSE, Phix).]
- The CFTC approved a proposal that modifies the circuit breaker price limit schedule for the domestic stock index futures contracts of the CME, KCBT, and NYFE to correspond with the NYSE proposal to increase its circuit breakers to 350 and 550 points. [61 FR 68722 (12/30/96).]
- The NYSE implemented a rule that requires index arbitrage equity trades to be entered "buy minus" when the DJIA advances 50 points from the previous day's close and "sell plus" when the DJIA declines 50 points from the previous day's close. [Release Nos. 34-28282 (7/30/90), 55 FR 31468 (8/2/90) (initial one year pilot program); 34-29854 (10/24/91), 56 FR 55963 (10/30/91) (permanent approval).]
- When the price of the S&P 500 futures contract falls 12 points below the previous day's closing value, market orders involving program trading in each of the stocks underlying the S&P 500 futures entered into the NYSE's automated order-routing system will be routed into a separated file for each of the stocks (NYSE sidecar file). Buy and sell orders for each stock will be paired in sidecar files for the next five minutes to determine the extent of the order imbalance. [Release No. 34-26198 (10/19/88), 53 FR 41637 (10/24/88).]
- The Market Reform Act of 1990 granted the commission the authority to issue rules on an emergency basis and, under extreme conditions, to order marketwide trading suspensions provided the president does not object. [Market Reform Act of 1990. Pub. L. No. 101-432 (1990); 15 U.S.C. § 78*l*(k).]
- The commission approved a proposal that authorized the NASD to halt OTC trading in exchange-listed securities when the primary market for the securities halts trading pending the dissemination of material news. [Release No. 34-25669 (5/5/88), 53 FR 16820 (5/11/88).]

The ITS plan needs to include a preopening notification routine for trading halts that occur as a result of an imbalance.

- The commission approved changes to the ITS plan and applicable SRO rules to include a preopening notification routine for all defined trading halts, including those resulting from an imbalance. [Release Nos. 34-29193 (5/15/91), 56 FR 23319 (5/21/91); 34-29194 (5/15/91), 56 FR 23318 (5/21/91); 34-29522 (8/5/91), 56 FR 38162 (8/12/91).]
- The commission approved changes to the SROs' rules that clarify that the ITS preopening application procedures must be used when establishing reopening prices after a circuit breaker trading halt occurs. [Release Nos. 34-38700 (5/30/97), 62 FR 30912 (6/5/97) (AMEX, BSE, CBOE, CHX, CSE, NASD, NYSE, and PSE); 34-38701 (5/30/97), 62 FR 30923 (6/5/97) (Phix).]

- The time period required for a primary market to provide an indication of interest after it has declared a trading halt for a security was reduced from 15 minutes to 10 minutes. [Release Nos. 34-38225 (1/31/97), 62 FR 5875 (2/7/97) (NYSE); 34-38546 (4/25/97), 62 FR 2451 (5/5/97) (CTA/CQ); 34-38549 (4/28/97), 62 FR 24519 (5/5/97) (AMEX).]

Increase transparency.

- The commission adopted Rule 11Ac1-4 to require the display of customer limit orders priced better than a specialist's or OTC market maker's quote or that add to the size associated with such quote. The commission also adopted amendments to Rule 11Ac1-1 to require a market maker to publish quotations for any listed security when it is responsible for more than 1% of the aggregate trading volume for that security and to make publicly available any superior prices that a market maker privately quotes through certain electronic communications networks. (The Order Execution Rules). [Release No. 34-37619A (9/6/96), 61 FR 48290 (9/12/96).]
- The NASD implemented various rule changes to facilitate the integration of the Order Execution Rules (reduced tier sizes to one unit of trading; displayed quotation sizes after SOES executions are decremented; split order execution permitted; eliminated the SOES limit order file; automatic quote updating allowed; SOES orders rejected when an ECN is the NBBO). [Release No. 34-38156 (1/10/97), 62 FR 2415 (1/16/97).]
- The commission adopted Rule 19c-5 under the Exchange Act to permit the trading of the same option in different markets. [Release No. 34-26870 (5/26/89), 54 FR 23963 (6/5/89).]

Increase accountability.

- The NYSE, the AMEX, and the PCX revised their specialist performance, evaluation, and improvement process to incorporate newly developed objective performance measures, codify their reallocation procedures, and establish minimum standards for specialist performance. [Release Nos. 34-27455 (11/22/89), 54 FR 49152 (11/29/89) (AMEX); 34-27803 (3/14/90), 55 FR 10740 (3/22/90) (NYSE); 34-27675 (2/5/90), 55 FR 4922 (2/12/90) (NYSE); 34-31596 (12/14/92), 57 FR 60549 (12/21/92) (NYSE); 34-33121 (10/29/93), 58 FR 59085 (11/5/93) (NYSE); 34-34906 (10/27/94), 59 FR 55142 (11/3/94) (NYSE); 34-35932 (6/30/95), 60 FR 35763 (7/11/95) (NYSE); 34-37667 (9/11/96), 61 FR 49185 (9/18/96) (NYSE); 34-37668 (9/11/96), 61 FR 49371 (9/19/96) (NYSE); 34-37770 (10/1/96), 61 FR 52820 (10/8/96) (initial PCX pilot program); 34-38372 (3/7/97), 62 FR 13421 (3/20/97) (NYSE); 34-38806 (7/1/97), 62 FR 36860 (7/9/97) (most recent extension of the PCX pilot program).]
- The NYSE and the AMEX clarified the restrictions concerning specialists' liquidating transactions. [Release Nos. 34-31797 (1/29/93), 58 FR 7277 (2/5/93) (NYSE); 34-38379 (3/10/97), 62 FR 13918 (3/24/97) (AMEX).]

- The NASD adopted rules providing greater limit order protection in the Nasdaq stock market. [Release No. 34-34279 (6/29/94), 59 FR 34883 (7/7/94).]
- The NASD prohibited Nasdaq market makers from trading ahead of any customer limit order in a Nasdaq security sent to it for execution from another broker/dealer. [Release No. 34-35751 (5/22/95), 60 FR 27997 (5/26/95).]
- The commission approved a NYSE/CME policy and circular prohibiting a member or person associated with a member or member organization from engaging in front running involving securities and stock index futures or options on stock index futures. [Release No. 34-27047 (7/19/89), 54 FR 31131 (7/26/89).]

Create a single specialist/market maker post where actual market baskets can be traded.

- The commission approved rule changes by the NYSE and CBOE to trade standardized baskets of stocks at an aggregate price in a single execution. [Release Nos. 34-27382 (10/26/89), 54 FR 45834 (10/31/89) (NYSE); 34-27383 (10/26/89), 54 FR 45846 (10/31/89) (CBOE).]
- The commission approved an OCC proposal to clear and settle a new CBOE market basket product through physical delivery of shares at each clearing member's designated clearing corporation. [Release No. 34-27389 (10/25/89), 54 FR 45872 (10/31/89).]
- NSCC changed its rules to enable it to clear and settle basket trades. [Release No. 34-27388 (10/26/89), 54 FR 45870 (10/31/89).]
- The Chicago Stock Exchange established rules to allow for the trading of standardized baskets and to trade a specific basket of stocks (the Chicago basket). [Release Nos. 34-33053 (10/15/93), 58 FR 54610 (10/22/93); 34-33058 (10/15/93), 58 FR 54388 (10/21/93).]
- The NYSE modified its rules regarding the trading of baskets by requiring the initiation of a discontinuous auction market when certain futures market circuit breakers take effect or when there would be a basket execution significantly away from the value underlying the index. [Release No. 34-28011 (5/11/90); 55 FR 20885 (5/21/90).]

Speed up the opening rotations in the options markets.

- The CBOE modified opening rotation procedures for OEX options to utilize lead market makers and supplemental market makers. This shortened the average length of OEX rotations from approximately 20 minutes to 5 minutes. [Release No. 34-25627 (4/29/88), 53 FR 16206 (5/5/88).]
- The CBOE adopted on a permanent basis auxiliary market opening procedures to accommodate increased order flow experienced on quarterly expirations of stock index derivative products. [Release No. 34-25804 (6/15/88), 53 FR 23474 (6/22/88).]

Review the impact of issuer repurchases and the possible need for amendments to Rule 10b–18.

- The commission's Division of Market Regulation declined to expand the exemption concerning block trades and trading volume. [No-Action Letter from Larry E. Bergmann, Associate Director, Division of Market Regulation, SEC, to Charles J. Plohn, Jr., Managing Director, Merrill Lynch, Pierce, Fenner & Smith Inc., dated 10/25/91 (File No. TP 91-16).]

Automation

Market makers need to develop and implement regular, comprehensive stress-testing programs for their automated systems to ensure sufficient capacity exists.

- The commission published two automation review policy statements (ARP I and ARP II) to provide the industry with, among other things, detailed guidelines on the independent review process for SROS' capacity planning, systems development, contingency planning, and security review programs. [Release Nos. 34-27445 (11/16/89), 54 FR 48703 (11/24/89) (ARP I); 34-29185 (5/9/91), 54 FR 48703 (5/15/91) (ARP II).]

Coordination among the markets should be improved, especially when systems are down and order flow may need to be sent to another market.

- The INFOE system was created. This "hoot and holler" teleconferencing system links the SEC, the CFTC, and the major securities and futures SROs to each other by using dedicated voice transmission lines. It is used during periods of market stress to disseminate simultaneously among the equity, options, and futures markets the latest information available concerning (1) the approach, implementation, or suspension of circuit breaker mechanisms; (2) securities experiencing delayed openings or trading halts; (3) order imbalances in NYSE securities disseminated as part of circuit breaker mechanisms; and (4) operational problems concerning the consolidated quotation system (CQS), Options Price Reporting Authority (OPRA), ITS, exchange order routing or order execution systems, or other exchange systems.
- In 1994, a similar teleconferencing system was implemented to link the SEC chairperson to the leaders of the nation's securities markets and clearing organizations.

Facilitate the ability of market makers to execute electronically against other market makers' quotations.

- The NASD required all Nasdaq national market securities market makers to participate in the SOES system, limited the number of valid excuses for market makers to withdraw from Nasdaq, and raised the penalty for unexcused withdrawal by a market maker from Nasdaq. [Release No. 34-25791 (6/9/88), 53 FR 22594 (6/16/88).]

- The NASD created SelectNet (originally named the order confirmation transaction service, OCT) to permit firms to access market makers over a computer link thereby obviating the need for voice contact. [Release No. 34-25690 (5/11/88), 53 FR 17523 (5/17/88).]
- The NASD modified SelectNet to allow order entry firms to preference a specific market maker and to "broadcast" an order through SelectNet to all market makers. [Release No. 34-28636 (11/21/90), 55 FR 49732 (11/30/90).]
- The NASD adopted rule changes that allow nonmembers to receive real-time access to view all orders "broadcast" through SelectNet. [Release No. 34-35482 (3/13/95), 60 FR 14806 (3/20/95).]
- The Pacific Exchange established electronic access memberships—automated system access privilege (ASAP). [Release No. 34-28335 (8/13/90), 55 FR 34106 (8/21/90).]
- The Boston Stock Exchange established an automated, small order communication, order routing, and execution system for member organizations known as BEACON. [Release Nos. 34-26029 (8/25/88), 53 FR 33565 (8/31/88) (initial 6 month pilot program); 34-27012 (7/10/89), 54 FR 30487 (7/20/89) (permanent approval).]
- The AMEX expanded the use of its Auto-Ex system to include all equity and stock index options traded on the AMEX. [Release No. 34-25996 (8/15/88), 53 FR 31779 (8/19/88).]
- The AMEX modified its rules and systems to permit the automatic execution of orders up to 599 shares entered into the PER system in select AMEX equities through the exchange's Auto-Ex system during periods of extremely high order flow. [Release No. 34-30757 (5/29/92), 57 FR 24067 (6/5/92).]
- The PCX created the Pacific Options Exchange trading system (POETS). [Release No. 34-27633 (1/18/90), 55 FR 2466 (1/24/90).]
- The Phix implemented the automated options market (AUTOM) system. This system, which is mandatory for specialists, provides for the automatic entry and routing of Phix-listed equity options and index orders to the Phix's trading floor. In addition, certain orders are eligible for AUTOM's automatic execution feature, AUTO-X. [Release Nos. 34-25540 (3/31/88), 53 FR 11390 (4/6/88) (initial pilot program); 34-38792 (6/30/97), 62 FR 36602 (7/8/97) (permanent approval).]
- The CBOE enhanced its electronic order routing system (ORS) to permit the inclusion of the following types of orders: all or none, immediate or cancel, fill or kill, minimum quantity, stop, stop loss, opening only, market on close, closing only, market if touched, not held, and with discretion. [Release No. 34-38702 (5/30/97), 62 FR 31184 (6/6/97).]
- The CBOE modified its rules to permit the use of proprietary brokerage order routing terminals and their related systems in the SPX trading crowd in order to expedite the process by which members can receive OEX orders.

Information systems should be established that incorporate information regarding the trade, the time of the trade, and the name of the ultimate customer in every major market segment so that developing problems can be diagnosed, potentially damaging abuses can be uncovered, and the nature and cause of a market crisis can be identified.

- The commission proposed Rule 13h-1 for comment, which would have established a large position reporting system, as contemplated by the Market Reform Act of 1990. In response to the comments received, the commission amended Rule 13h-1 and reproposed it. [Release Nos. 34-29593 (8/22/91), 56 FR 42550 (8/28/91); 34-33608 (2/17/94), 59 FR 7917 (2/22/94); Market Reform Act of 1990. Pub. L. No. 101-432 (1990).]
- The commission adopted Rule 17a-23 under the Exchange Act to establish record-keeping and reporting requirements for broker/dealers that operate automated trading systems. Registered broker/dealer sponsors of these systems are required to maintain participant, volume, and transaction records, and to report system activity periodically to the commission. [Release No. 34-35124 (2/20/94), 59 FR 66702 (2/28/94).]

The options exchanges need to review their rules regarding market maker participation in small order execution systems.

- The CBOE modified its rules to ensure adequate market maker participants in the retail automatic execution system (RAES). [Release Nos. 34-25995 (8/15/88), 53 FR 31781 (8/19/88) (initial pilot); 34-28088 (6/1/90), 55 FR 23620 (6/11/90) (permanent approval).]

Other automation initiatives.

- The NYSE modified its individual investor express delivery service (IIEDS) to provide that market orders of individual investors of up to 2,099 shares always will have priority delivery to specialists posts through the exchange's SuperDOT system ahead of all other orders at all times. [Release No. 34-27600 (1/9/90), 55 FR 1749 (1/18/90).]
- OPRA implemented systems modifications that allow the announcement of new series through computer formatted messages thus eliminating the time-consuming and error-prone process of transcribing needed to announce a new series.

Clearance and settlement

Shorten the five day settlement process for securities transactions.

- The commission approved Rule 15c6-1 under the Exchange Act which established $T+3$ as the standard settlement time frame for broker/dealer trades. [Release No. 34-33023 (10/6/93), 58 FR 52891 (10/13/93).]
- Conforming changes to Reg T were implemented. [59 FR 53565 (10/25/94).]
- The MSRB required that all broker/dealer trades in municipal securities, other than trades done on a "when, as, and if issued" basis, settle within three business days. [Release No. 34-35427 (2/28/95), 60 FR 12798 (3/8/95).]

- The commission approved the DTC same-day funds settlement system, which expanded DTC's certificate immobilization and book-entry delivery services to certain securities settling in same-day funds, such as municipal notes and auction rate preferred stock. [Release No. 34-26051 (8/31/88), 53 FR 34852 (9/8/88).]
- In February 1996, the payment systems for securities transactions and principal and interest payments converted from next-day funds settlement to same-day funds settlement in order to eliminate overnight credit risk. [Release Nos. 34-35720 (5/16/95), 60 FR 27360 (5/23/95) (DTC); 34-36843 (2/14/96), 61 FR 6672 (2/21/96) (modifying DTC's procedures relating to receiver authorized delivery processing); 34-36866 (2/21/96), 61 FR 7290 (2/27/96) (NSCC); 34-36868 (2/21/96), 61 FR 7570 (2/28/96) (PCC); 34-36875 (2/22/96), 61 FR 7846 (2/29/96) (initial SCCP temporary approval); 34-36876 (2/22/96), 61 FR 7841 (2/29/96) (initial Philadep temporary approval); 34-37440 (7/15/96), 61 FR 37948 (7/22/96) (modifying DTC-NSCC Fund/SERV interface agreement to accommodate the conversion to a same-day funds settlement system); 34-38100 (12/30/96), 62 FR 1018 (1/7/97) (extension of temporary approval for Philadep and SCCP); 34-38281 (2/13/97), 62 FR 8073 (2/21/97) (clarifying Philadep's procedures); 34-38282 (2/13/97), 62 FR 8074 (2/21/97) (clarifying SCCP's procedures).]
- A direct registration system was implemented. [Release Nos. 34-37931 (11/8/96), 61 FR 58600 (11/15/96) (DTC); 34-37933 (11/8/96), 61 FR 59269 (11/21/96) (Philadep); 34-37937 (11/8/96), 61 FR 58728 (11/18/96) (NYSE).]
- The NYSE and the NASD modified their rules to require that members use securities depositories to confirm, affirm, and settle institutional trades in corporate equity securities for delivery against payment or receipt against payment. [Release No. 34-25120 (11/13/87), 52 FR 44506 (11/19/87).]

Coordinate the settlement process across markets.

- The major U.S. clearing organizations established the Securities Clearing Group. This is a voluntary organization of clearing agencies designed to increase coordination and cooperation between clearing agencies in overseeing the financial and operating condition of the participants' common members. [Release Nos. 34-26300 (11/21/88), 53 FR 48353 (11/30/88) (full text of SCG agreement); 34-27044 (7/18/89), 54 FR 30963 (7/25/89) (DTC, MCC, MSTC, NSCC, OCC, Philadep, SCCP); 34-28044 (5/23/90), 55 FR 22122 (5/31/90) (MBSCC and BSECC); 34-28157 (6/28/90), 55 FR 28115 (7/9/90) (GSCC); 34-29639 (8/30/91), 56 FR 44116 (9/6/91) (PTC).]
- Uniform book entry requirements were adopted. [Release Nos. 34-32455 (6/11/93), 58 FR 33679 (6/18/93) (AMEX, BSE, CHX, NASD, NYSE, Phix, PCX); 34-32640 (7/15/93), 58 FR 39260 (7/22/93) (MSRB); 34-36778 (1/26/96), 61 FR 3741 (2/1/96) (CBOE).]
- Uniform depository eligibility requirements were adopted. [Release Nos. 34-35798 (6/1/95), 60 FR 30909 (6/12/95) (AMEX, BSE, CHX, NASD, NYSE, Phix, PCX); 34-36778 (1/26/96), 61 FR 3741 (2/1/96) (CBOE).]

A single mechanism should be developed for clearing stocks, stock index futures, and stock options to facilitate the smooth settlement of intermarket transactions, allow intermarket exposure to be assessed accurately, and remove inhibitions on the collateralization of intermarket positions.

- The collateral management service (CMS) was developed to provide information regarding participants' clearing fund, margin, and other similar requirements and deposits, including excess or deficit amounts and comprehensive data on underlying collateral. [Release Nos. 34-36091 (8/10/95), 60 FR 42931 (8/17/95); 34-36431 (10/27/95), 60 FR 55749 (11/2/95).]
- In order to facilitate participation in CMS, the major U.S. securities clearing organizations modified their rules to authorize the release of clearing data. [Release Nos. 34-36431 (10/27/95), 60 FR 55749 (11/2/95) (MBSCC); 34-36597 (12/15/95), 60 FR 66570 (12/22/95) (GSCC); 34-36743 (1/26/96), 61 FR 2551 (1/19/96) (SCCP and Philadep); 34-37608 (8/26/96), 61 FR 46498 (9/3/96) (DTC); 34-38313 (2/19/97), 62 FR 8810 (2/26/97) (PTC).]
- The risk management system (RMS) was developed to facilitate participants' ability to evaluate the risk profile of certain positions in debt and equity securities, securities options, and futures contracts in light of certain theoretical market movements. [Release No. 34-30346 (2/6/92), 57 FR 5195 (2/12/92).]
- The institutional delivery (ID) system was enhanced by adding electronic mail features and interactive capabilities such as the notice of order execution and institutional instructions, prime broker option, the advice of confirm correction/cancellation feature, and the authorization/exception processing feature. [Release Nos. 34-34199 (6/10/94), 59 FR 31660 (6/20/94); 34-34779 (10/3/94), 59 FR 51465 (10/11/94); 34-35971, 60 FR 37696 (7/21/95); 34-36050 (8/12/95), 60 FR 41139 (8/11/95).]
- MSTC and DTC expanded the interface to DTC's Interactive Institution Delivery System (IID) to include interactive inquiry and affirmation capability and to facilitate access to DTC's Standing Instruction Database (SID). [Release No. 34-35656 (4/28/95), 60 FR 24938 (5/10/95).]
- The commission permanently approved the NSCC's centralized, automated clearance and settlement system for mutual funds known as the *mutual fund settlement, entry, and registration verification service* (Fund/SERV). [Release No. 34-25416 (11/20/87), 52 FR 45418 (11/27/87).]
- The NSCC added the Networking service to the Fund/SERV system to centralize and standardize the exchange of customer account level activity information between broker/dealers and mutual fund processors. [Release No. 34-26376 (12/20/88), 53 FR 52544 (12/28/88).]
- DTC enhanced its link to Fund/SERV by allowing NSCC members who are not direct Fund/SERV participants to access this service through DTC. [Release No. 34-27904 (4/13/90), 55 FR 15047 (4/20/90).]
- NSCC modified Fund/SERV to automate the processing of mutual fund underwritings and tender offers. [Release No. 34-28573 (10/23/90), 55 FR 45700 (10/30/90).]

- NSCC increased the flexibility of Fund/SERV to permit the inclusion of no-load funds. [Release No. 34-31937 (3/1/93), 58 FR 12609 (3/5/93).]
- NSCC modified its rules to allow unit investment trusts to be processed through Fund/SERV. [Release No. 34-38632 (5/14/97), 62 FR 28721 (5/21/97).]
- Delta Clearing Corp. modified its rules to allow brokers who have been approved by Delta to submit trade reports for options transactions on behalf of participants. This should increase the number of trades that are incorporated into the national clearance and settlement system and thus obtain the benefit of Delta's guarantee and risk management system. [Release No. 34-38796 (6/30/97), 62 FR 37326 (7/11/97).]

Integrate clearing.

- OCC and Comex established a cross-margining program. [Release No. 34-31414 (11/6/92), 57 FR 53943 (11/13/92).]
- OCC and ICC established a cross-margining program. [Release Nos. 34-26153 (10/3/88), 53 FR 39567 (10/7/88); 34-30041 (12/5/91), 56 FR 64824 (12/12/91) (expanded cross-margining program to include nonproprietary, market maker positions).]
- OCC and the CME established a cross-margining program. [Release Nos. 34-27296 (9/26/89), 54 FR 41195 (10/5/89); 34-29991 (11/26/91), 56 FR 61458 (12/3/91) (expanded cross-margining program to include nonproprietary, market maker positions).]
- OCC and the Board of Trade Clearing Corporation established a proprietary cross-margining program. [Release No. 34-29888 (10/31/91), 56 FR 56680 (11/6/91).]
- OCC and the Kansas City Board of Trade Clearing Corporation established a proprietary cross-margining program. [Release Nos. 34-30413 (2/16/92), 57 FR 7830 (3/4/92); 34-32708 (8/2/93), 58 FR 42586 (8/10/93) (expanded cross-margining program to include positions held for market professionals.)]
- OCC, CME, and ICC established a trilateral cross-margining program. [Release No. 34-32534 (6/28/93), 58 FR 36234 (7/6/93).]
- OCC conformed the agreements governing nonproprietary XM accounts of market professionals in the OCC-ICC-CME program, the OCC-ICM XM program, and the OCC-KCC XM program to the revised distribution scheme in the new appendix to the CFTC's bankruptcy rules. In addition, the terms of the agreements governing the proprietary and nonproprietary XM accounts in the OCC-KCC XM program were made consistent with those used in the OCC-ICC-CME XM program and in the OCC-ICC XM program. [Release No. 34-36819 (2/7/96), 61 FR 5594 (2/13/96).]
- OCC, CME, and CCC established a trilateral cross-margining program. [Release No. 34-38584 (5/8/97), 62 FR 26602 (5/14/97).]
- OCC included equities in its theoretical intermarket margin system. [Release No. 34-28928 (3/1/91), 56 FR 9995 (3/8/91).]
- OCC created a small-cap index product group for cross-margining purposes. [Release No. 34-32020 (3/19/93), 58 FR 16438 (3/26/93).]

Confirm all trades on trade date.

- The NYSE and the AMEX, in conjunction with the NSCC, adopted rules that require members to compare or close out all regular way equity trades by the close of business on $T+1$ and supplemented these rules with automated trade resolution systems that assist members in resolving uncompared trades efficiently. [Release Nos. 34-28285 (7/30/90), 55 FR 31930 (8/6/90) (NYSE); 34-27851 (3/27/90), 55 FR 12759 (4/5/90) (AMEX); 34-27074 (7/28/89), 54 FR 32405 (8/7/89) (NSCC).]
- The commission approved rule changes that fully implemented next-day comparison of exchange and OTC corporate securities trade and the automated resolution of uncompared trades. [Release Nos. 34-27598 (1/9/90), 55 FR 1748 (1/18/90) (NYSE); 34-27809 (3/16/90), 55 FR 11074 (3/26/90) (AMEX).]
- The NASD developed the automated confirmation transaction (ACT) service. ACT matches nonautomated OTC trades in an automated system and then forwards the trades to NSCC for processing. [Release Nos. 34-27229 (9/7/89), 54 FR 38484 (9/18/89); 34-28583 (11/21/90), 55 FR 46120 (11/1/90); 34-30415 (2/26/92), 57 FR 7829 (3/4/92).]
- The CBOE established procedures for its intraday trade match system. [Release No. 34-3000 (11/26/91), 56 FR 63531 (12/4/91).]

Reassess basic volatility assumptions and margin formulas.

- OCC began utilizing its theoretical intermarket margin system for calculating member margin on equity options (Equity TIMS). [Release Nos. 34-28928 (3/1/91), 56 FR 9995 (3/8/91); 34-37985 (11/25/96), 61 FR 64406 (12/4/96) (permanent approval).]
- OCC modified the margin intervals relating to nonequity options positions to alleviate the excessive margin required for out-of-the-money nonequity options positions in unusually volatile market conditions. [Release No. 34-25174 (12/4/87), 52 FR 47474 (12/14/87).]
- GSCC, based on its assessment of historical data, found that certain components of its clearing fund formula were overly conservative. In response, it adjusted this formula to ensure appropriate risk protection for GSCC, while providing members with increased liquidity. [Release No. 34-37368 (6/25/96), 61 FR 34912 (7/3/96).]

Augment the ability of clearing organizations to satisfy the obligations of defaulting market participants.

- The commission granted OCC the authority, in the event of a market emergency, to defer liquidation of a defaulting clearing member's positions and to execute hedge transactions to protect against a decline in open positions. [Release No. 34-27104 (8/8/89), 54 FR 33642 (8/15/89).]

- The clearing agencies modified their rules to permit the execution of cross-guarantee agreements with other clearing agencies, including futures clearing organizations. [Release Nos. 34-38410 (3/17/97), 62 FR 13931 (3/24/97), (OCC); 34-37616 (8/28/96), 61 FR 46887 (9/5/96) (MBSCC, GSCC, ISCC); 34-38350 (2/27/97), 62 FR 10601 (3/7/97) (NSCC); 34-38604 (5/9/97), 62 FR 27097 (5/16/97) (PTC).]
- The clearing organizations executed cross-guarantee agreements. [Release Nos. 34-33548 (1/31/94), 59 FR 5638 (2/7/94) (DTC-NSCC agreement); 34-38624 (5/13/97), 62 FR 27286 (5/19/97) (clarifying DTC-NSCC agreement to include futures clearing organizations); 34-39020 (9/4/97) (agreements between NSCC-ISCC, NSCC-GSCC, and NSCC-MBSCC); 34-39022 (9/4/97) (NSCC-OCC agreement); 34-38604 (5/9/97), 62 FR 27097 (5/16/97) (PTC-MBSCC agreement).]
- MBSCC modified its rules to explicitly state that MBSCC has a lien on all property placed in its possession by its participants in order to ensure that MBSCC can cover a participant's unpaid obligations to MBSCC. [Release No. 34-38598 (5/9/97), 62 FR 27091 (5/16/97).]
- GSCC expanded its rules to allow GSCC to issue a comparison of a transaction between a solvent and an insolvent member based solely on data submitted by the solvent netting member, subject to certain prerequisites. [Release No. 34-38636 (5/14/97), 62 FR 27818 (5/21/97).]

Clarify and confirm the rights and duties of parties to the clearing and settlement process.

- The GSCC changed its rules to clarify that comparisons issued by it to GSCC members for compared trades are binding contracts. [Release No. 34-26565 (2/22/89), 54 FR 8417 (2/28/89).]
- DCC clarified the terms *trading limit* and *exposure limit*. [Release No. 34-38646 (5/15/97), 62 FR 28085 (5/22/97).]

Increase the availability of timely information to participants in the settlement process concerning payment obligations and cash flows.

- The NSCC and the SCCP modified their rules and systems to provide earlier settlement guarantees of continuous net settlement trades. [Release Nos. 34-27192 (8/29/89), 54 FR 37070 (9/6/89) (initial plot program); 34-37381 (6/28/96), 61 FR 35289 (7/5/96) (permanent approval).]
- OCC modified its systems to distribute clearing reports to members electronically. [Release No. 34-31992 (3/12/93), 58 FR 14606 (3/18/93).]
- MBSCC has established the comparison only system (COS). COS is a limited system that allows principals to compare trade data. [Release No. 34-38697 (5/30/97), 62 FR 30918 (6/5/97).]

Capital requirements

Increase the minimum financial requirements on market participants.

- The NYSE raised the minimum dollar amount for specialists' capital from $100,000 to $1 million and increased the measure based on the trading unit position to three times its 1987 level. [Release No. 34-25677 (5/6/88), 53 FR 17286 (5/16/88).]
- The AMEX raised its capital requirements from $100,000 to $600,000. [Release No. 34-25863 (6/28/88), 53 FR 25225 (7/5/88).]
- The NYSE raised the capital requirements for members who execute transactions on the floor but are not otherwise covered by the higher capital requirements from $50,000 to $100,000. [Release No. 34-26176 (10/13/88), 53 FR 41009 (10/19/88).]
- OCC increased the initial and minimum net capital required of its members from $150,000 initial/$100,000 maintenance to $1,000,000 initial/$750,000 maintenance. [Release No. 34-26840 (5/19/89), 54 FR 23004 (5/30/89).]
- The NYSE deleted a restriction in NYSE Rule 98 that prohibited an approved person of an NYSE specialist unit from acting as a managing underwriter for a distribution of any security in which the associated specialist was registered. This facilitated the ability of large, diversified firms to enter the specialist business. [Release No. 34-26125 (9/28/88), 53 FR 39395 (10/16/88).]
- Competing specialists were allowed on the BSE's trading floor. [Release No. 34-34078 (5/18/94), 59 FR 27082 (5/25/94).]
- The AMEX, the CBOE, the NYSE, the PCX, and the Phix implemented a "10 up" requirement for options contracts (ensures a minimum market depth of 10 contracts for nonbroker/dealer customer orders (1,000 shares)). [Release Nos. 34-27235 (9/11/89), 54 FR 38580 (9/19/89) (AMEX); 34-26924 (6/13/89), 54 FR 26284 (6/22/89) (CBOE); 34-28897 (2/19/91), 56 FR 7736 (NYSE) (2/25/91); 34-24580 (6/11/87), 52 FR 23120 (6/17/87) (Phix); 34-31824 (2/4/93), 58 FR 8078 (2/11/93); (PCX); 34-34891 (10/25/94), 59 FR 54653 (11/1/94) (expanding PCX guarantee to 20 contracts); 34-36601 (12/18/95), 60 FR 66817 (12/26/95) (increasing the maximum order size eligible for automatic execution on the Phix to 50 contracts); 34-37521 (8/2/96); 61 FR 41675 (8/9/96) (modifying the PCX's rules to codify some related floor policies and to clarify certain related provisions); 34-38420 (3/19/97), 62 FR 14488 (3/26/97) (clarifying the term *broker/dealer* in the PCX's rule).]
- OCC increased the minimum required contribution by members to OCC's clearing fund from $10,000 to $75,000 for the stock fund and from $50,000 to $75,000 for the nonequity fund. [Release No. 34-27480 (11/28/89), 54 FR 50553 (12/7/89).]
- In order to provide further investor protection in the event of a failure of a retail broker, the Securities Investor Protection Corporation (SIPC) has taken action to increase the size of its fund—the SIPC fund has grown to $1.1 billion (an increase of 190% from 1987). In addition, SIPC has secured additional lines of credit of $2 billion.

Improve risk monitoring capabilities.

- The commission approved Rules 17h-1T and 17h-2T, which, together with Form 17-H, established a risk assessment record-keeping and reporting system for registered broker/dealers concerning certain of their associated persons. The Division of Market Regulation is preparing a study that evaluates the effectiveness of the risk assessment rules. The division plans to present the study to the commission in 1997. [Release No. 34-30929 (7/16/92), 57 FR 32159 (7/21/92).]

Re-examine the minimum net capital required of broker/dealers that carry customer accounts, those that introduce customer accounts on a fully disclosed basis to another broker/dealer, and those that are market makers in OTC securities.

- The commission amended the Net Capital Rule to gradually increase the minimum net capital requirements for certain registered broker/dealers. [Release No. 34-31511 (11/24/92), 57 FR 56973 (12/2/92).]
- The commission amended the Net Capital Rule to permit broker/dealers to employ theoretical option pricing models in determining net capital requirements for listed options and related positions. [Release No. 34-38248 (2/6/97), 62 FR 6474 (2/12/97).]
- The commission issued a concept release soliciting comments on a broad range of issues regarding the capital standards imposed by the Net Capital Rule on broker/dealer participation in the derivative products markets. [Release No. 34-32256 (5/4/93), 58 FR 27486 (5/10/93).]

The provision in the Net Capital Rules that allows some options market makers that are not exempt from the Net Capital Rule to avoid under certain circumstances the haircuts on their options positions should be eliminated.

- The commission amended the Net Capital Rule to make it applicable to certain specialists that formerly were exempt from the rule but continued to exempt options market makers on national exchanges under certain conditions. [Release No. 34-32737 (8/11/93), 58 FR 43555 (8/17/93).]

Limitations should be placed on the withdrawal of equity from market makers' accounts.

- The commission amended the Net Capital Rule to prevent the withdrawal of net capital by broker/dealers under certain circumstances for the benefit of certain persons related to the broker/dealer without first notifying the commission at least two business days before the withdrawal of capital. [Release No. 34-28927 (2/28/91), 56 FR 9124 (3/5/91).]

Increase the margin requirements.

- The AMEX, the CBOE, the NYSE, the PCX, and the Phix raised the basic and minimum formula percentages for both index and equity options. Generally, broad-based index options = premium + 15%; equity and narrow-based index options = premium + 20%; the minimum required margin was raised an additional 5%. [Release Nos. 34-25701 (5/17/88), 53 FR 20706 (6/6/88); 34-27075 (7/28/89), 54 FR 32409 (8/7/89); 34-27159 (8/21/89), 54 FR 35958 (8/30/89); 34-27186 (8/25/89), 44 SEC Docket 848.)]
- The Federal Reserve Board amended Regulation T to delete certain rules regarding options transactions in favor of rules to be adopted by the options markets and approved by the commission. [61 FR 20386 (5/6/96) (Federal Reserve Board); Release Nos. 34-38710 (6/2/97), 62 FR 31638 (6/10/97) (AMEX); 34-38709 (6/2/97), 62 FR 31643 (6/10/97) (CBOE); 34-38708 (6/2/97), 62 FR 31650 (6/10/97) (NYSE); 34-38707 (6/2/97), 62 FR 31652 (6/10/97) (PCX); 34-38729 (6/10/97), 62 FR 32669 (6/16/97) (NASD); 34-38735 (6/11/97), 62 FR 33147 (6/18/97) (Phix).]
- Margin requirements for OTC options were modified. [Release No. 34-36948 (3/11/96), 61 FR 10832 (3/15/96).]

International coordination

Increase coordination with regulators in other countries by developing trading links, clearance and settlement links, and other similar arrangements by implementing international trade and quote reporting mechanisms, by ensuring adequate financial oversight systems exist, and by forming effective enforcement and surveillance relationships.

- The commission signed formal information sharing agreements with a number of countries. [International Series Release No. 354, 50 SEC Docket 0878 (12/9/91) (Argentina); International Series Release No. 599, 55 SEC Docket 0840 (10/20/93) (Australia); International Series Release No. 7, 43 SEC Docket 0206 (7/1/88) (Brazil); International Series Release No. 6, 43 SEC Docket 0186 (1/7/88) (Canada); International Series Release No. 548, 54 SEC Docket 0737 (6/3/93) (Chile); International Series Release No. 662, 56 SEC Docket 1980 (4/29/94) (China); International Series Release No. 331, 49 SEC Docket 2002 (10/10/91) (Costa Rica); International Series Release No. 932, 61 SEC Docket 0932 (2/11/96) (Egypt); International Series Release No. 932A, 61 SEC Docket 2180 (4/11/96) (Egypt); International Series Release No. 320, 49 SEC Docket 1746 (9/23/91) (European Community); International Series Release No. 116, 45 SEC Docket 724 (12/14/89) (France); International Series Release No. 691, 57 SEC Docket 734 (7/22/94) (Germany); International Series Release No. 863, 60 SEC Docket 1458 (10/5/95) (Hong Kong); International Series Release No. 864, 60 SEC Docket 1464 (10/5/95) (Hong Kong); International Series Release No. 129, 46 SEC Docket 1076 (6/22/90) (Hungary); International Series Release No. 376, 51 SEC Docket 0183 (3/24/92)

(Indonesia); International Series Release No. 324, 49 SEC Docket 1780 (9/26/91) (IADB/UNECLAC); International Series Release No. 934, 61 SEC Docket 0933 (2/13/96) (Israel); International Series Release No. 934A, 61 SEC Docket 2185 (4/9/96) (Israel); International Series Release No. 112, 44 SEC Docket 1319 (9/20/89) (Italy); International Series Release No. 547, 54 SEC Docket 0347 (5/5/93); International Series Release No. 5, 43 SEC Docket 184 (5/23/86) (Japan); International Series Release No. 137, 46 SEC Docket 1715 (5/23/90) (Luxembourg); International Series Release No. 181, 47 SEC Docket 1128 (10/18/90) (Mexico); International Series Release No. 115, 45 SEC Docket 715 (1/12/90) (Netherlands); International Series Release No. 321, 49 SEC Docket 1747 (9/24/91) (Norway); International Series Release No. 899, 60 SEC Docket 2671 (12/5/95) (Russia); International Series Release No. 794, 58 SEC Docket 3006 (3/2/95) (South Africa); International Series Release No. 429, 51 SEC Docket 2839 (7/8/92) (Spain); International Series Release No. 322, 49 SEC Docket 1764 (9/25/91) (Sweden); International Series Release No. 2, 43 SEC Docket 141 (8/31/82) (Switzerland); International Series Release No. 626, 55 SEC Docket 2600 (11/3/93) (Switzerland); International Series Release No. 4, 43 SEC Docket 176 (9/23/86) (U.K.); International Series Release No. 323, 49 SEC Docket 1767 (9/25/91) (U.K.); International Series Release No. 806, 59 SEC Docket 0698 (5/1/95) (U.K.).]

- The NASD implemented the Nasdaq international service to support an early trading session in London. Its hours coincide with the business hours of the London financial markets. It is primarily designed to accommodate international trading by institutional investors in the United States, United Kingdom, and other parts of Europe. [Release Nos. 34-29812 (10/11/91), 56 FR 52082 (10/17/91); 34-32471 (6/16/93), 58 FR 33965 (6/22/93); 34-33037 (10/8/93), 58 FR 53752 (10/18/93); 34-36359 (10/11/95), 60 FR 53820 (10/17/95).]

Notes

1. In response to the extraordinary events of October 1987, President Reagan created the Task Force on Market Mechanisms (Task Force) on November 5, 1987. The Task Force was chaired by Nicholas F. Brady. Its purpose was to

    > review relevant analyses of the current and long-term financial condition of the U.S. securities markets; identify problems that may threaten the short-term liquidity or long-term solvency of such markets; analyze potential solutions to such problems that will both assure the continued functioning of free, fair, and competitive securities markets and maintain investor confidence in such markets; and provide appropriate recommendations to the President, to the Secretary of the Treasury, and to the Chairman of the Board of Governors of the Federal Reserve System.

    The Task Force issued its report, known as the *Brady report*, two months later.
2. The Securities and Exchange Commission's (SEC or commission) Division of Market Regulation (division) conducted a comprehensive study of the causes, effects, and regulatory ramifications of the 1987 market break. Rather than attempt to identify the precise combination of investor psychology, economic developments, and trading strategies that caused the precipitous decline, the division instead sought to

reconstruct the relevant trading activity and analyze how the trading systems for stocks, options, and futures may have contributed to the speed and depth of the decline. The division issued its report in February 1988.

3. The Working Group on Financial Markets (Working Group) was established by President Reagan on March 18, 1988, to provide a coordinating framework for consideration, resolution, recommendation, and action on the complex issues raised by the market break in October 1987. The Working Group was, and still is, composed of the Secretary of the Department of the Treasury and the chairpersons of the Securities and Exchange Commission, the Board of Governors of the Federal Reserve System, and the Commodity Futures Trading Commission (CFTC).
4. Securities Exchange Act Release No. 33023 (Oct. 6, 1993), 58 FR 52891 (Oct. 13, 1993) (citing *The Market Reform Act of 1989: Joint Hearings on S.648 Before the Subcomm. on Securities and the Senate Comm. on Banking, Housing, and Urban Affairs*, 101st Cong., 1st Sess. (Oct. 26, 1989)).
5. Ibid. (quoting "Remarks by Alan Greenspan Before the Annual Convention of the Securities Industry Association" (Nov. 30, 1988)).
6. Ibid. (quoting E. Gerald Corrigan, then-president, Federal Reserve Bank of New York, "Luncheon Address: Perspectives on Payment System Risk Reduction," in *The U.S. Payment System: Efficiency, Risk, and the Role of the Federal Reserve System* (1990), pp. 129–130).
7. The NDFS system was used primarily for the money settlement of equity, corporate debt, and municipal debt transactions. The SDFS system, prior to the conversion, was used primarily for the money settlement of transactions in commercial paper and other money market instruments.

References

Bachmann Task Force, *Report of the Bachmann Task Force on Clearance and Settlement Reform in U.S. Securities Markets*, Washington, DC: May 1992.

Group of Thirty, *Clearance and Settlement Systems in the World's Securities Markets*, March 1989.

Presidential Task Force on Market Mechanisms, *Report of the Presidential Task Force on Market Mechanisms*, Washington, DC: January 1988.

U.S. General Accounting Office, *Financial Markets: Preliminary Observations on the October 1987 Crash*, Washington, DC: January 1988.

U.S. Securities and Exchange Commission, *Fifty-Fourth Annual Report*, Washington, DC: 1988.

U.S. Securities and Exchange Commission, *Fifty-Fifth Annual Report*, Washington, DC: 1989.

U.S. Securities and Exchange Commission, *Fifty-Six Annual Report*, Washington, DC: 1990.

U.S. Securities and Exchange Commission, *Fifty-Seventh Annual Report*, Washington, DC: 1991.

U.S. Securities and Exchange Commission, *Fifty-Eighth Annual Report*, Washington, DC: 1992.

U.S. Securities and Exchange Commission, *Fifty-Ninth Annual Report*, Washington, DC: 1993.

U.S. Securities and Exchange Commission, *Sixtieth Annual Report*, Washington, DC: 1994.

U.S. Securities and Exchange Commission, *Sixty-First Annual Report*, Washington, DC: 1995.

U.S. Securities and Exchange Commission, *Sixty-Second Annual Report*, Washington, DC: 1996.

U.S. Securities and Exchange Commission, Division of Market Regulation, *The October 1987 Market Break*, Washington, DC: February 1988.

U.S. Securities and Exchange Commission, Division of Market Regulation, *Market Analysis of October 13 and 16, 1989*, Washington, DC: December 1990.

U.S. Securities and Exchange Commission, Division of Market Regulation, *Market 2000: An Examination of Current Equity Market Developments*, Washington, DC: January 1994.

U.S. Securities and Exchange Commission, Office of Economic Analysis, *Triggering the 1987 Stock Market Crash: Antitakeover Provisions in the Proposed House Ways and Means Tax Bill?* Washington, DC: May 1989.

Working Group on Financial Markets, *Interim Report of the Working Group on Financial Markets*, Washington, DC: May 1988.

Shadow Financial Regulatory Committee Statements

Reflecting the *Journal's* interest in promoting an indepth analysis of public policy issues, we publish the quarterly statements of the Shadow Financial Regulatory Committee on a regular basis.

Journal of Financial Services Research 13:3 317–318 (1998)

Shadow Financial Regulatory Committee Press Release

December 19, 1997

The Shadow Financial Regulatory Committee is proud to recognize the establishment of a European Shadow Financial Regulatory Committee. The new European Comittee will serve the same function as the U.S. committee of analyzing economic, financial, regulatory and legislative forces affecting the financial services industry from a public interest point of view focusing on safety and efficiency. The European committee will focus particularly on the important and rapid changes arising from the European Union and a single currency. The European committee held its first organizational meeting in Maastricht (the Netherlands) on November 22 and 23, 1997, and will hold its next meeting in Brussels (Belgium) in March. Two of the committee's members attended the December 7–8 meeting of the U.S. committee in Washington, DC, to brief the group of its agenda and to observe the operation of its U.S. counterpart.

The members of the European committee are leading professors of banking and law in countries included in the European Union. The organizing members of the committee include

Harald Benink, Maastricht University, Maastricht, the Netherlands
Christian de Boissieu, University of Paris I, Paris, France
Franco Bruni, Bocconi University, Milan, Italy
Jordi Canals, University of Navarra, Barcelona, Spain
David Llewellyn, Loughborough University, Loughborough, United Kingdom
Niels Thygesen, University of Copenhagen, Copenhagen, Denmark
Clas Wihlborg, Gothenborg University, Gothenborg, Sweden
Heinz Zimmerman, Hochschule St. Gallen, St. Gallen, Switzerland

Members from Germany and other countries will be added in the near future.

Press Release

December 19, 1997

Professor Charles Calomiris has joined the Shadow Financial Regulatory Committee effective with its next quarterly meeting March 1, 1988. Calomiris is the Paul M. Montrone Professor of Finance and Economics at Columbia University, and a visiting scholar at the American Enterprise Institute. Previously, he taught at Northwestern University, the Wharton School at the University of Pennsylvania, and the University of Illinois. Calomiris received his Ph.D. from Stanford University. Calomiris has been published widely in both journals and books. He has been a consultant to numerous private firms and government agencies in the United States and abroad, serves on the editorial board of a number of academic journals, including the *Journal of Financial Services Research*, and is a research associate at the National Bureau of Economic Research.

Journal of Financial Services Research 13:3 319–324 (1998)

Statement No. 141
Strategic Plans of the Federal Financial Institution Regulatory Agencies

December 7, 1997

The Government Performance and Results Act of 1993 required all government agencies to produce a strategic plan by September 30, 1997. Its objective was to make the agencies pay more attention to their long-run goals and priorities, and express them in specific terms so that performance could actually be measured.

The act required the plan to include a mission statement, goals and objectives for the period 1997 through 2002, approaches and strategies to achieve those goals, a discussion of external factors affecting the plans, a discussion of the relationship between strategic objectives and annual goals, and a program to evaluate actual performance. The committee reviewed the plans of the Board of Governors of the Federal Reserve System (FRB), The Office of the Comptroller of the Currency (OCC), The Federal Deposit Insurance Corporation (FDIC), The Office of Thrift Supervision (OTS), and The National Credit Union Administration (NCUA). Each agency's plan, of course, reflected its unique statutory role. This statement will focus principally on the safety and soundness supervision and regulation section of each agency's plan.

In general, the plans do not achieve the objectives of the act and need considerable improvement in their quality and substance. There are two primary deficiencies: (1) The plans do not expressly set priorities among a variety of goals, and (2) the goals mentioned do not reflect any link to a coherent strategy.

For example,

- The plan published by the OCC does not describe how the agency's significant efforts to extend national bank activities through subsidiaries relate in any way to its other goals or to its long-term vision for the banking industry.
- The FDIC's plan does not even mention the Federal Deposit Insurance Corporation Improvement Act of 1991 (FDICIA), the most significant legislation to come out of the S&L and banking disaster. The underlying concept of FDICIA is that the FDIC should assure the safety and soundness of insured banks by insisting on and policing strong capitalization. Its strategic plan should reflect this objective.
- The Federal Reserve Board's banking discussion paid little attention to the board's plans for administering the Bank Holding Company Act. The board's recent interpretations of the act have reduced the Glass-Steagall Act to a minor annoyance—an action with which we agree—and have opened up significant areas of data processing activity to bank holding companies. This must reflect a series of assumptions by the board about the future of the financial industry and

the role of bank holding companies in that future. What these assumptions are and what the board plans to do in the future are nowhere described in its strategic plan.

General observations

To fulfill the congressional objective,

- All the plans should discuss the implication of regulatory policies for industry market share and trends in market share, and vice versa. None do.
- All the plans should describe how the agency intends to implement the mandates and requirements of FDICIA.
- All the plans should discuss how reliance on risk management relates to capital standards and the enforcement of those standards.
- All the plans should discuss institutional consolidation in terms of implications for the industry and consumers of financial services, not just staffing of the agencies.

Statement No. 142
Congress and Financial Reform

December 7, 1997

Again this year, despite considerable efforts almost to the last day of the session, Congress failed to pass financial reform legislation. This has happened so often in recent years that it calls into question the ability of Congress to change national policy in this area and leads many observers to believe that it is better to rely on actions by regulators than to bother with legislation.

Under these circumstances, it may be time for congressional leaders—some of whom became deeply involved this year in an effort to craft compromise legislation—to take a step back and consider whether the approach they have been taking is ever likely to bear fruit and whether it might not be better to scrap the current bill and start over.

H.R. 10, the bill that moved through Congress this year, was a classic illustration of the old joke that a camel is a horse put together by a committee. By the time it had passed through the House Banking and Commerce Committees, the bill was a complex welter of compromises and adjustments. The contending interests—large banks, small banks, foreign banks, securities firms, insurance companies, insurance agents, S&Ls and S&L holding companies, and diversified financial services firms—each got something it wanted in an ultimately unsuccessful effort by Congress to gain their support. No one appears to have asked why all this trading was a benefit to the public.

In the committee's view, a primary cause of the failure this year— as in years past—was the fallacious notion that banks must be separated from the rest of the commercial world. Misplaced allegiance to the so-called separation of banking and commerce has made it impossible for Congress to create the two-way street that would meet the needs of all the players and best serve the interests of consumers.

Under a two-way street approach, all the contending interests would be able to compete with one another, with consumers the ultimate beneficiaries. Banks and bank holding companies could engage in securities and insurance activities, just as securities firms and insurance companies could acquire banks. Any company could enter the financial services industry, just as any company engaged in financial services could extend its activities into areas that its management considers more likely to be profitable. Insurance companies could not reasonably complain about banks entering their business if they were free to enter the banking business, and banks could not reasonably complain about the freedoms enjoyed by securities firms if they also could form affiliations without regulatory approval. In other words, many of the interindustry disputes that made legislation impossible last year would be eliminated and the way cleared for healthy competition. Existing laws, such as Section 23A and 23B of the Federal Reserve Act, applied to bank transactions with subsidiaries as well as affiliates—coupled with a requirement that nonbank activities be separately capitalized—would prevent transfer of the benefits, if any, of the federal safety net to the nonbanking operations.

On the other hand, Congress can continue on the course it has followed for the last three years—a fruitless search for the formula that will satisfy all the contending interests. Even if such a formula could be found, it would be only a temporary solution. The markets and consumer demand for services will continue to evolve, forcing changes in business strategy on the members of what today we call the *financial services industry.* In a few years they will be back again before Congress, asking to renegotiate the most recent deal.

The only permanent solution is to eliminate the artificial and unnecessary restraints that arise from the mistaken idea that banking must be separated from commerce. Once this concept is abandoned, Congress can create the competitive two-way street that will lead both to permanent financial reform and the benefits that consumers always get from competition.

Statement No. 143
Sweep Accounts and the Prohibition on Paying Interest on Reserve Balances and Demand Deposits

December 7, 1997

In its planning document prepared for the Government Performance and Results Act, the Federal Reserve Board notes that the use by banks of sweep accounts may complicate its implementation of monetary policy. The committee finds no justification for this conclusion. Furthermore, it does believe that sweep accounts present a potential risk to the FDIC's insurance funds. To the extent that these accounts sweep demand deposits into overnight repurchase agreements, they strip the banks of their highest quality assets, for example, Treasury securities. This is not in the best interest of the FDIC or the taxpayer.

Moreover, the Federal Reserve argues that the incentive for banks to offer sweep accounts would be reduced if Congress authorized the payment of interest on reserve balances. Although payment of interest on reserve balances is desirable, the Fed's reasoning is incorrect. The incentive of banks to offer their customers interest yielding sweep accounts comes from the prohibition of interest payments on demand deposits, not on bank reserves. Sweep accounts are an inefficient way of paying interest on business demand deposits. The prohibition of interest payments on demand deposits is a remnant of the Banking Act of 1933 that has long outlived any supposed usefulness, and should be repealed. Paying interest directly on demand deposits is both more efficient and safer for the banking system than encouraging bank use of sweep accounts.

GPSR Compliance

The European Union's (EU) General Product Safety Regulation (GPSR) is a set of rules that requires consumer products to be safe and our obligations to ensure this.

If you have any concerns about our products, you can contact us on ProductSafety@springernature.com

In case Publisher is established outside the EU, the EU authorized representative is:

Springer Nature Customer Service Center GmbH
Europaplatz 3
69115 Heidelberg, Germany

Batch number: 10816040

Printed by Printforce, the Netherlands